Competition Obedience:
A Balancing Act

by
Judy Byron & Adele Yunck

Photographs by Karen Taylor
Illustrations by Kimberly Hundley & Adele Yunck

JABBY Productions
Ann Arbor, Michigan
Mentor, Ohio

Competition Obedience:
A Balancing Act

by
Judy Byron & Adele Yunck
Photographs by Karen Taylor
Illustrations by Kimberly Hundley & Adele Yunck

Published by: JABBY Productions
3676 W. Ellsworth Rd.
Ann Arbor, MI 48103

Library of Congress Catalog Card Number: 98-91768
ISBN 0-9664574-0-4

First Edition, Second Printing, 1999
Printed in the United States of America

To my family, for all their love and support.

— Judy

To my father, Robbins Burling,
for his unflagging encouragement,
his humor, and his editing skills
and
to Fritz, Chris, and Ryan,
for their patience in waiting until
"after The Book is done!"

— Adele

Table of Contents

Preface

B efore I read Judy and Adele's manuscript for this book, I had decided to treat myself to a new puppy. I hadn't started a puppy in eight years and had all kinds of what I thought were new and creative ideas about laying down a foundation for obedience, herding and agility. I began reading the manuscript and discovered that they'd stolen all my best stuff. Or I'd stolen theirs.

Bob Self has said that there's nothing new in dog training. But this book *is* new. Its organization, completeness, and attention to solid, positive foundation work put it in a class by itself. It represents more than just years of successful training. It also reflects a commitment to effective teaching shared by few other competitors. Although no book can tell you everything you need to know about competition obedience, this one comes as close as any I've ever read.

This is a big book. Don't be intimidated by it. You can devour it whole, or you can graze for tips and solutions to specific problems. If you find by grazing that you have holes in your foundation training, the book will help you fill them.

Competition Obedience: A Balancing Act addresses the fundamental problem faced by all modern obedience trainers — finding the right mix of rewards and corrections that work best for you and your dog. Of course, your dog is the best judge of this. Share what you learn here with him. I think he'll like this book.

Margie English
Purdys, NY

About the Authors

Judy Byron

I got my first dog in 1971. She was a Standard Poodle and I knew she would need to be well behaved, especially since we had three small children at the time. There was not much choice of classes and all training was done by beginning each exercise with a jerk on a choke collar. I used this type of training until I had the opportunity to train with Ted Aranda in 1986. He presented a truly wonderful program in alternative methods of training with his teaching of operant conditioning methods.

I have been a member of Cleveland All-Breed Training Club and Buckeye Tracking Club since the early '70s and once was more active than I have been for the past few years. I taught for Cleveland All-Breed for a number of years, but left there to run my own school in 1982. I taught competitive obedience and tracking until I became ill in 1997. Unfortunately I have not been able to teach much since then.

My husband and I own a home in Florida and try to split the year between Florida and Ohio. The past several years have been difficult ones for me and my family. I have been struggling with a severe illness and its treatment. I would love to be able to train and show again, but this may not be possible.

My dogs have included the following:

🐾 Standard Poodle *Tiffany* (Byron's Black Pearl Am CDX), 1971-1985. There was a woman training a Dalmatian where I was training and this dog could do hand signals! I remember telling my instructor that I could get my dog to do that and get all the titles in one year. Ha! I had a lot to learn! Tiffany earned her CDX and had a lot of trouble jumping. I also discovered that female dogs and I did not get along very well. I placed her in a pet home where she lived many happy years. Alas, I never did get to show off her hand signals.

🐾 Standard Poodle *Whizzer* (Hariann's Satan Solo Am/Can UD Am/Can TD/TDX) - Multiple Dog World Awards, 1974-1987. Whizzer was one of those once in a lifetime dogs. In spite of the jerk and yell method of training, he was always willing and always gave me everything he had. He was OTCh. pointed and had to be retired at the age of seven because of two ruptured vertebrae from jumping 36 inches with very straight shoulders.

🐾 Toy Poodle *Killer* (Poodhall Achilles Heel Am/Can UD), 1978-1992. Killer was my son Steve's dog. Steve did most of the training, but I was there for constant reinforcement. Killer was not an easy dog to train and by the time he got his UD, he was smaller than Steve's feet since Steve was a teenager and growing rapidly!

🐾 Field Spaniel *Bekki* (Ch. Jester's Bertschwood Bekki Am/Can UDT), 1975-1988. Dog World Award in Open. Bekki was the first of her breed to earn all these titles. Bekki was the only bitch I have ever enjoyed training as much as I do my males! She was one in a million and had I known about food training with her, I suspect she could have and would have done all the work while walking on her hind legs and backwards! She was a truly food-motivated dog.

🐾 Miniature Poodle *Gus* (Ch. Mavro's Go For The Gusto Am/Can UD), 1983-1997. Multiple HIT's. Gus was a game little dog and one I ruined by correcting him when he didn't understand an exercise. I have never forgiven myself for the way I got him through Utility; I became even more enthusiastic about training the "new" way because of Gus.

🐾 Standard Poodle *Cutter* (Bolbec's A Cut Above Am/Can CDX), 1988-1993. Dog World Award in Novice in the USA and Canada. Cutter was the first dog I trained with Ted Aranda and he struggled with me to learn all the new ways. He was a very sensitive dog and never very healthy. He died of heart block at the age of five.

🐾 English Springer Spaniel *Brig* (Society's Brigadier General Am/Can/Ber CD, Am/Can TD), 1990-1992. Dog World Award in three countries, Multiple HIT's. First place, Novice Division, World Series, 1992. Brig was my OTCh. dog *not* to be. He was the number one Springer in the USA, Canada, and Bermuda when we showed in Novice. Unfortunately, he was both dog and people aggressive and had to be put down at a very young age. I still get teary eyed thinking about him.

🐾 Whippet *Alec* (Paris Smart Alec Am/Can CDX), 1992- . Dog World Award in Novice. Alec has taught me more about dog training than all of my past dogs put together! He is very smart, very sensitive, but becomes extremely stressed in the ring. He is easy to train, likes to train, and learns quickly. Working to give him the confidence he needs to show has been our biggest challenge. Had I trained him before the methods used in this book, we would have been lucky to get through Novice. He is fully trained in Utility

Judy and her current dog buddies, Alec and Clark.

and will be shown as soon as I am well enough to do so. He has a good attitude and a good foundation, so I am confident he will do well.

🐾 Whippet *Clark* (Seafire Superman), 1997- . Whippets are dogdom's best kept secret so don't tell anyone! Clark is sweet and smart, and loves to work. He is far less worried about the environment than Alec so I believe he will enjoy showing more. Time will tell as he is only about halfway trained through Utility and not proofed for anything!

I have been married to Barry for 36 years. We have three sons, Michael, Stephen, and Matthew, and three daughters-in-law, Wendy, Reggie, and Lori. The true lights of my life are my five grandchildren, Alex, Zoë, Katie, Teddy, and Jack!

Adele Yunck

I got my first dog, Casey, in 1985 and quickly became obsessed with obedience training. I began teaching for the Ann Arbor Dog Training Club in 1987 while still working as a Software Engineer and started Northfield Dog Training in 1990. I teach classes and private lessons at home in Ann Arbor. Although I teach puppy classes regularly, my main interest is teaching competition obedience classes. My dogs have included:

🐾 Australian Terrier *Casey* (U-CD Hott Pursuitt on the Farm Am/Can UD), 1984-1997. When I first got Casey, I wanted to earn a UD. I had no idea what that would entail, but we did eventually reach that goal. The most important lesson that Casey taught me was perseverance! She earned a couple of HIT's, my very first one and one at the first obedience trial ever held at an Australian Terrier National Specialty, coming out of three years of retirement to beat her "brother" Rio.

🐾 Flat-Coated Retriever *Tramp* (Am/Can Ch. Am/Can OTCh. U-CD Grousemoor Some Like It Hot TD, WC), 1985-1994. Tramp joined our family one year after Casey. While her Novice career was not especially brilliant, she went on to earn multiple HIT's and HC's, and over 250 OTCh. points. She taught me a lot about the importance of balanced training and, like Casey, about persevering in spite of repeated NQs. She placed in the 1988 Open and 1993 Top Dog divisions at the World Series. She became a member of the Flat-Coated Retriever Hall of Fame in 1991 when she earned her WC title.

- Australian Terrier *Rio* (Ch. OTCh. U-CD Free For All on the Farm UDX, TD, Can CDX), 1988-1996. Rio earned his breed's first OTCh. title in 1995, and my first UDX that same year. He earned multiple HIT's and HC's and placed in the 1992 Open divisions at a Gaines Regional and World Series. He was an ambassador for his breed throughout his show career. He was a sunny little dog, and showed many people that little dogs are *cool*.

- Flat-Coated Retriever *Treasure* (Ch. OTCh. Grousemoor Forget Me Not UDX, OA, NAJ, Can CDX), 1992- . Treasure's Novice show career will be hard to top. She has earned multiple HIT's in both AKC and CKC Novice and Open. She won first place at the 1996 Pup-peroni Central Regional Novice division, second place at the 1996 World Series Open division, and second place at the 1996 Classic Novice division. Since the book's first printing, Treasure completed her OTCh., her UDX, her NA, her OA and NAJ. Treasure is a lovely, sweet-tempered dog, and I look forward to showing her for many more years.

Adele and her current dog buddies, Treasure and Java.

Border Terrier *Java* (Riverside Magen's Starbucks NA, NAJ), 1997- . Java is pure fun! He is quick, wickedly smart, and so far, loves to play the obedience game. As Rio did before him, Java seems to shout "Pick me, pick me!" when I need to demonstrate an exercise in a class. He zipped through his Novice agility titles with ease and was scheduled to debut in obedience in Novice in the fall of 1999. Above all else, he is a joy to have around and a splendid companion.

My husband Fritz and I have been married for 15 years and have two sons, Chris, 10, and Ryan, 7. In the summer, I can often be found puttering around in my large organic garden.

Acknowledgements

When Adele started training her first two dogs, she was fortunate to have Gail Dapogny as her mentor. Gail trained with Ted Aranda, who was influential in introducing food into competition obedience training in Michigan. Ted presented the first dog training seminar Adele attended and it filled in a number of gaps in Adele's understanding. These methods became the basis for her training program.

When Ted moved to Ohio, he helped Judy change her training program from correction–based to positive motivation and operant conditioning with balanced corrections. Though we don't live close to each other, we have similar training foundations. Thanks, Ted! As you will see, however, our training method is a composite of many excellent trainers. We did not intentionally copy any material. If this has happened, we sincerely apologize for the oversight.

A big thank you also goes to our students and their dogs. They have taught us so much, both about what works and what doesn't work. We appreciate their faith in us as teachers. Many have also studied diagrams and read pieces of this manuscript for clarity.

Thanks to our dedicated proofreaders who helped us wrestle our words into this book: Barry Byron, Terri Clingerman, Kathy Crislip, Margie English, Sandy Ganz, Jane Jackson, Paula McIntyre, AnnaMarie Mondro, Debbie Spence, and Fritz Yunck. An extra-large measure of thanks goes to Adele's father, Robbins Burling. For someone who doesn't even like dogs, his contribution to this book was enormous. He gave us many giggles with his humorous interpretations of what he perceived as "foreign" terms. An excellent writer and noted author, his editing skills helped us to improve ours.

Two very talented artists contributed mightily. Karen Taylor patiently took all of the photographs in one long day. Our sometimes fuzzy ideas were brought to life in the illustrations drawn by Kimberly Hundley. It seems fitting that these two gifted women have been friends with each other since they were in elementary school. In addition to their obvious skills, they are a joy to work with. Thanks for sharing your talents, ladies!

Thanks also to the handlers and their dogs who patiently posed for the photographs:

- Marilyn Burhop and Keeshond *Cindy* (Cindy CD).

- Elly Burke and Shetland Sheepdogs *Bijou* (U-CDX Eska's Ultimate Legacy UD) and *Parker* (U-CDX Moribrook In The Park CDX).

- Judy Byron and Whippets *Alec* (Paris Smart Alec Am/Can CDX) and *Clark* (Seafire Superman).

- Marcia Cavan and Pharaoh Hound *Bristol* (Ch. Galadrial's Dream Weaver UD, F.Ch., SC).

- Raissa Hinman and Alaskan Malamute *Sister* (U-CD Mountain Home's Goldsmoke WTD, Can CD).

- Jan Sinclair and Greyhound *Brendan* (U-CD Brendan CD) and Norwich Terrier *Rocky* (Sho-Me Ketka's Rolling Rock).

- Adele Yunck and Flat Coated Retriever *Treasure* (Ch. OTCh. Grousemoor Forget Me Not UDX, OA, NAJ, Can CDX) and Border Terrier *Java* (Riverside Magen's Starbucks NA, NAJ).

The biggest thanks must go to our own dogs, both past and present. They are truly the most important teachers we have had.

Introduction

T he motivation to write this book came from our students, as well as our fellow obedience trainers on the Internet. We had tremendous support for what we were doing with our own dogs and what we were recommending to others. We thank them for that support and hope they will not be disappointed in what we have written.

We realize there are many areas where good instruction is not available. In addition, a number of people cannot afford to travel long distances to attend seminars. This book is for them.

Why This Book?

This book is written primarily for competition obedience trainers. We hope that anyone training a dog will get *something* out of it, but we train for competition, and that is our goal for you who are reading this. We compete primarily in American Kennel Club (AKC) events, although we have both put United Kennel Club (UKC) and Canadian Kennel Club (CKC) titles on our dogs.

We begin training each new dog with the goal to earn at least a *Utility Dog* title. We believe it is never too early to start getting ready for Utility. The foundation for Utility is laid along with the foundation for Novice and Open work.

We firmly believe that with the right dog, within the breed of your choice, you can accomplish whatever you wish to accomplish in competition obedience. Your goals are yours, though we think you should aim as high as you and your dog are capable. Some people are limited by time and money, some by physical constraints. By using the following training methods faithfully, you should achieve a level of performance of which you can be proud. Above all, you and your dog should be happy and enjoy training. This is our goal when we train our own dogs. Isn't that what a sport is all about?

Dogs and handlers both come in two genders, but we need to be clear about which we are referring to, so we will arbitrarily use "she" and "her" for the handler and "he" and "him" for the dog. We trust that neither female dogs nor male handlers will take offense.

Commands are given in small capitals, such as SIT and STAY. The formal exercise names are given in italics with leading capitals, such as *Scent Discrimination* and *Drop on Recall*. Our exercise names are also in italics, but without the leading capital, such as *dizzy spin* or *heel start*.

A Balancing Act

Teaching, proofing, and showing a dog in obedience requires the proper balance of positives — food, toys, play, praise — and negatives — verbal and physical corrections. We use lots of food, toys, and play throughout our dogs' training careers. We also use appropriate, fair corrections to build the consistency required for the obedience ring.

Dog training is both a science and an art. We consider the various principles of learning theory to be the science. Many trainers are unaware of these principles even though they apply some of them every time they train their dog. A number of excellent books on this theory are now available to dog trainers (see Appendix B).

The art of training is finding the proper balance of positives and negatives for each dog. It is knowing when to help the dog because he is confused, adding a fair correction because he has chosen not to obey a command, and releasing the dog at just the right moment for the best effect. It is knowing when to pressure the dog and when to back off.

One of the best ways to learn the science and art of dog training is actually to train your dog! With each new dog you train, you will refine your understanding of both sides of the equation. We continue to be amazed at how consistent application of this learning theory produces results. We think the balancing act is fascinating. We hope you will find it so as well.

Some Points to Ponder While Reading

- In order for a dog to train and show well, he must have a solid foundation. The foundation work, for the most part, is found in the early chapters. Teaching a proper foundation takes a long time. Don't rush it. The time invested will be returned when you do advanced work.

- Mental attitude is everything, both yours and the dog's. We try to always think and act positively when working with our dogs, either in training or showing. We want to see a happy dog during training, showing, and all times in between.

- Timing is critical for success. Timing is something that is very hard to teach and explain. When do you use the food? When do you use praise? When do you use a correction?

- Be aware constantly of what your dog is telling you. Is he confused? Is he unsure? Is he not understanding? Is he choosing not to do the exercise? If you do not know "why," you cannot know "how." You cannot fix a problem you don't understand!

- Training a dog for the obedience ring takes a lot of time, in hours, days, and years. Remember, this is not a race. Great dogs do not happen overnight. Many long hours go into their training.

- Dogs should never be afraid to be wrong and neither should the handlers. Being wrong often teaches one how to be right.

- FOOD is only a four letter word.

- CORRECTION is not a dirty word.

- STRESS *is* a four letter word with six letters. Work is play and play is work. This attitude about training should make going in the ring just another "walk in the park!"

We send you our best wishes for a wonderful ring performance.

Happy training!

Judy and Adele
September, 1998

Why Competition Obedience?

Why would you want to pursue competition obedience training? What is an obedience title? How do you earn one with your dog? What is it all about?

Obedience trials are events which are sanctioned by a governing body. In the United States, this is most often the American Kennel Club (AKC) or United Kennel Club (UKC). Trials are sponsored by clubs throughout the country and are usually held year round. Many people train their dogs for obedience trials with the goal of earning various titles.

One of the fine things about obedience is that there are attainable goals for almost everyone. If you are a competitive person, have a dog with reasonable ability, and are willing to work hard, you can aim for high scores and class placements. Perhaps you are not interested in competing, but enjoy the challenge of earning titles. As long as your dog does the minimum work required, you can earn obedience titles. There are as many goals as there are trainers. Many trainers start out being thrilled with a passing score (Adele began this way) and then get bitten by the competition bug.

Consider your dog's temperament, conformation, and work ethic, and set realistic goals. While we think you should aim high, it is wise to keep in mind the difficulty of training a shy dog or one who is very sensitive to his environment. It is not impossible to earn titles with this type of dog; it just takes more careful and thorough preparation. You should also be realistic about your abilities as a trainer and handler.

Solid obedience training is necessary when participating in many other performance events, such as Agility, Flyball, Herding, Hunt Tests, and Lure Coursing. An obedient dog is also a more enjoyable companion in the home. We have found that the training required for advanced obedience strengthens our relationship and deepens the bond with our dogs.

People of all ages, from children to senior citizens, can and do compete in obedience. There are few other sports with such a diversity of exhibitors.

The Structure of Obedience Competition

There are three different class levels at an obedience trial: *Novice, Open,* and *Utility.* When you and your dog enter an obedience ring, you have 200 points to your credit. If you exit the ring with at least 170 points, and more than 50% of the points available for each exercise, you pass, or *qualify,* that day. When you receive a qualifying score from three different judges, your dog has earned a title at that level. A passing score is called a *leg* and you need three legs to earn a title. You may continue to show at a given class level for some period of time after finishing your title. This period of time depends on the sanctioning body.

The *Companion Dog* title, or *CD,* is earned in the Novice class. The *Companion Dog Excellent* title, or *CDX,* is earned in the Open class. The *Utility Dog,* or *UD,* is earned in the Utility class.

The following lists show the exercises that make up the three different class levels in an AKC obedience trial.

The *Novice* class comprises these exercises:

Heel on Leash and Figure Eight	40 points
Stand for Examination	30 points
Heel Free	40 points
Recall	30 points
Long Sit (1 minute)	30 points
Long Down (3 minutes)	30 points

The *Open* exercises:

Heel Free and Figure Eight	40 points
Drop on Recall	30 points
Retrieve on Flat	20 points
Retrieve over High Jump	30 points
Broad Jump	20 points
Long Sit (3 minutes)	30 points
Long Down (5 minutes)	30 points

The *Utility* exercises:

Signal Exercise	40 points
Scent Discrimination Article 1	30 points
Scent Discrimination Article 2	30 points
Directed Retrieve	30 points
Moving Stand and Examination	30 points
Directed Jumping	40 points

The classes are further divided into A and B sections. Anyone may show a dog in the B classes, while the A classes are more restricted. Novice A is for handlers and dogs who have never earned an obedience title. Open A and Utility A are for dogs who have not yet or only recently earned a CDX or a UD. Obedience judges and handlers who have earned an *OTCh* (explained below) must compete in the B classes.

Once your dog has earned his UD title, he can continue to compete in Open B and Utility B to earn the *Utility Dog Excellent,* or *UDX* title, and the *Obedience Trial Championship,* or *OTCh.*

The *UDX* is earned by passing both Open B and Utility B on the same day at ten separate trials. You must first earn your UD to compete for this title. Scores are not critical, but you must pass every exercise in both classes. This title recognizes the consistent team.

The AKC *Obedience Trial Championship* is the only AKC obedience title that is based on competition. Once a dog has completed his UD, he can start accumulating OTCh points. Championship points are earned by winning first or second place in Open B or Utility B. The number of points earned depends on the number of dogs competing in that class. The dog must:

- Earn at least 100 points.
- Win a first place in Open B.
- Win a first place in Utility B.
- Win a third first place in either class.
- Win these three first places under three different judges.

In addition to the "regular" classes (*Novice, Open,* and *Utility*), some trial-giving clubs also offer some or all of the following "non-regular" classes: *Graduate Novice, Veterans, Brace, Versatility, Team,* and *Graduate Open.* The non-regular classes are just for fun and no titles can be earned in these classes.

Rules and Regulations

Each organization that awards obedience titles has a rule book which explains the rules that are to be followed by exhibitors. These rule books contain the exercises needed to earn a title at each level, an explanation of perfect exercises, and how points might be lost for various types of errors. We urge you to get a copy of the rule book for the organization in which you'll be showing. You will find it invaluable.

The rule books also explain when a judge must give a failing score. This is also called *non-qualifying* or *NQing*. New exhibitors often view NQing as a ghastly experience. Experienced exhibitors usually realize it is just part of the game. Most dogs, shown long enough, are going to fail at least one exercise.

There is a big difference between *non*-qualifying and being *dis*qualified or excused. When you or your dog NQ an exercise, you finish the remaining exercises in the class. When you are excused or disqualified, you may not finish and must leave the ring immediately. If you are excused by three AKC judges because your dog attacks or attempts to attack another dog, your dog is no longer eligible to compete in AKC obedience trials. There are various other reasons why you might be excused or disqualified. Be sure to read your rule book! We also recommend that you read a booklet from the AKC called *Obedience Guidelines for Judges*. One copy of this and the regulations is available free from the AKC on request (see *Appendix B*).

The AKC rule book describes the *principal features* of each exercise. These are the most important parts of the exercise and you must perform them correctly or you will not pass it. The rule book also differentiates between *substantial* and *minor* deductions. A *substantial* deduction is usually three or more points taken from your score. A *minor* deduction is .5 to 2.5 points taken from your score. A judge cannot make a deduction of less than .5.

Placements are usually given to the four dogs and handlers with the highest scores within each class. Some trial-giving clubs also give other prizes, typically based on breed, group, or other titles earned. In the case of a tie for any prize in an AKC trial, each dog and handler perform individually a Novice *Heel Free* exercise. This is known as a *runoff*.

When the judging is complete for a given class, the judge calls all the exhibitors who passed back into the ring for the awards. Each team that has passed receives a qualifying ribbon.

At the end of a trial, two overall awards are given. *High in Trial* or *HIT* is given to the dog and handler with the highest qualifying score in the regular classes. *High Combined* or *HC* is given to the dog and handler with the highest combined score from the Open B and Utility classes. In Canada, a *Best in Trial* is awarded to the winner of a runoff among the first place winners from all of the regular classes.

Point Systems

In addition to prizes won at individual trials, there are various point systems maintained by different groups around the country. One such system is the *Delaney system*. Every dog who gets one of the four placements in a class receives one Delaney point for every dog defeated. If there are ten dogs competing in a class, first place earns nine points, second place eight points, and so on.

First & Foremost points are awarded for any qualifying score in Open or Utility. The number of points depends on the score: a score of 200 nets eight points, down to one point for a score in the 170–174.5 range.

Score	Points
200	8
198-199.5	7
195-197.5	6
190-194.5	5
185-189.5	4
180-184.5	3
175-179.5	2
170-174.5	1

The *Kennel Ration Dog of the Year* award is given out each year to the person who earns the most OTCh points. This is one of the most prestigious awards available to obedience competitors in the United States.

Matches

Matches are events where the primary purpose is to practice for obedience trials. There are two types of matches: matches for fun and *sanctioned matches. Fun matches, show and go's*, or simply *matches* allow training; you may give your dog a treat or time to play with a toy as a reward for a good performance. You may also need or want to correct him for errors.

Sanctioned matches are run exactly like obedience trials. Prizes are awarded, though still no titles. Sanctioned matches may serve as practice for an AKC sanctioned club and are required before that club may hold a licensed obedience trial. They may also be given by clubs already sanctioned by the AKC as part of fulfilling their AKC membership requirements. Sanctioned matches are not as useful for training purposes because they are typically run like a regular trial (i.e., no food or training in the ring).

Tournaments

In addition to trials and matches, a number of obedience tournaments are held each year. To qualify for most of these, you must have earned three scores in approved trials with a minimum average, typically 193 or higher. Titles are not usually earned in tournaments (UKC's *Top Gun* is an exception). There are generally three or four class levels of competition in which the Novice, Open, or Utility exercises are performed. Exhibitors show two to six times, depending on the tournament and class. Up to ten placements are given in each division, based on total score.

Among the most popular tournaments are what used to be known officially as the *Gaines Obedience Championships* but are now the *Pup–Peroni Obedience Championships*. Informally, they are called *Regionals* or *The Classic*. Three Regional tournaments, an Eastern, a Central, and a Western, are held each year. To enter a Regional, you must have three scores averaging 193 or higher. The Classic is the year-end "finals" of the Regionals. Anyone with the required scores (currently three scores averaging 195 or higher) can enter the Classic, but spaces are reserved for those teams who place at each of the Regionals. The groups sponsoring these tournaments raise money for several years before the event in order to hold a great party with obedience as the excuse! Exhibitors are treated in grand style, and the ring conditions are marvelous.

One of our favorite tournaments is the *Detroit-Windsor Dog Obedience Association World Series.* This tournament is held every summer in Michigan and is the longest continuously running tournament. The entry requirements are similar to the Regionals.

One of the most exciting parts of the *World Series* is participating in or spectating the runoffs. One final score for each exhibitor remains secret. Anyone who is tied for a top-ten placement in a division goes to a hidden room. Each exhibitor comes out one at a time to run off. All judges from the division are in the ring, one calling commands and the others scoring. Two normal-sized rings are combined into one that is 40' X 100'. Typically, the judges dream up devilishly hard patterns, and the exhibitors have no advanced knowledge of what they will be. A long *fast* and a long *slow* are common.

The preparation required for an obedience tournament differs from a normal trial. Stamina is a plus, as is consistency of passing each exercise. They are exciting events, and it is prestigious to earn a placement at one of them.

Equipment

I n this chapter, we discuss all the equipment we use in our training. If there is something we have left out, it is probably because we don't use it!

Much of the equipment we use needs to be ordered from a company specializing in dog obedience equipment. We list a few of the well-known suppliers, but this does not mean there are not others equally as good. These are simply our favorites.

MAX 200 Dog Obedience Equipment Co.
114 Beach St.
Bldg. 5
Rockaway, NJ 07866
1-800-446-2920
web site: www.max200.com

J and J Dog Supplies
P.O. Box 1517
Dept. F
Galesburg, IL 61402
1-800-642-2050
web site: www.jandjdog.com

Sylvia's Tack Shop (specializes in small dog equipment and the Micro Prong collar)
4333 11th St. A
Moline, IL 61265
309-797-9060
e-mail: tacbox@aol.com

Joe Feist (specializes in extremely well-made [and expensive] scent articles and dumbbells, both wood and plastic)
2581 Crafton
N. Canton, OH 44720
330-494-2301

General Equipment

- *Leashes in various lengths and widths*, depending on your height and the height and weight of your dog. We recommend a minimum of one four- to six-foot and one two- to three-foot leash in the proper width. At the present time, a six-foot leash is required to show a dog in Canada. A one-quarter-inch wide by three feet long leash is a good size for a small dog. When training a larger dog, a wider leash may be necessary, though longer isn't usually needed. When Adele showed her Australian Terrier, Rio, in Novice, she showed him on a leash made from a bootlace and a small clip (bought from one of the above suppliers).

- *Retractable Leash.* They are available from some veterinary supply houses. A retractable leash is either a cord or web with a snap to attach to your dog's collar. It extends to either 16 or 26 feet and can be locked or rewound with the push of a button. We use one when training a variety of exercises.

- *Tab.* Three- to six-inch strip of leather attached to a clip. We don't use these ourselves but occasionally recommend them to students to help control their dog off-leash.

- *String leash.* Three-foot piece of nylon string attached to a small clip. We use string leashes to help aid off-leash work.

- *Collars.* A buckle collar is our main choice for training. We use and recommend pinch or prong collars as needed for control. We seldom train with a slip collar (also known as a choke collar), though we may use one for showing in trials. Check your regulations for what type of collar may be used in the ring.

- *Jumps.* Needed for *Retrieve Over High Jump* (Open), *Broad Jump* (Open), and *Directed Jumping* (Utility).
  Generally speaking, you can train for a short time without owning jumps. We teach jumping early so if you are serious about training, get a set of jumps. We recommend a lightweight set of four-foot wide PVC jumps. These are portable and allow you to train away from home when you are teaching and proofing. If you don't want to buy jumps right away, you can make facsimiles using boards, bricks, and PVC piping. You will need a high jump, a broad jump, and a bar jump to train your dog for Open and Utility.

- *Dumbbells.* Needed for *Retrieve on Flat* (Open) and *Retrieve Over the High Jump* (Open).
  Dumbbells come in either plastic or wood and in a variety of shapes and sizes. Correct sizing is discussed in the *Retrieve* chapter.

- *Scent Articles.* Needed for *Scent Discrimination* (Utility).
  Scent articles are available in single bar, double bar, and triple bar. Quality varies widely, as does price. You will need a minimum of six leather and six metal articles. If you plan to show in Canada, you will also need a set of six wooden articles. We each own a minimum of two sets per dog or size of dog. Two sets are needed if you want a clean set for each trial of a double show weekend. Also, when proofing, we often put out more than one set.

- *Baby Gates.* Important for desensitizing dogs for *Heeling* and *Recalls* in Novice and Open, *Retrieves* and *Broad Jump* in Open, *Directed Jumping* and *Directed Retrieve* in Utility. Most serious obedience trainers own at least two ten-foot baby gates and three stanchions to support them. Many own a whole ring or at least two sides to replicate the ring in training. Gating is now available in wood or PVC. The PVC gates are free-standing and very convenient to use, and we highly recommend them.

- *Treats and Toys.* Available at various pet stores and grocery stores as well as specialty stores. You will need a variety of toys and food to train using our methods. Some dogs are happy throughout their obedience work with hot dogs and a tennis ball. Others need a variety of food and toys to maintain their interest.

  Examples of popular training toys include:
  - Balls.
  - Bumpers.
  - Frisbees.
  - All styles of squeaky toys.
  - All styles of tug toys.
  - Pieces of rubber hose (red radiator hose works well, as does clear tubing used for fish tanks).
  - Whatever your dog loves (be creative!).

Training treats include:

- Hot dogs.
- Cheese (string cheese works well).
- Roll-Over™.
- Oinkeroll™.
- Moist and Meaty™.
- Tender Chops™.
- Pup-Peroni™.
- Macaroni or other small pasta (cooked al dente).
- Small pieces of leftover chicken or other meat or soft snack food.

Some dogs will work happily for Cheerios™ or other dry cereal. It is important to find the special treat that keeps *your* dog motivated and interested, even in distracting places. It usually helps to use a variety of food in your training.

Use the smallest piece of food that motivates your dog. It should require little, if any, chewing.

Hardware or Discount Store Items

- *White work gloves.* For the Utility *Directed Retrieve.* They don't need to be completely white, just predominantly white, cotton work gloves. You need three for the ring, but extras are recommended for training. White gloves are also available through the obedience specialty catalogs. Most people with small dogs use smaller gloves.

- *Wire mesh* (also known as chicken wire). This has many uses, including keeping the dog away from a part of a jump, like the right corner of the broad jump, or backing the dog off on a front when he insists on coming in too tight.

- *Rubber mat* or *peg board.* For tying articles for scent work, if this is how you choose to teach articles.

- *Nylon light line.* Approximately twenty to thirty feet long and one-quarter to one-half inch diameter. It is used for distance control. Boating line works well.

- *Wood dowels.* Can be cut to any length and bought in any circumference. These are usually twenty to thirty inches long and three-eighths to one-half inch wide depending on the size of your dog. They are used as *heeling* aids or *front* and *finish* aids. They may also mark the drop spot on the *Drop on Recall* or keep the dog from moving forward on the *Signal Exercise.* Shorter lengths (six- to eight-inches) may be used for retrieving and go-outs.

- *Plastic gutters* cut into three or four foot lengths may also be helpful for the above work of marking the drop or making a chute for a *go-out.*

- *Athletic cones* similar to those used to mark soccer fields. These can be used as *Figure Eight* posts or as objects to weave around while heeling.

- *PVC piping.* Can be cut to size with a hacksaw and used with ninety-degree joints to make chutes. A white piece, with three-inch stripes of black electrical tape, makes an excellent jump stick.

- *Clothespins.* Teach the dog to touch one with his nose and you can use it in a variety of ways such as a *go-out* target. Clothespins can also be used for a lazy jumper who ticks the high jump (see *Jumping* chapter).

Miscellaneous Items

- *Metronome.* Available at music stores (ones that sell instruments). There are two types: pocket sized or wristwatch. Helps you develop rhythm during heeling.

- *Bait bag.* For holding training treats.

- *Small plastic containers with lids* (for jackpots).

- *Plastic lids of various sizes.* Used for *go-outs* and *marking.*

- *Hula-hoops.* For *Figure Eight* work and to teach a *sit* at a distance. Also used to help with your dumbbell aim.

- *Clicker.* Used as a conditioned reinforcer (see *Methods* chapter).

- *Ponytail holders and bells.* Use these on the front legs of dogs who shift their feet during *sit-stays.*

Methods

B efore we go into the mechanics of how we teach specific exercises, we want to discuss our general approach to training. The basic theories we use are fairly simple, but can seem overwhelming to a new trainer. When we first started training with these methods, there was very little written on them specifically for dog trainers. Fortunately for all of us, there are now a number of excellent books available that go into far more detail about reinforcement and training with food than we do here. You will find a list of recommended reading in Appendix B. Our intent is to give you an overview of how we apply these theories to our training. ***Please take the time to read and thoroughly understand this chapter before continuing to train your dog.*** Subsequent chapters will guide you through the application of these methods to the formal obedience exercises.

Getting Started

We approach any new exercise in basically the same way:

- Break the exercise into small parts. For a worried dog or one new to training, these parts may be quite tiny.

- Teach each part separately.

- Combine two parts when the dog understands the individual parts.

- Keep combining until you have an entire exercise.

- Vary which part of the whole exercise gets reinforced (positive and/or negative). Most dogs have weak areas and these may fluctuate depending on your focus in training.

- Pay attention to the *balance* of food and corrections.

Training with Food

We use a lot of food during our training sessions. Food helps hold the dog's attention. *The more attentive your dog, the faster his training progresses.* The proper use of food gives your dog clear information about what he is doing. It helps pinpoint his correct actions.

We try to use food that is nutritious and something different from his regular meal time fare (see *Equipment* chapter for suggestions).

Each piece you give should be as small as possible. You'll often want to give several pieces at a time and don't want to fill your dog up too soon. Overfeeding may also produce weight gain.

Food Delivery

You must teach your dog to take food gently. If he is lunging toward the food, you are probably moving your hand too fast or holding your hand too far away from his mouth. Hold the food firmly between your thumb and index finger, but don't give it to him unless he takes it gently. If he insists on trying to bite, say something like "Ouch!" Then let him try again. If he continues to bite, you may have to give him a bonk on the nose just after you say "Ouch." Usually the dog with the temperament to continue to "bite the hand that feeds him" can handle a few bonks! Don't do this with a timid puppy or you may create a hand-shy dog.

Practice holding several small treats and feed them to your dog one after the other. One large chunk of food that he can nibble, such as a whole hot dog, may also work well. The goal is to teach him to take food gently, even when the food is visible. This exercise also gives you the practice you need to handle the food smoothly.

Use the food like a magnet. If it gets too far from your dog's mouth, it loses its power. If you keep the food at mouth or nose level, he will follow it closely with his head and the rest of his body will follow.

Teach your dog to track the food smoothly. This means he should be able to follow your hand until it comes to a stop. He then gets to take the food. Initially, move the food slowly enough to allow him to keep up with it easily. As he catches on, move your hand faster. This helps speed up his responses. This food-following technique becomes more important later, particularly when introducing heeling and finishes.

Modeling

Modeling is a common method of dog training. Modeling is defined as placing your dog in the desired position and then praising. This technique works for many dogs, but we try to keep our hands off the dog as much as possible. Some dogs strongly object to being forced into position and will resist. Techniques such as targeting or luring (see *Levels of Food Use* later in this chapter) usually result in faster learning, although sometimes physical help is necessary to speed up initial learning. We use modeling most often when we introduce the *down.*

If you plan to add physical corrections later, some gentle physical guiding as the dog learns the exercise may help him understand the point of a correction later on.

Voice

Your voice is one of the most important forms of communication you have with your dog. People often overuse it and their dogs tune them out. It is important to remember that you must not talk in the ring during the exercises while the dog is working. During heeling, you may give a verbal cue each time the judge says "Forward," but that is all. The dog should trust silence. *Silence should mean "Keep it up, you are doing the right thing."*

Trainers sometimes get into the bad habit of talking to their dogs during training, particularly while heeling, to "jolly" the dog along. They then go into the ring and are silent, which often causes the dog to "shut down." He will appear stressed and may stop working. The dog sees the handler behaving differently and responds by slowing down, wandering off, or simply tuning out. One cure for this is to practice your heeling in a more silent and formal manner. This doesn't mean you can't play and be talkative when you release your dog! Nor does it mean that when the dog is first learning, you shouldn't talk to him.

Random, unexpected releases and reinforcements during training can carry you successfully through a ring performance. Remember that releasing is not the same as praising.

The tone of your voice is often more important than the words you use. You can say all sorts of terrible things in a "praising" voice and have your dog respond in a happy way. Most dogs respond well to high-pitched, excited talk, typically paying better attention and speeding up. Growling, low-pitched sounds often inhibit the dog and are more useful for communicating a correction.

You will notice that throughout teaching and training, we suggest that you command or tell your dog to do something. Do not *ask* your dog to perform. Use a soft voice and a commanding tone. Dogs gain confidence from being told what to do, not from being asked if they would like to do it.

Reinforcement Training

We all learn via reinforcement. A *reinforcer* is any stimulus that causes a behavior to occur more frequently (Fig. 4.1). There are positive and negative reinforcers. A positive reinforcer immediately *follows* a correct response, such as giving food to a dog right after he comes to you. A negative reinforcer *precedes* a response, such as a jerk on a leash that causes the dog to come. *If the timing of the reinforcer is poor, whether positive or negative, your results will not be what you desire.* For example, you are teaching your dog to sit. He sits and you dig around in your pocket for a treat. You finally produce one and give it to him, but by the time you do, he is standing instead of sitting. Instead of reinforcing a sit, you have just reinforced a stand.

A stimulus is truly a reinforcer only if it causes a behavior to happen more frequently. For most dogs, food is a successful and useful positive reinforcer, but if the dog doesn't like a particular treat, it won't work to reinforce his behaviors.

Some dogs work for any kind of food, even if they've just finished a meal. Others require a more careful selection of treats. Switching to a food that your dog likes better or training him when he is hungry will often dramatically improve his behavior.

Method	What it does	When it happens	Example
Positive Reinforcement: add something good	Increases behavior	After behavior	Praise dog while coming; give a treat when dog gets to you.
Negative Reinforcement: remove something bad	Increases behavior	Before behavior	Jerk on leash until dog begins moving in your direction.

Figure 4.1

Punishment Training

The technical meaning of a *punisher* is anything which *decreases* the frequency of an action (Fig. 4.2). Just as there are both positive and negative reinforcers, so there are also positive and negative punishers. Using a positive punisher means you are adding something unpleasant to decrease a behavior. A collar pop to stop barking is a common positive punisher. Using a negative punisher means you are taking away something desirable or removing privileges. An example is removing your dog's toy for growling during play. If the unwanted behavior is not decreasing, the punisher isn't working.

Method	What it does	When it happens	Example
Positive Punisher: add something bad	Decreases behavior	During behavior	Spray barking dog in face with water to interrupt barking.
Negative Punisher: remove something good	Decreases behavior	During behavior	Close curtains so dog can't see what is making him bark.

Figure 4.2

Corrections

We are convinced that adding corrections is a necessary part of building reliability for the ring, but adding them improperly can create a poor attitude in your dog. A correction is any adjustment, usually physical, which causes the action you desire. It can be something as gentle as folding the dog's back legs under him to help him sit, a small "pop" on the leash, or an ear pinch for the retrieve. *Corrections do not have to be severe and should always increase the quality of the desired action.* We do not add a correction to a command until we are 100% sure the dog understands the reason he is being corrected. The method we use for adding corrections is called "escape and avoidance."

Escape and Avoidance

This is the stage in training when your dog learns that he must obey a given command or face the consequence (a correction). You are conditioning respect into the cue. We do not begin this stage until we have taught the exercise with positive reinforcement.

In the *escape* phase, you give a command and then a correction before your dog has a chance to respond. He should respond to *escape* any further correction. He learns that there is a choice he can make. This is negative reinforcement. We also call this an *automatic correction. Do not correct if your dog responds immediately.*

It is essential that you precede any correction with a command.

In subsequent situations, your dog *avoids* the correction altogether by responding promptly. It is extremely important to reinforce his efforts. From this training, your dog learns he has control over his actions and can predict and understand yours. This builds trust.

As a rule, you should not give food during the escape phase. Immediately after a correction, you should verbally praise the dog for the desired behavior, but the use of food should be a clear signal to him that his performance is correct or improved. Instead of feeding after a correction, immediately give the dog another chance to do it right *without* a correction. This effort earns a treat. If you start with the mildest correction, followed immediately by lots of praise, most dogs learn how to handle the correction and do not lose confidence.

Types of Corrections

You must temper physical corrections to fit your dog's temperament and size. Sometimes changing collars can make a difference in your dog's response to your corrections. A change from a buckle to a pinch collar can make a radical difference in the dog's response.

When using a correction which is intended to motivate your dog to action (a negative reinforcer), start with a mild correction, like a light tug on a buckle collar. Increase the level of correction as necessary until you find the right level for your dog. Don't get into "nagging," which means using frequent, insignificant corrections that don't change the dog's performance.

When using a correction as a punisher to eliminate a behavior, start with a strong correction.

If your dog is not responding more frequently and correctly after you add a correction, the correction clearly is not working as a reinforcer. If he is responding even less frequently than before the correction, it is serving as a punisher.

Praise should immediately follow your correction. This is extremely important! *Do not make corrections in anger.* Cultivate a playful attitude about corrections: "Whoops, I gotcha! Let's try again." If you find your dog quits after a correction, help him or review the teaching steps.

A correction should motivate your dog to action, not shut him down. You should see a sharper focus, better attitude, and a decrease in response time.

It is more meaningful and infinitely more fair to give the dog a cue just prior to the correction. This cue can be either a verbal command or a hand signal. Silence in the trial ring should mean, "You are doing the right thing. Keep it up!" rather than "Look out, I may jerk your collar any time now!" Trainers often overlook this important point. By physically correcting your dog from silence, you teach him to mistrust silence.

Too many people get in the bad habit of "babbling" to their dog — keeping up a constant flow of words at the dog, whether cue words or verbal praise. While this is helpful when first lengthening the time and distance your dog can work, he comes to depend on this. He must be weaned off extra talking before showing. Don't depend on your voice to get a ring performance from your dog!

Conditioned Reinforcer

It is never too soon to start training your puppy or adult dog. The first goal is for your dog to "learn to learn." We begin our training by introducing a *conditioned reinforcer*. A conditioned reinforcer (CR) is simply a word or sound that begins as a neutral sound to the dog. We use it to pinpoint what we specifically like about what the dog is doing. The sound tells the dog he is right and signals that food is coming. Our favorite conditioned reinforcer is the word "*ready.*" We like to use *ready* as it is a word not generally used around the house and you can also carry it quite nicely into the ring where the judge asks you repeatedly "Are you ready?" The word "*yes*" is another excellent CR. Many people use the word "*good.*" This is fine as long as you don't dilute the meaning by frequent use in normal conversation.

Clickers are currently in vogue as a CR. A clicker is a small device that produces an audible "click" when you push it. This click is usually distinct, even in noisy environments. Some people can produce a click faster than they can say a word. Any tool which improves your timing will help your training. We have both used a clicker, although we are so accustomed to using a verbal CR that we tend to use the word more often. The two drawbacks to the clicker are that (a) it requires a free hand and (b) it must be totally eliminated before you show the dog. When training an exercise such as the retrieve, we hold the dumbbell in one hand and a handful of treats in the other. This doesn't leave a hand for the clicker. We prefer to use words for the following reasons:

- Words are portable and you don't lose them.
- You can use your word with a different tone of voice, depending on your dog's effort; neutral for the average effort or excited for better efforts.

A clicker may work better for some people or for some dogs. If your dog responds poorly to your voice or worries at the slightest change in the tone of your voice, using a clicker might be more efficient for you.

To introduce the CR, begin pairing the word *ready* (or the word or sound of your choice) with food. Several times a day, say *ready,* and give your dog a little piece of food. This causes the word *ready* to mean two things. At first, it means that food is coming. Later it will mean that what he is doing when he hears the word is desirable and food is coming.

*Use your conditioned reinforcer **before** you give a treat.* Use it before you move your hand towards your dog (Fig. 4.3). This is a critical point in using food which many trainers overlook. When you feed before the CR (conditioned reinforcer), you are reinforcing your dog for eating. Not much need for that!

Start with small successes and build on them. Try to find some action to reinforce at least every five to ten seconds. For example, you have decided you want to teach your dog to sit using a conditioned reinforcer. The bouncy, enthusiastic dog or puppy is the perfect candidate for the "*waiting game.*" Stand quietly with your dog on a leash and have a handful of treats. Most dogs with any interest in food will try to figure out how to get it. Pay close attention to the dog's actions. Often, he will jump on you, paw you, and nudge the hand with the treats. Quite often, he will also sit. As soon as his bottom hits the floor, use your conditioned reinforcer. Your CR helps the dog pinpoint what is pleasing you. After you have used the CR, give the dog a treat. Let the dog get up. Wait for another sit. Repeat the above steps.

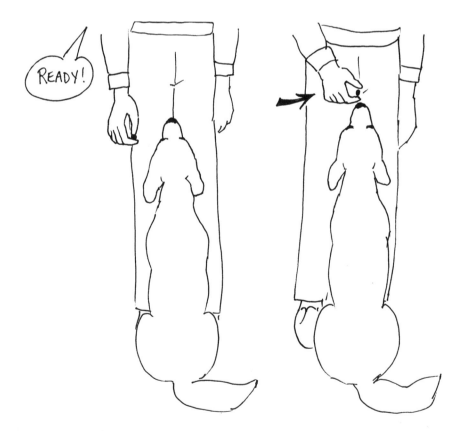

Figure 4.3 Use your conditioned reinforcer before you give a treat. Use it before you move your hand towards your dog.

As the dog figures out the game, you will see an increase in the frequency of the sits, as well as a decrease in other actions. This shows that your food is serving as a positive reinforcer for sit (i.e., the dog sits more often when you use food). Most dogs continue to push for more food by offering either the correct behavior or what they perceive to be the correct behavior.

Levels of Food Use

We use four levels of food as a reward. The way the food is used and the level used at any given time depends on the exercise being taught and where your dog is in his learning progression. The following is the approximate order in which we use food in our training.

- *Guiding* or *Luring:* The food is in sight to guide the dog into position. The dog gets the food for a correct response.

- *Constant Reinforcement or Singles:* The food is out of sight (hidden in your hand), but you reinforce the dog (you use your conditioned reinforcer and give a piece of food) for each correct response

- *Variable or Random Reinforcement — Doubles, Triples, and more:* The dog does two, three, or more correct responses before getting a treat. Use your conditioned reinforcer each time the dog offers the desired response and feed after two, three or more responses. You may also wait before giving any CR or food to the dog until after the series of repetitions. In other words, he must do two or more repetitions with no feedback from you. This is how the dog gains an understanding of the task. It helps him learn to try again, instead of giving up because no food came immediately from the treat dispenser (you). When the dog quickly does the behavior again, you can almost see the wheels turning in his head. You can see him working to figure out what is getting you to feed him. Be patient. Wait to see if he will offer an action for you to reinforce.

- *Selective Reinforcement:* You reinforce the dog only for the *best* performances of the task. This is an excellent time to use *jackpots*, discussed later in this chapter.

When you begin to require *doubles* and *triples*, mix in *singles* as well. Once you start to vary the reinforcement, you will see a wider range of responses from the dog. He will use your response to his actions to define the exercise. The following are examples of incorrect behavior seen when teaching *sit* this way:

The dog:

- Stands and stares.
- Barks.
- Jumps on you.
- Nudges you with his nose.
- Slaps you with his paw.
- Sniffs the floor briefly.

Sometimes these are signs of frustration, but they usually mean he wants to keep playing the game. Try to ignore these extra responses and wait for something closer to your goal behavior. If your dog has to wait too long between reinforcements, he may give up and do something he finds reinforcing. Wandering off to sniff the floor is common. If this happens often, relax your standards of what is immediately acceptable. Reinforce anything that resembles your goal behavior, sometimes backing up two or more steps in the process. This should jump-start the dog back to work.

If waiting him out isn't getting the desired response, do something to produce an action you can reinforce. You might:

- Use a food lure to guide the dog into position.
- Make a hand motion.
- Physically position the dog.

You may have assumed that your dog understood better than he really did. *Dogs are very honest about telling you what they do or do not know.*

Changing Levels

When teaching, it is important to move away from singles (constant reinforcement) as soon as the dog shows an understanding of the word and action. This may be in as little as one session or as long as a week or more. The sooner the dog learns that food will not always be there for every try, the sooner you can move to selective reinforcement. When you first start withholding food, reinforce about half your dog's responses. Some responses are going to be a bit slower than others. Don't reinforce the slower ones. Repeat and reinforce when the dog tries harder. Gradually go to a random schedule by reducing this ratio to one out of four or more. Pay close attention to which responses more closely resemble your goal. Become increasingly more selective about which efforts you reinforce with food. Suppose your dog sits, but more slowly than you would like. Use your CR, but don't feed. This gives the dog valuable information by telling him he is correct, but not quite as correct as you would like him to be.

Dogs trained this way become confident early in their training. They are usually willing to try harder. They also learn that making mistakes is okay, and that you will help them when they need it.

Initially, your conditioned reinforcer must occur within a split second of the desired behavior. The dog needs immediate feedback for confidence (i.e., he is right!). The food should follow within a couple of seconds. When you go to a random schedule, the CR should immediately follow the correct behavior, but you might not give food each time.

Jackpots

The term *jackpot* means a positive reinforcer that is much larger than usual, and one that comes as a surprise to your dog. We recommend that you use jackpots in this fashion: reserve a small portion of your dog's normal meal (1/4 to 1/2 of the meal, depending on the dog), and put it in a small, covered, plastic container, sometimes with a small portion of leftovers or canned dog or cat food. Use a container that you can tuck into a pocket or the waistband of your pants. We sometimes split the jackpot into two or three smaller portions. When your dog performs an exercise which is particularly hard for him to the best of his current ability, give him the whole jackpot! You might even pair a word with it (we use JACKPOT). We have used jackpots with almost all of the obedience exercises. We have found that our dogs get very energized after a jackpot, often performing subsequent exercises far better than normal. After jackpotting in practice sessions, including at fun matches, over the course of a number of weeks, we have found that it carries over to the obedience trial ring, and helps motivate the dog through an entire routine. When we return to the crate after showing successfully, the dog gets a jackpot.

We also use a less-formal jackpot when teaching a new exercise. When the dog makes a sudden and large improvement in performance, we give a handful of treats rather than just one. This often helps the dog clarify his understanding of the exercise and he may perform more consistently at this new level.

Adding Cues

We use cues to tell the dog what he should do. Cues can be verbal commands, hand signals, or body posture. Most people add cues too soon. We teach an exercise with food before we add a cue. Dogs are action oriented, while people are word oriented. Many beginning trainers repeat (and repeat and repeat) a verbal cue to the dog during initial training of an exercise. The dog tunes out the cue as unneeded noise. Listen to what you are saying to your dog. **Wait to add the cue until just before you think he will respond.** This prevents dilution of the cue.

When you get to the ring, the dog must respond to your first cue. He must also wait for you to give the cue. When you see the dog responding to your cue regularly in training, vary how often you give the cue. Don't reinforce any responses which happen without a cue.

Emotional Balance

It is important to find the right balance of positive and negative rein-forcement in training. Each dog requires a slightly different application. We refer to this type of balance as *emotional balance.* Negative reinforcement helps ensure a prompt response to your first command as required in the obedience ring. Positive reinforcement helps the dog perform in an animated, yet relaxed manner. We believe both types of reinforcement are important, although the obedience regulations place the importance on prompt response. Without this, all the animation in the world doesn't get you a passing score. And a passing score **is** the first requirement.

Recognizing Stress

It is important for you to be able to read your dog's stress level during training. Observe his ears, eyes, and general body posture. Yawning, licking his lips, avoiding eye contact, or at worst, trembling, are all ways that dogs show stress. A dog who is stressed leaves sweaty paw prints on the floor. He pants excessively and looks worried.

A dog who is overly stressed may work slowly and in an inhibited way. He may freeze up completely or run away from the situation. Other dogs "stress up" and get hyperactive when stressed. This is not the type of performance we are working towards! Generally, we want to greatly reduce stress before attempting to teach him anything. If the fear is due to a scary noise in the environment, you may need to move your dog farther away from the noise, gradually habituating him to it. You can speed this process along by using your CR and food just after the noise. This method is called *counter conditioning* and is a valuable tool when training a "stressy" dog. Your dog will eventually associate the scary sound with food, which should cause him to relax rather than worry.

Balance Points

Each of the exercises you perform in a trial ring is composed of many pieces. We refer to these parts as *balance points*. For example, the Novice *Recall* has the following points:

- Set up in heel position.
- Wait.
- Come.
- Sit in front.
- Finish, moving from front position to heel position.

You must teach each of the parts individually before expecting the dog to do two or more together. The more complex the final goal, the more separate balance points there are. If one point gets out of balance, the dog typically either anticipates or fails to perform on the first command. Anticipation usually means you have reinforced that particular balance point too much. Reinforce the previous balance point more often. Failure to perform on the first command sometimes means that you have reinforced the previous point too often. It might also mean that the dog doesn't really understand what to do. Reinforce the failed part more often.

For a complete listing of the *balance points* for all AKC exercises, see Appendix A

Training Frequency and Repetitions

How often should you train? How many repetitions should you do before moving on to another exercise? Each dog differs, so you must listen to what your dog is telling you. Think about the following:

❑ **Energy level**

- Does your dog need a lot of physical exercise every day? If so, you should be able to train with more repetitions and longer sessions. This type of dog thrives on daily training sessions.
- Is he a couch potato? You must keep the sessions short, with fewer repetitions. Spending every other day physically exercising a lazy, hard-to-motivate dog, instead of skill training will keep the training sessions fresher and more interesting.

❏ Physical conditioning

- Does your dog tire quickly? Do you spend time conditioning him aerobically apart from obedience training? This can be trotting with you while you run, bike, or roller blade, or jumping multiple jumps. Swimming is excellent exercise. Play retrieving is helpful for conditioning the dog for the short bursts of speed needed in the ring. The medium to large dog usually requires more than a brisk walk to gain proper conditioning.

❏ Age

- Many puppies can only work for short amounts of time (e.g., 5 minutes) so do several brief training sessions rather than one long one. Older, more experienced dogs can work for much longer periods, from 15 to 60 minutes.

❏ Attention span

- This is not solely dependent on your dog's age, but also on his level of conditioning. Sometimes an unaltered adolescent dog's attention span shrinks during this difficult age.

❏ Stage of growth

- A puppy may go through awkward growth stages which make performing even a simple *sit* or *down* difficult. Wait for these stages to pass rather than trying to train through them.

❏ Weight

- Is your dog too fat? Many dogs are. A fat dog is much less enthusiastic about training for food than one who is kept lean and physically fit. *You should not ask a fat dog to jump.*

Try doing six to twelve repetitions of a given exercise before moving on to the next one. The dog will tell you when you are doing too many repetitions because his desire fades. Stop before this happens. A release and play break part way through the repetitions may help keep his enthusiasm high. A beginning dog requires far more breaks than an experienced one.

An important rule of thumb is to train one thing at a time, as much as possible. If too much time passes between each repetition of a given exercise, you lose continuity. We commonly see beginning trainers make this mistake. For example, we describe how to train a variety of movements in the *Power Steering* chapter. Many of these movements require that the dog start in a certain position, often sitting or standing in heel position at the handler's left side. (See the *Heeling* chapter for a complete description of heel position). Because the beginner spends an inordinate amount of time getting the dog into the starting position, doing six repetitions can take a long time. A more experienced trainer helps the dog get into the desired starting position, quickly adjusts her position to the dog's, and gets on with the exercise she is training. She does not expect the dog to do all the positioning himself. This allows more repetitions of the exercise in a shorter period of time. Keep in mind the part you are working to improve and concentrate on training that piece only.

Proofing

Proofing is defined as increasing the difficulty of an exercise to determine a dog's weaknesses in that exercise. It is a way to help your dog define the parameters of an exercise. It is used and explained in each chapter as the exercises progress. Proofing is an important part of preparing your dog for the trial ring and should be considered absolutely necessary before showing.

We do not carry proofing to an extreme and we use much harder proofing with an advanced dog than a beginner. We *expect* the dog to make mistakes when we introduce proofing. Since we expect these mistakes, we are ready to help the dog be right, usually with a quiet verbal reminder or gentle physical help.

Chaining

A long string of behaviors, which follow one after the other, is called a *behavior chain*. Each successive step in a behavior chain reinforces the previous step.

An example from obedience is the *Retrieve Over the High Jump*. On your command to JUMP, your dog jumps the jump, picks up his dumbbell, jumps back over the jump, and sits in front of you, holding his dumbbell until you take it.

Before a behavior chain is possible, your dog must understand how to perform each of the individual pieces, or links, in the chain. You then begin to put two or more parts of an exercise or two or more exercises together. In the above example, your dog must know how to set up for the *Retrieve Over the High Jump,* respond to the JUMP command, jump the jump without errors, pick up the dumbbell quickly and without fumbling, return over the jump, and sit in front holding the dumbbell without mouthing. Each of these links must be trained separately before putting two or more of them together. You should practice using food delay with two links as soon as the dog shows a clear understanding of what you are asking of him.

Backward Chaining

If you build a behavior chain by training the final segment first, then the final two segments, continuing backwards, you are *backward chaining.* You work from the less known to the better known, and this gives your dog more confidence as he works further into the chain. For our earlier example of the *Retrieve Over the High Jump,* begin by training the final segment first — the *sit in front and hold* — followed by the *carry over the jump,* to the *sit in front and hold.* Next, add the *pickup* of the dumbbell so your dog picks up his dumbbell, jumps the jump, and sits in front and holds. Keep adding earlier links until you have completed the chain.

Backward chaining is valuable when training the more complicated exercises, such as the Utility *Signal Exercise,* and when putting together an entire ring routine. It is discussed further in the *Signals* chapter and *Are You Ready?*

In this chapter, we have attempted to give you an overview of what our training methods entail. We have tried to remind you how to use your voice, food and most importantly, the conditioned reinforcer or CR. We hope that by applying these methods, your training will be easier and more fun. We wish you good luck!

Puppies

When buying a puppy or dog, you should consider two things. The first is which breed or breeds you like. The second is what type of work you want the dog to perform. For obedience competition, the so-called obedience breeds — Golden Retrievers, Border Collies, Australian Shepherds, Shetland Sheepdogs, Poodles, Doberman Pinschers, etc. — are very popular.

Still, many people who are interested in obedience competition want a different breed from these popular ones. We believe that you can train a dog of almost any breed to be competitive, providing you carefully choose the breeder, the dog, and the training program.

The right breeder is not necessarily one whose dogs have obedience titles in their background, but someone who is sympathetic to your needs and who breeds dogs with a strong work ethic. Owners prove this work ethic by earning titles in such areas as hunting and field work, herding, lure coursing, earth dog trials, and tracking. Your job will be to channel this work ethic into the area of competition obedience.

Within every breed, there are examples of successful dogs and duds. You should choose from a successful line and if you are serious about obedience competition, choose a puppy with strong food, play, and chase drives, as well as good social attraction to humans.

The puppy who will do well in obedience is the same type who will do well in the breed ring. He has a "winning" attitude. We also like a dog who looks as if he could be a champion, even if we never earn that title with him. The puppy or dog should be highly motivated by food and toys. He should retrieve or at least show an interest in an object tossed nearby. Even the most independent breeds have individuals who fit this bill. An independent, uninterested puppy will usually not make a good competition obedience dog without a *lot* of extra work. The puppy should follow his owner with very little encouragement and not be afraid of loud noises or walking on different surfaces. *The most desirable characteristic is confidence.* Caution is okay, but fear is not! Temperament characteristics are usually present in a puppy at seven weeks and they will not change a lot with training. The breeder can be of real benefit by exposing the puppy to loud sounds, different footing, and frequent handling.

Judy's Whippet puppy, Clark, was very independent when he was three months old. Judy took the advice of a good friend and excellent trainer, Margie English, and tied Clark to her during the day with a six-foot leash. Clark had to be interested in Judy or at least follow her around all day. Judy found this method worked well with this pup. He is now confident and very bonded to her. He takes all new situations in stride and is a secure, happy dog.

Choosing Your Breeder

The choice of a breeder is a vital first step in the process of selecting a puppy. Look for a breeder who provides a written guarantee against genetic health defects for the life of the puppies she breeds. Reputable breeders should require you to return any puppy or dog to them if you decide, for any reason, that you cannot keep him.

A puppy raised in a clean home or kennel is likely to be easier to housebreak. The puppy should already have had his first shots and be free of worms before leaving the breeder.

Our puppies have ranged in age from seven weeks to nine months when they joined our families. Sometimes, we have visited a puppy and his littermates many times before taking him home. Other times, there have been few visits. Some of our puppies have been picked for us by the breeder, other puppies have literally picked us.

Puppy Goals

Our main goals in the first few months after a new puppy comes home are to teach him:

- To be quiet and relaxed in his crate.
- Where he should and should not eliminate.
- To learn how to learn.
- To tolerate and enjoy grooming and being handled from head to toe.
- The rules for playtime.
- What he can and cannot chew or bite.
- What a leash is for.
- That other people, puppies, and dogs are nice to be around.

Puppies have an amazing capacity to learn. Even if you aren't consciously teaching your puppy something, he is learning at a rapid rate. If you don't guide him, he can learn a lot of bad habits, such as house soiling, obnoxious barking, biting, digging, and object stealing. Many people still think you can't start training a puppy until he is six months old. If you wait until your puppy is that old, you have wasted valuable training time. So, let's get started!

Crate Training

A crate is a plastic or metal box with a door. We use them to confine our dogs as puppies, to keep them safe, and as an aid in housebreaking. We crate our dogs in the car for safety. Usually, we have two crates set up at home; one in the living area and one in the bedroom. The puppy will spend much of his early life in a crate, and most puppies are happier when they can see their owners. The crate will eventually be his resting place at obedience trials and dog shows, so he should learn to be quiet and relaxed in one early in his training.

The crate should be just big enough for your puppy to stand up, turn around, and lie down. If it's any larger, he can eliminate at one end and sleep at the other. This would defeat one purpose of a crate, which is to teach your pup to keep his living and sleeping area clean.

Confinement helps keep your puppy from chewing on items such as electrical wires, carpeting, house plants, sofas, and curtains, any one of which could hurt or kill him. Although we prefer to rent or borrow a smaller-sized crate, you can save money by buying one crate in the size you will need for the full grown dog and block off part of it with cement blocks. As he grows, simply enlarge the living area.

Only put items in the crate that may be safely eaten or chewed. What is in the crate belongs to the puppy! Remember that bedding or papers can make sleeping in a wet crate comfy, so sometimes the pup may need to sleep on the bare metal pan to discourage eliminating in his crate.

Many puppies are very vocal when first confined to a crate. They may bark, whine, howl, or scream — not a fun experience! They must learn to be quiet. Here are some general suggestions to help you with the crate-training process:

- Feed him his meals in the crate. Start by leaving the door open and progress to shutting it for brief periods.

- Toss treats or special toys in the crate that he can discover for himself. Kongs™ or hollow bones, filled with a little cheese or peanut butter, are generally well-received!

- Do *not* let him out when he is noisy. An exception is made for quiet whining when he has just awakened; this usually means he needs to go outside to eliminate.

- A spray bottle with water in it can be used to spray a noisy puppy after a stern QUIET! command.

- Banging on the side or top of the crate, if the water doesn't work, is sometimes warranted.

- Though some puppies like the taste, lemon juice squirted in his mouth will often quiet a noisy puppy. You should open the crate door when doing this to avoid spraying the pup in the eyes.

- Crate him for short periods when you are home.

Do not crate him 20+ hours a day! While the crate is a useful tool, overuse borders on abuse. Understimulated and underexercised puppies can get into mischief. Keep yours busy with obedience training!

Housebreaking and Feeding

Your puppy's toilet habits will totally consume your time for the first few weeks he lives with you. If you are starting with a seven or eight week old puppy, that time may be much longer than a few weeks. Your puppy will probably need to eliminate any time he wakes up, right after he has eaten, and right after confinement. For some puppies, it is as often as every ten to fifteen minutes! This is probably the most important training you will do during the first few weeks that you have your new pup at home. To have a "clean" dog for the 12 to 14 years that he will live with you, it is well worth it.

Think about housebreaking from your puppy's point of view. Any time he relieves himself, this elimination is reinforced because the uncomfortable feeling of a full bladder or bowels goes away. He gets similar reinforcement whether he eliminates in grass or on carpet. You must give him frequent opportunities to eliminate *where you want him to* — *outside*. It is usually easier to housebreak a puppy in the summer, as it is quicker to dash out the door when you don't have to put on boots, coat, hat, and gloves.

Put a leash on your pup, carry him outside, and set him down in the area where you want him to eliminate. If you don't carry him outside, he may eliminate on the floor as you are struggling to get him outside. We teach him to eliminate while on a leash because we plan to travel away from home and want this type of control. We have heard of dogs who were so convinced that they could *only* eliminate in their own yard, off lead, that they would "hold it" for an entire weekend — not particularly good for their health! Help your puppy generalize this by taking him to several different areas outside, in addition to your yard, where he may eliminate. Be sure to carry a plastic bag for cleanup!

Use a unique word or phrase as a command for your puppy to eliminate. Words such as GO POTTY and HURRY UP are examples. Judy introduces a signal to this exercise, which is pointing the right index finger toward the ground. This is the puppy's first hand signal as well as his first words. In the beginning, outside is for elimination only; playing occurs inside. When he does eliminate outside, praise profusely and give a tidbit of food.

Confine your pup in his crate when you are unable to keep your full attention on him. This helps prevent mischief and accidents. If you witness an accident, say NO! in a loud, stern voice and carry him outside. Stay with him to see if he completes the deed, praise him if he does, and put him in his crate while you clean up. *Do not* let him see you clean up the spot and *do not* hit him! **Housebreaking is best achieved by preventing accidents rather than punishing.** Most puppies only remember for a few seconds after doing anything (good or bad), so punishing after the fact does no good. You must catch him in the act of eliminating in the wrong place and interrupt it with your NO! to get the message across.

At night, have your pup's crate beside your bed so that when he cries, you can get up and take him outside immediately. Say only your potty and praise words. Do not talk, play, or entertain him in any way. He must understand that night time is for quiet and not for play.

If you work away from your home, it is more difficult, but not impossible, to housebreak your puppy. If you cannot get home during the day, you will need to have someone come at midday to feed and potty your puppy until he is four to six months old. Young puppies cannot go all day without eliminating and having a midday meal. If there is no one to let your puppy out during the day, you will probably have to set up an exercise pen with a bed at one end and papers on which he can eliminate at the other. We do not like using the house for a bathroom, but there are circumstances where it can't be helped. You may also want to leave some dry food for the puppy for a midday meal. If you must be away from home for long hours, with no one to help you at midday, you may want to consider buying a well-socialized older puppy.

We feed young puppies — those less than four months old — three times a day. We feed a measured amount at each meal and stay with the puppy while he eats. What isn't gone in ten minutes is either thrown out or saved for the next meal. Take your pup outside immediately after a meal, as eating stimulates the elimination process. We don't feed "free choice" mainly because we each have more than one dog. We feed our older puppies and adults twice a day and regulate the amount, according to how much food we are using in training with that particular dog.

How much should your puppy eat? It depends on what kind of food you are feeding him, his breed, his age and his activity level. Let your dog's actual weight be your guide. A fit adult dog's ribs should not be buried under a thick layer of fat. He should have a waistline and his backbone, as well as his ribs, should be easily felt when you run your hands down his back or sides.

Any time you switch to a new food, gradually mix more of the new food with the old. We generally switch a puppy to adult food between four and ten months. Check with your breeder and veterinarian for guidance. Many owners of some larger breeds feed adult food from the beginning. This is thought to help slow the growth of the puppy and seems to be beneficial in preventing some later bone and joint problems.

Early Training

Training starts the day you bring your puppy home. The time to play, train, or groom is after your pup has eliminated. We suggest that you do only one of these activities per session. All of his time out of the crate should be directed by and focused on you. This is a very important part of the bonding process. While Adele does allow contact with her other dogs at this time, Judy restricts the time her pup interacts with other dogs in the household. She believes this is the time for him to bond to her, not to other dogs.

Judy has found this to be especially important with her Whippet, Clark. Although he loves all humans he met, his preference was for other dogs and in particular his Whippet "brother," Alec. He played with Alec a few times a day and, as he matured and learned, he got used to being called away from play to receive reinforcement from Judy. He learned that his first duty was to her, and when that was fulfilled, he could play. Many dogs never have a problem adapting to people after being allowed to socialize with other dogs. It is important for you to decide how your particular puppy needs to be trained. If he ignores you when other dogs or puppies are around, restrict his social contacts until he bonds to you.

Your puppy should get used to being playfully batted around with your hands and feet. There may be a time in later training when you will want to use your hands and/or feet for minor adjustments. He should not be afraid. You can either attach a leather shoelace to his collar or play tug with it. This can simulate the later use of a leash. To get a little tug reaction, let him see it move over and around him.

Grooming and Handling

After your pup has been outside and eliminated successfully, bring him inside and begin his grooming sessions. Sit on the floor and start to gently handle him. Think of all the ways he will be handled and groomed as an adult. Pay special attention to his feet and muzzle. He should allow you to examine his teeth and to clip one or two toenails each day. Have a supply of treats handy, and give them to him for his acceptance of your handling. Teach him to have his coat brushed, ears cleaned, teeth brushed, and if he is a breed that requires trimming or clipping, get him used to the required equipment during these sessions. Even if your puppy is not destined for the breed ring, you will want to present a well-groomed partner to the obedience judge.

Begin to get him used to being stroked all over, as he will have to accept at least two different exams in the obedience ring. Work with him using a ruler or a dowel held against his side in preparation for possible measurement in the ring (Fig. 5.1). Start by letting him sniff the dowel, using your CR and food when he is brave. Gradually, move the dowel or

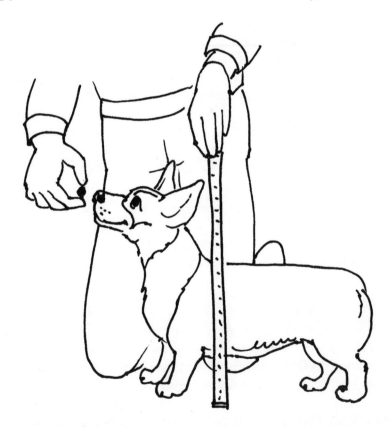

Figure 5.1 Accustom your puppy to a ruler held against his side in preparation for possible measurement in the ring.

ruler closer to his side, reinforcing with your CR and food his confident acceptance. Do everything slowly and gently, gradually building his confidence for these new activities.

Name Attention

You are allowed to use your dog's name before most verbal commands in the obedience ring. If your dog looks at you when he hears his name, he is much more likely to obey the command that follows. To teach *name attention*, say your puppy's name, and reinforce him with food the instant he looks at you. Practice this in a variety of places.

Judy doesn't always use her dog's name in the ring. When she teaches the command words, she does not use the dog's name. In the ring, if there is a need for extra attention, she uses it where permitted. Adele often uses the name before moving commands. Neither of us use it when giving STAY or WAIT commands.

Leash Training

Use a plain buckle collar. An adjustable nylon one works well since puppies grow fast. Attach a cheap leash or a short piece of rope to the collar and let the puppy drag it during play for a few days. Make sure you are always on hand to supervise these play periods, as you don't want your pup to get tangled. He should learn now that dragging a leash is okay. This is an important lesson for later training. In a few days, pick up the leash and begin to walk where he wants to walk; follow him. If you encourage him with food, he should willingly go with you. Do not force him to walk with you. Lower your expectations and concentrate more on encouraging him.

We frequently walk a puppy on a retractable leash. It does not tangle in his legs as easily as a regular leash and gives him a little constant pressure on the collar. Both the retractability and the tension will be used in later training.

On the Road

Sometime during his first week in your house, you should take your pup to your veterinarian's office. Take him in, let anyone who is there feed him and play with him, and then take him home. A few days later, take him again, and let your vet examine him and perhaps give him a treat. No shots are given at this visit. These visits are establishing a pleasant memory for your pup, who will have to go there many times in his life when it may not be so pleasant. We take our puppies everywhere we can during the first few weeks to get them used to new experiences. Hardware stores, pet food supermarkets, most kinds of dry goods stores, and strip malls will usually allow dogs. Your puppy should not meet any groups of dogs until his inoculations are at a level agreed upon by you and your veterinarian. These early trips and positive associations with other people help your puppy adjust to the outside world. Ideally, he should meet most life situations by the time he is 14 weeks old. Socialization does not stop at this age; it continues throughout life, but it is very important to concentrate on early socialization. *As with most training, the first impression is the one which will stay with your dog for his lifetime.*

During this early socializing period, he should ride in the car and learn that it is fun. If he is a little car sick at first, drive him to the corner and back, then feed him a dry biscuit. If he continues to be nervous about the car, just put him in the car, start the engine, turn the engine off, take him out, and give him a treat. He will soon learn to associate car rides with eating and enjoyable outings. Our dogs ride in crates in the car. This keeps them out of trouble and helps prevent accidents caused by a rambunctious, exploring dog. It is also much safer for them in case of an accident. If your car isn't large enough to hold a crate, consider buying one of the seatbelt type harnesses for your dog.

Play Retrieving

Start your puppy play retrieving as soon as he shows interest in carrying an object. If he's stealing everything in sight, use it to your advantage! Have two toys. Throw one a short distance. When he brings it back, throw the other. If he doesn't bring it back, but runs off to chew it or play by himself, make a big fuss with the toy you are holding: wiggle it along the floor, squeak it if it squeaks, and tease him with it. This should all be done close to you while you are sitting on the floor. If all your teasing doesn't get him to play with you, keep a leash attached and reel him in gently, praising the entire time.

Make a fuss over your pup before taking one toy and tossing the other. When he is little, always exchange one toy for another or for food. Sometimes let him win the game by keeping the toy for a bit. This can help bolster his self confidence. To end the game, slip him a piece of food when you take the toy away for the last time. One of the retrieve toys we introduce at this point is a metal article. A bent spoon works well if you don't have any "real" scent articles yet (see *Equipment* chapter). It accustoms your pup to carrying metal in his mouth. We also use a piece of cloth like a washcloth or a garden glove. This is to get him used to all the types of materials that he will have to carry in the obedience exercises.

Play a little tug-of-war. Let him win this game as well. Because he is getting new teeth between four and six months, be careful with the tug game, as you may accidentally help him shed his teeth prematurely. During these play games, you must teach him that biting flesh is not acceptable. NO BITE!, NO TEETH!, or OUCH! is the command and he must learn this early. If he does not respect your verbal command, this may be the time to use a little force to get the point across quickly. Squeeze his muzzle until he squeaks as you use the command. When he stops his mouthing, praise profusely, give him a treat, and substitute something he is allowed to chew on. Don't continue in a negative vein. If he continues to want to bite, "change the subject." Maybe it is time for a nap or another trip outside. Tired puppies or puppies who have to eliminate will often start biting more than usual. Remember, the attention span in young pups is only about five minutes.

New Surfaces

During this early puppy training period, you should expose your puppy to the many surfaces upon which he may walk as an adult: grass, rubber matting, linoleum, concrete, carpet. Do this slowly and with food, never forcing him through any area where he seems unsure.

We also introduce stairs about this time. If you don't have stairs in your home, try to find some on which to practice since your pup will surely have to navigate them in his lifetime. One of Java's early exposures to stairs was at a hotel, where he had to go up and down multiple times a day. He was nine months old at the time.

To teach your puppy to go up a staircase, start by putting him on the second step from the top, while you stand below and behind him. Place a bit of food on the top step and let him scamper up to get the food. Try it with two steps, then three, and so on. To teach him to go down, do the same at the bottom of the steps. Go to the bottom, put the pup up one step, and call him down to you using food. Progress to two steps when he appears confident. **If your puppy shows any reluctance, practice patience in your training; do not force any behaviors.** Figure out what makes your pup want to do the task you have asked of him. Usually the right type of food will work wonders. Follow this up with pats and hugs. Adele's Treasure and Java were both well over six months old before they would negotiate her basement steps, so don't worry if your puppy takes a while to do so.

Going to School

As soon as your pup has finished his series of inoculations, he should go to school. Choose a puppy kindergarten class, conformation class, or both. Conformation class can be a marvelous way to socialize and train a puppy. There are other dogs, people to examine him, and food! Just make sure the instructor is gentle and doesn't expect a lot of obedience from your pup.

The puppy kindergarten class should be *motivational* and should allow you some freedom to work with your pup as you see fit. The class should encourage bonding and attention to you, as well as socialization with puppies and people. Above all, puppy class should be fun!

When done carefully, off-leash playtime in puppy class can be very beneficial, especially for the more retiring puppy. Handled poorly, free play produces puppies who ignore their owners or are afraid of more dominant puppies. The play school type of atmosphere can deteriorate quickly into a free-for-all or bigger pups picking on smaller ones. Adele teaches a recall-from-playtime, with a treat and a return to play as a reward for a quick response to the COME command (see *Fundamental Words* chapter). Puppies who are too slow go back on leash to prevent the slow or non-response.

Before enrolling in any obedience class, visit the school and observe the training methods. Talk to the students, observe the behavior of the dogs and, of course, talk to the instructor(s). You should look for an instructor who has had success with many breeds, either his or her own dogs, and/or dogs in the school. You should look for students who seem genuinely pleased to be there — people *and* dogs! You should visit local obedience trials or matches and see how the instructor's students handle their dogs both in and out of the ring and how the dogs respond to their owners. If the dogs seem unhappy, the people yell at their dogs, or the instructor doesn't believe in food, find another instructor. If the instructor has had success using his/her methods, and you like the way the instructor handles the dogs and the trainers, sign up!

This is the time you need to develop your own training philosophy. What will you accept in training as far as food use or corrections? We believe that some *compulsion*, or force, *is* needed during training. You need to consider when and where or *if* you will use it. We call this *BALANCED TRAINING*. We constantly seek the right balance of positive and negative motivation. This is what our training methods address.

Fun Matches

In addition to classes, we recommend taking your pup to practice matches. The first time you go to one, let him walk around and get used to the environment. Don't sign up just yet. You are trying to form a positive association with dog shows and do not want any adverse circumstances to occur if you can avoid it. Walk him around the grounds, do a little training if you feel he is relaxed, and let other people pet and feed him. These activities tell your puppy that this is a marvelous place to be.

When he has been to a match or two and you are sure he is relaxed, enter him in conformation in the age class for his breed. Conformation is the "beauty" portion of a dog show. Feed him, have a good time, and let the judge examine him. You are not there to win, but to teach and socialize your puppy and learn what makes either of you nervous and what helps you both relax. If you have fun and relax, so will he.

Some have even suggested taking puppies into the obedience ring at fun matches and show and go's and luring the puppy through a short obedience routine. A word of caution from Judy: she realized too late that working Alec in a match, even with food in sight, was still too stressful. In the future, she will go into the ring, play a bit, and leave. This gets the dog used to the ring with absolutely no demands made on him until he is entirely comfortable. Some dogs need more of this than others. If your dog seems stressed or nervous, he is the type of dog who requires a good deal more play time in a new environment than one who takes everything in stride. Keep this in mind for the entire career of your dog.

In our opinion, matches are for training, learning, and proofing. Enter for practice so you don't get caught up in the competition. You want to help your puppy learn to love the environment and if you are worrying about winning, this will not happen. He takes his cues from you. First and foremost, this is a sport and it's supposed to be *fun*!

Fundamental Words

I n this chapter, we introduce the basic vocabulary necessary for all competition obedience exercises. We teach these words with the dog up close, within three feet of us. These words give you control of every exercise that you will eventually teach your dog for competition obedience. Although we prefer certain words to cue certain actions, you may choose any words you like, as long as you are consistent in their usage. We recommend that you select words which sound different from one another.

These fundamental words are the foundation for *all* of your obedience work. They will give your dog the confidence to move in any direction, as well as to understand why he is right or wrong. Study these words well, and spend enough time on each one to be sure your dog understands each word thoroughly. It is important for your dog to understand them separately, because we will use them in combination with other words later in training.

The following list briefly explains the commands and concepts we cover within this chapter:

- OKAY: Release word.
- SIT: Quickly tuck the rear end to the floor.
- DOWN: Lie down in a sphinx position (not rolled onto a hip).
- COME: Get to me as quickly as possible.
- STAND *(kick-back stand):* Move from a sit to a standing position without moving the front feet.
- LEAVE IT: Don't sniff or touch a piece of food or other enticing object.
- WATCH *(Attention):* Look at me until I tell you to do something else.
- *Find heel:* Get to heel position quickly.

- MARK: Stare intently at an object or piece of food until commanded to GET IT.
- TOUCH: Touch a target (a plastic lid or small towel) with a front paw or nose.

Release

One of the first words we teach a dog is how to release from an action or position. Choose a word that you don't use a lot in regular conversation. We use OKAY and have nearly eliminated it from our non-dog training vocabulary. *Dogs need a release word to end an exercise or a part of an exercise, to offer a rest in the middle of repetitions, or simply to relieve stress.* Playing is also a good stress reliever, and we introduce it early as part of our training sessions. We want our dogs to think work is a form of play. Training should be fun!

The dog should come up onto his hind legs to get a treat or a toy when he hears the release word. By releasing to his hind legs, you can be fairly certain he is truly relaxed. If you do not want your dog jumping on you, teach him to put his paws up on your arm instead. Do this by teaching him to jump up for a treat held in your outstretched hand. Most dogs will willingly come up for food. Be aware that if you let your dog jump up during training, he is more likely to do so at inconvenient times. Make sure to give consistent verbal and physical cues (your arm extended out at your side, for example) when jumping on you is allowed.

To teach the release word, lure your dog up onto his hind legs using a piece of food. Use your conditioned reinforcer (CR) and give him the food when he does it correctly. You can add the release command as you do this since your dog is likely to do it. We also teach some type of play maneuver as a release. One of Judy's favorite play releases is to have her dog jump over her leg when she holds it out. Adele has her dog stand on his hind legs with his front feet on her and walk forward while she backs up (Fig. 6.1). A "high five"— a paw slap on a hand — is another favorite. Any of these releases may be used in the obedience ring since they require no extra props.

Sit

The general meaning of SIT is "quickly put your bottom on the floor." When training for competition obedience, we distinguish between a *tuck sit* and a *rock sit*. When a dog does a *tuck sit*, he brings his rear toward his front legs (Fig. 6.2); when he does a *rock sit*, he backs his front legs toward his rear (Fig. 6.3). A dog who rocks back into a sit puts himself out of the correct position. He ends up sitting too far back when you halt

Figure 6.1 A favorite release is to have your dog stand with front feet against you and walk forwards while you walk backwards.

during a heeling pattern or too far away from you when he sits in front. Examples of breeds who tend to have rock sits are some of the long-backed breeds, such as German Shepherd Dogs, Corgis, Dachshunds, and Dobermans.

There are several ways to teach your dog how to sit correctly. We recommend that you teach SIT the following way:

Plan "A:" Hold a piece of food in front of and just above your dog's nose. Raise it slightly until the dog lifts his head; this usually makes him sit. As soon as his bottom hits the floor, use your CR and give a treat. Repeat this many times. *We prefer to see the behavior first before adding the associated command.* If you are more comfortable using a command from the beginning, go ahead. Do not, however, get into the habit of repeating SIT, SIT, SIT! Remember that the command doesn't mean anything to your dog at this point.

If your dog rocks back, *do not* use your CR or feed. Begin again. **It is important that you neither give commands twice nor reward an exercise that is not what you want. Ignore wrong behavior and**

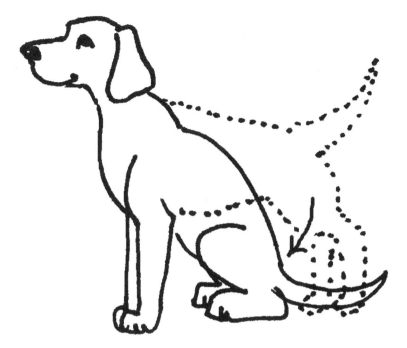

Figure 6.2 The dog brings his rear feet towards his front feet in a *tuck sit.*

Figure 6.3 The dog moves his front feet back towards his rear when he does an incorrect *rock sit.*

praise correct behavior! Your dog should not become stressed since you have shown no emotion. It is important to remember to keep the food in front of his nose. If you push the food toward him, you encourage a rock sit. In order for your dog to tuck and still get the food, hold the food still, in front of and slightly above his nose (Fig. 6.4).

If, after two or three repetitions, your dog does not catch on and is still doing a rock sit, go to plan "B."

Plan "B:" Hold a piece of food in the same place as before. Place your free hand just above his tail and slide your hand over his rear as you scoop him into the *tuck sit* (Fig. 6.5). If your dog *tuck sits*, simply say the command, use your CR, and feed. If your dog does not *tuck sit* naturally, do not reinforce the wrong *sit*.

Sometimes the dog only does a small part of the behavior you are training. Reward these efforts to keep the dog wanting to "play the game." If the treats aren't coming quickly enough, many dogs choose to do something more interesting, such as sniffing the floor or wandering off.

Figure 6.4 Plan "A:" Hold the food slightly above your dog's nose to encourage a *tuck sit*.

An example of rewarding the dog's effort is to reinforce him as soon as his rear feet move forward — even slightly. A complete *sit* is not necessary. Use your CR and then give a treat. Gradually wait for an action that is more like the complete *sit*. If you follow this rule carefully, your dog will understand more quickly and more thoroughly what you want him to do.

A fairly common problem, especially with puppies, is a "flopped-on-a-hip sit" (Fig. 6.6). If your dog constantly flops over on a hip, reinforce the sit with your CR *before* the flop occurs. Some dogs and puppies may need separate work to strengthen the hip muscles in order to sit straight. Such a dog may also require an extra command such as SIT UP or SIT STRAIGHT (see *Scoot Fronts* in *Combination Words* chapter). Use a piece of food to lure him forward until he is no longer on his hip. By getting him to put more weight on his front legs, he is more apt to stay "up" on his sit. Sometimes a puppy will outgrow this stage within a few weeks. If you are having trouble, wait a couple of weeks and try again.

If your dog sits slowly, require a sit in return for "life rewards" — going for a walk, getting dinner, getting petted, or before retrieving a toy. If he doesn't sit within a certain amount of time, walk away — "Sorry, no sit, no dinner!" Try again after a short break. You will probably see more willingness to work as your dog begins to understand the game.

Figure 6.5 Plan "B:" Slide you hand over your dog's rear as you scoop him into a *tuck sit*.

Figure 6.6 This puppy is doing an undesirable "flopped-on-one-hip" sit.

Adding Corrections to the Sit

When your dog demonstrates that he truly understands the meaning of the SIT command, be prepared to correct him for a slow response. When we say "truly understands," we mean that your dog sits promptly most of the time when you tell him to. Some suggested corrections for a slow sit are:

- Pop up and release the leash.
- Poke, slap, or pinch the top of your dog's rump.

If you correct your dog (the *escape* phase), repeat the exercise immediately to give him a chance to succeed and earn a treat (the *avoidance* phase). If you are correcting more than half the time, you are advancing too fast. Back up a step or two in your training.

Down

We teach two different down positions. The dog rolls onto one hip when he does a correct *hip down*. We use the *hip down* for the Novice and Open *Down-stay* exercises (Fig. 6.7). We will explain the *hip down* in the *Stays* chapter.

When your dog does a correct *sphinx down*, he has both hind legs folded evenly under his body and his front legs are straight out in front (Fig. 6.8). The action of going from a *stand* to a *sphinx down* is sometimes called the "fold back" or the "accordion down." We prefer the *sphinx down* for the Open *Drop On Recall* and the Utility *Signal Exercise*. The dog will be asked to do another action following this down, such as another recall or a sit, and it is easier for him to get up quickly from the *sphinx* than from the *hip down*.

We teach the *sphinx down* for a period of time before introducing the *hip down*. The reason for this is to make sure the dog understands the *sphinx* position before introducing the *hip down*.

Adele introduces the *down* with the dog in a sitting position. Judy does not teach the dog to *down* from a *sit*, the long term goal being to prevent the dog from erring during the *Sit-stay* exercises and lying down when he is supposed to be sitting. She starts instead from a *stand*.

Use the food as a magnet in front of your dog's nose. When you teach the down from a sit, slowly move your hand straight down to the floor (Fig. 6.9). If your dog stands up from a sit when you do this, you are

Figure 6.7 The "rolled onto one hip" down.

Figure 6.8 The sphinx down.

probably moving your hand too far ahead of him. It helps some dogs to make an "L" pattern with the food (i.e., straight down to the floor, then along the ground away from the dog's nose). As soon as his elbows are on the floor, use your CR, and give a treat while he is in the down. Don't give the CR until the dog is completely down — elbows and rear.

If your dog resists going down, start by reinforcing his first head movement toward the floor. Next reward him as soon as he moves a front foot forward slightly, then when he moves both front feet forward, and so on, until he finally goes down. You might also try using your free hand to put gentle pressure on his shoulders.

Another method for the resistant dog, most often small dogs, is to sit on the floor with your knees raised. Lure your dog under your knees with food, lowering your knees on subsequent tries until he must lie down to get to the food (Fig. 6.10). This is a form of the "commando" crawl. Most dogs will go down willingly for a food lure once they understand what you want.

When you teach the *down* from a *stand*, your dog should either go down head first or drop as a single unit. Instead of moving your food straight down, move it on a diagonal line from his nose to the floor between his front feet (Fig. 6.11). This causes his head to drop along with the rest of his body, rather than his rear followed by his front. If your dog leaves his rear in the air, move your food more slowly and add slight hand pressure to his rear. Sometimes simply stroke him from his shoulders to his tail to get his rear down faster. Do not push!

If you push or pull a dog in one direction, he tends to push or pull in the opposite direction.

Figure 6.9 Slowly move your hand to the floor, going straight down to the floor.

Figure 6.10 Lure the dog under your knees with food.

Try using one finger between the shoulder blades as a gentle re-minder to go *down*. Make sure you use your CR the instant the dog's whole body is on the floor. The food can be given after the CR, as usual, but the timing of the CR is critical to reinforce the *down*. Many dogs feel threatened by being in the *down* position. By using the CR and feeding immediately, you can allow the dog to get up right away. In order to help him want to stay down longer, try giving him a handful of food on the floor following the CR. The use of the food on the floor can be used later as a jackpot, if needed.

Some dogs flop back into a *hip down* when you are trying for a *sphinx down*. If this happens, pull the food forward along the floor a short distance from his nose, just as he goes down. This should help him shift his weight forward over his elbows instead of back on one hip. You will need to experiment with the food placement to get the desired result which is a quick, smooth *sphinx down*. If your dog rolls onto a hip, release him immediately and do not reinforce. If possible, use your CR quickly when your dog is in the correct position and before he rolls. He will begin to understand that his motion and his final position are of equal importance.

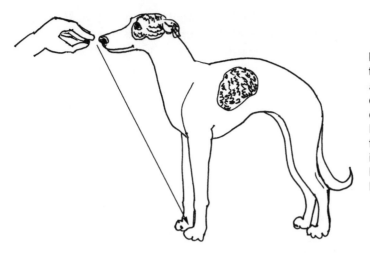

Figure 6.11 When you teach the *down* from a *stand,* your dog should either go down head first or drop as a single unit. Instead of moving your food straight down, move it on a diagonal line from his nose to the floor between his front feet.

Different Surfaces

It is important to teach your dog to *down* on different surfaces. This is especially true for the "naked" breeds that don't have much hair to protect them. When your dog goes down well on "soft" surfaces like carpet, grass, or mats, it is time to teach him to go down on concrete, asphalt, wet grass, stones, snow, and ice. This may sound cruel, but when you command a *drop on recall* at a trial and your dog doesn't like the surface, you will be glad you proofed for it.

Fading the Lure

Many people have trouble eliminating the hand cue for DOWN (i.e., the food lure or the fake food lure). Some dogs catch on quickly, but after spending months working to fade the hand cue with Treasure, Adele thought there had to be a better way. And there is! Many dogs can learn it in a couple of ten to fifteen minute sessions.

Kneel on the floor near your dog, with a large supply of treats close at hand. Lure him into a down a few times and CR and treat as soon as his elbows and rear hit the floor. You might start by reinforcing any type of down, but your main goal is the *sphinx down.* Ignore all other behaviors.

Once he has eaten the treat, release him. **We try not to use one behavior when teaching another, so you would not want to command him to SIT or STAND — even if they are in his vocabulary.** If he gets stuck in the *down,* toss a piece of food a short distance behind him. The food toss also allows you to get your next treat ready without him seeing what you are doing.

Hold another treat in your closed fist and place your fist on the floor in front of your knees (Fig. 6.12). Note: You are no longer luring. Some dogs will lie down fairly quickly. Others will try a variety of other behaviors, such as pawing at your hand, nose butting, sitting, barking, and so on. Do your best to ignore everything that isn't a *down* and try not to laugh! As long as your dog keeps doing something, other than standing and staring, keep your hand still. If he gives up and walks away, he needs help. Lure him into the *down*, but use a more subtle hand motion than before.

Above all, be patient! Notice there is no mention of a command at this stage. Keep quiet, other than using your CR and food when your dog goes down. You can often see the wheels turning in his head as he figures out what behavior will earn the food. This is a good example of "waiting out" the behavior, and he will figure it out if you can just be quiet and patient.

Once he *downs* regularly with your closed fist on the floor, move your fist to your knee. Again, if you do not get a quick response, help your dog by putting your fist back on the floor. When you see a regular response with your fist near your knee, move it a few inches higher up your leg. You should gradually inch your fist toward your waist, while still kneeling or sitting on the floor. Let your dog tell you by his responses when he needs less help. If you move your hand higher and get no response, move it back a bit lower — but don't give in too soon! Let the wheels turn a little longer before you help him.

Figure 6.12 Place your fist on the floor in front of your knees.

Eventually, you should be standing when your dog offers the down. One of the easiest ways to make this transition is to move from the floor to a chair before standing. Wait to add your command until you are seeing the type of *down* you like. ***A good rule of thumb is to add a command when you are reasonably sure your dog will do "behavior X" (in this case, a sphinx down) within five to ten seconds.***

The Splat Drop

Adele has taught both Treasure and Java to put their chins on the floor when doing a drop (a friend dubbed it the *splat drop*). She has two reasons to teach it this way — one silly and one serious. The silly reason is that it looks cute when the dog puts his head down. The serious reason is that it leaves little doubt in the judge's mind about whether or not he is completely down. Adele decided to do this because Rio, like many dogs, tended to drop with his head held in the air. Many judges walked around to examine his drop, checking carefully to see if his elbows were all the way down. Fortunately, he always remained down, but this extra time taken by the judge added unnecessary suspense to the exercise.

If you want to add the *chin-on-the-floor drop*, do this:

Sit on the floor with your dog in a *sphinx down*. Hold a treat, hidden in your fist, and place your fist on the floor six to twelve inches in front of the dog's nose. The dog should lower his head to sniff your hand. Use your CR the instant his head dips and give him the treat from your closed fist. Gradually fade the food-in-the-fist aid and wait for a head dip to occur before reinforcing. If you do this early in your dog's *down* training, the head dip becomes an integral part of his *down* exercise.

Adding Corrections to the Down

When your dog shows you that he truly understands the meaning of the DOWN command, be ready to correct him for a slow or incorrect response. Some suggested corrections for the *down* are:

- Pop toward the floor using a leash or your hand in his collar.
- Pat or slap your dog on the shoulders.
- Use pressure with one finger between the shoulder blades.

If you correct your dog (the *escape* phase), make sure you give him a chance to be right the next time (the *avoidance* phase).

The pat or slap on the shoulders may be used later during the *Signal Exercise* when you may need to use a correction with a signal. If you have praised your dog for going down correctly using a few fairly hard pats on the shoulder for praise, it is not a severe correction.

Come

The word COME is one of the most important words you will ever teach your dog. This command can be a lifesaver! His response should be immediate, direct, and fast; a trot or gallop. He should come close enough to you to be petted and fed. It is important to *keep* your dog near you after he comes to you. Continue to talk and play with him, as well as feeding him, so he enjoys staying close and doesn't lose interest and wander away.

It is easy to begin teaching the word COME. The problem with the command arises when a trainer uses the word while the dog is out of reach, both mentally and physically. He soon learns to ignore the command.

Begin with your dog on a leash and have a good supply of *interesting* food in your hand and/or pocket. We try to always have a ready supply of food when training our dogs, especially when they are puppies. Show your dog a treat, say COME, and lure him to you with it. Use your CR and give him a treat.

Do not introduce the "front" yet, which is when your dog sits in front of you at the end of the recall. The goal is for speed at this point, and a *front* will probably slow your dog down. Teach the *front* separately and don't incorporate it into the total exercise until your dog has a solid *wait* and a fast, focused *recall*. The *Fronts and Finishes* chapter details the teaching of the *front* exercise.

Bring your dog to the center and front of your body from the begin-ning. Do not hold the food over to one side, as this only contributes to off-center recalls. Position your hand so the back of it is centered against your legs and hold the food an inch or two above the height of your dog's nose. Either vary which hand holds and gives the food or use both hands together. We prefer to use two hands to start.

We usually include the verbal COME command from the beginning, unlike the *down* and *sit* training. This is because most dogs will follow food, and therefore respond correctly. Coming toward you is much easier than sitting or lying down, especially for a young puppy. If you have a dog who doesn't follow food easily, wait until he learns how to do this before adding your command.

As your dog becomes more familiar with the command, back away slowly as you say the word COME. The moment he starts toward you, use your CR, and give him the food when he gets to you. COME, at this point, does not mean to sit in front, but merely the act of moving toward you. If you keep the hand holding the food against your legs, as we've suggested, the dog has to come all the way to you to get the food. Again, pet, play, or feed for a few seconds to keep the dog near you. Scratch his tummy or back — or do whatever he enjoys to keep him near you. Do not let him wander off and go into business for himself!

As your dog figures out the mechanics of this new command, move away from him faster. The increase in speed will cause him to come faster and farther before getting his reward. Be careful when you back up! A safer move than backing up is to turn and walk or run away. Keep your eyes on your dog as you do this by glancing over your shoulder.

Restrained Recalls

A *restrained recall* is when one person holds the dog while another person calls him. Once the dog gets to the caller, that person then restrains him and the other person calls him back. It's a great way to tire out a puppy!

Restrained recalls also build speed and distance into the recall. Start doing them as soon as your puppy is coordinated enough to gallop. Since there is no *stay* involved, even young puppies enjoy doing them.

Have your helper hold your dog, who should be off-leash in a safe area. We prefer to hold the dog with our hands around his chest, rather than by the collar. As your dog gets the idea of the exercise, the holder can do some on-again, off-again pressure backwards on his chest. This tends to excite most dogs and results in a faster recall.

Show your dog a piece of food and either walk briskly or run away from him. When working with a very young puppy, keep the distance short (six to eight feet) in order to maintain his attention. As soon as you turn around, stoop down and call his name. As soon as his attention is focused on you, command COME! He should race to you! Praise enthusiastically the moment he starts toward you. This helps him remember what he is doing. When he arrives, give him a treat, and pet and play for a few seconds before moving on to the next recall. Then you can hold him and have your helper call him back, or return him to your helper and do another recall yourself. Puppies love this game and quickly learn to do long, fast, focused recalls.

Don't forget to use your CR with the recall. This will be one of the first times your dog will not receive the food immediately upon hearing the CR. **The CR is given when the dog leaves the other person, not after he gets to you. You are rewarding prompt response to the command COME.**

You should occasionally do this exercise with your dog dragging a short leash. This teaches him to run and play while on a leash, which may be needed for future training. Many dogs, especially those who have been corrected unfairly in training, get upset when a leash is attached. This fun game teaches them not to worry about it.

Food-Toss Recalls

Add some fun to your recall training by tossing a treat or toy between your legs at the end of the recall. This helps keep your dog running fast all the way to you. When first introduced to this game, some dogs are reluctant to run between your legs. Don't toss your treat until he has started through them. Also, don't toss the treat very far, perhaps only two or three feet. If necessary, teach him to go between your legs as a separate exercise.

Another way to have fun is to turn in one direction or the other as your dog gets to you and let him jump up for the food. This works well for someone with short legs and a tall dog! You might also try lifting one leg up as your dog runs through.

A follow-up game to this is to run forward after you have thrown the food and the dog has gone through your legs. Turn around and, as soon as he has eaten his treat, call him again. We call this type of recall a *food-toss recall*. You may tire of the game more quickly than your dog does! Some trainers are concerned that allowing their dog to eat any food from the floor will cause problems later. You will proof for this later in your training, but we believe the benefits of the exercise outweigh the potential problems. We use food tosses for many exercises.

Chase Recalls

A *chase recall* is one in which you call, turn, and run away until your dog catches you. Most dogs like this game as it gives them a chance to use their natural chase instinct.

Adding Corrections

When adding any correction for the recall, we use a leash pop on a buckle collar. This directs the dog toward you with pressure on the back of his neck. Be sure to reinforce him for a prompt response. You may also want to attach a long rope or line to his collar before turning him loose in a fenced area like your backyard. This gives you control when you call him as you can pick up the end of the line and pop him toward you if he fails to respond to the command. Never let him get into the "catch-me-if-you-can" mode. This is not a game and can quickly deteriorate into a situation where your dog doesn't respect either the command or you. The retractable leash works well when you call your dog to you while walking him.

We add a correction early when teaching the recall. Remember that this exercise can save your dog's life and you should imprint the command COME early in his training. You should expect him to respond the first time and every time he hears the command. When your dog responds well each time he hears the COME command, he is ready for an *automatic correction*, which is one that you give immediately after a command, but before the dog has an opportunity to respond. Praise as soon as he responds, but don't give him food. This is the *escape* phase. Repeat the command as soon as he is a short distance away from you, and if he responds quickly without a correction, CR and give him a treat. This is the *avoidance* phase.

Kick-Back Stand

There are four different times your dog must stand in obedience:

- The Novice *Stand for Exam.*
- Stand for measuring at the start of the AKC Open and Utility classes. This is not a formal exercise for which you earn points and it is now optional as to whether the judge measures your dog or not. Some judges still measure, so you should train your dog to accept it.
- The Utility *Signal Stand.*
- The Utility *Moving Stand.*

When setting up for the Novice *Stand for Examination*, the rules permit you to help your dog, including positioning his feet as you might in the conformation ring. Usually, however, a dog will set himself up more comfortably than if you physically position him.

The stand for measuring is very informal. Some dogs get very stressed when a stranger hovers over them with a ruler in his hand, so it is an exercise you should shape carefully.

Some trainers teach what we call a "creeping stand" to their Novice dog. The dog is allowed to walk forward many steps when standing up. While this does not usually mean a point deduction in Novice, it can be a big problem in Utility. If your dog has learned to creep forward on the Novice stand, he will creep on the Utility stands as well, which will result in points off your score. To avoid this problem, we teach the *kick-back stand*, where the dog's front feet remain in place and his hind feet move backwards. In other words, the dog lifts his rear until he is standing. Our first goal is for the dog to understand that standing up earns food. We then refine it to a *kick-back stand*.

Start with your dog in a sit. Hold food in your right hand and slowly lure him forward just enough to get him to lift his rear (Judy never moves the food forward. She teaches the *kick-back stand* from day one). Your dog should move no more than ten inches if he is a medium to large dog and a shorter distance if he is a small dog. CR as soon as he is up and give him the treat. Work on this phase until he stands quickly. If your dog takes more than a step or two forward, you are probably moving your hand too far away from his nose. When it is likely that your dog will *stand* when you show him the food, introduce a STAND command.

Once your dog has the idea of standing, move to the *kick-back stand*. Sit your dog. Stand facing his right side, about halfway between his nose and tail. Put your right foot in front of your dog's front paws to block any forward motion (Fig. 6.13). Hold a piece of food in your right hand by his nose. Command STAND, gently touch his rear toes with your left foot or tickle his tummy with your left hand. As soon as he lifts his rear, CR and give him a treat. Keep your right hand still! Focus on your dog's front feet. If they are moving forward, you need to block them better and move your hand less. If anything, push the food into his nose to encourage *no* forward movement.

Some dogs keep their front feet still, but swing their rear sideways away from you as they stand. If your dog does this, work against a wall or other barrier to prevent this unwanted motion.

If you want to teach your dog to stand on command only (i.e., without any hand signal), make sure you give the command first, followed by the physical prompt (the food lure in your hand). Gradually reduce the amount of food you use for the physical prompt and increase the number of repetitions before feeding.

After your dog understands what to do, begin to extend the length of time he must stand before he gets the food. Use only your CR when he stands up and delay the food longer each time. The formal *Stand–stay* is covered in the *Stays* chapter.

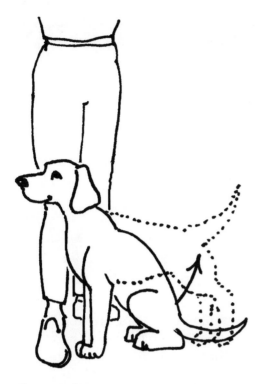

Figure 6.13 To work on the *kick-back stand*, stand facing your dog's right side, about halfway between his nose and tail. Put your right foot in front of his front paws to block any forward motion.

Leave It

LEAVE IT is an important command which we teach early in the dog's obedience career. When first taught, it means "don't touch a piece of food on the ground." As the dog becomes more familiar with the term, you may use it to mean "leave another dog alone" or to stop him from getting into something that may be dangerous for him. We usually use mild compulsion with this exercise, since it may be a lifesaving exercise. It is important for your dog to understand early that LEAVE IT means *right now*.

Teaching LEAVE IT lays the groundwork for the *Stay* exercises. Your dog learns to show some restraint in the presence of enticing objects. You may also want to use LEAVE IT later in your training to keep your dog focused during his stays.

Start to teach LEAVE IT with your dog either sitting or standing. He should be wearing a buckle collar with a leash attached. You may restrain him either by the leash or with your hand in his collar. Use your CR and feed him a couple of pieces of food to let him know you have the food. Place a piece of food on the floor about three feet away and command LEAVE IT. Most dogs try to lunge at the food. When your dog lunges, use your verbal correction AH-AH, along with mild restraint on the collar, usually a small tug backwards. If you have a wild, determined dog, don't be as mild! This sort of dog usually requires a firmer hand. As soon as your dog shows some restraint and hopefully turns to you for direction, CR and feed from your hand. He does *not* get to eat the food from the floor when he has heard LEAVE IT.

Set up again, this time asking for a bit more restraint from your dog before using the CR and the food. When done correctly, dogs quickly learn to remain in place, stare intently at the food, and turn to you for their reward.

When your dog shows restraint with the food at a distance of a few feet, move it closer to him. Once he can restrain himself with the food right in front of him, begin to work with him in the *down* position with the food a foot or two away. Train *leave it* until he ignores the food when it is directly in front of his nose when he is in a *down*.

Attention

It is vital for you to have your dog's attention during training. He must pay attention to you and ignore everything else going on around him. Teaching your dog new exercises in a familiar environment allows him to focus on you and not his surroundings. Your dog will become more secure when he has learned to be attentive. The surroundings, which previously may have frightened or distracted him, are now not his responsibility. When he needs direction or help, he looks to you.

Attention does not necessarily mean staring into your eyes. Many dogs can't move with their heads up, so you may need to train one focal (or attention) point for heeling and a different one for when your dog sits in front of you. Focal points are discussed thoroughly in the next section. We recommend that you start to teach attention with your dog sitting in front of you, as it is easier to tell what he is doing in this position.

The following list shows stages dogs go through during attention training:

- Dog completely ignores his person.
- Dog occasionally glances at his person, but spends much of his time watching what is going on around him.
- Dog glances at his person frequently, sometimes maintaining his attention for seconds at a time, but any mild distraction causes a loss of focus and the dog turns to look at the distraction.

- Dog focuses on his person for seconds at a time, but mild distractions cause fast glances away. His focus usually returns quickly to the handler. Big distractions cause a loss of focus on the handler.

- Dog focuses well, keeps his head in his attention position, but his eyes move away, sometimes focusing on a distraction. From a distance, it is hard to tell that the dog has lost focus.

- Dog focuses well, makes quick, darting glances with his eyes while his head remains still, but quickly returns his eyes to his handler.

- Dog focuses very well, in spite of big distractions, staring harder at his person when a distraction occurs. His eyes bore holes in you!

If your dog falls into the first category, you have your work cut out for you! Start by carrying food with you at all times. Any time your dog glances in your direction, use your CR and give him a treat. Do this for about a week. You should see a dramatic improvement. Require your dog's attention before you do anything fun with him. Before you throw a toy for him, make him look at you. Before going out for a walk, he should sit and look at you. Stop occasionally when you are out for a walk and wait for him to look at you before moving again. Use your CR any time he looks at you. You may pair it with food, but you may just wish to use the walk as your main reinforcement. When you feed him his meals, stand holding the bowl of food. Wait until he looks at your face, use your CR, and then put down the bowl. Think of other *life rewards* (discussed earlier in the SIT section) you can use to get what you want from your dog.

If your dog has passed beyond stage one, hold three or four small pieces of food in each hand and stand facing him. When training a small dog or puppy, you may wish to sit in a chair or on the floor. *Ultimately, your dog should sit squarely and centered in front of you and stare intently at your face.* His front feet are mere inches from your toes; your hands are relaxed at your side. While the dog's position is not critical at this point, be aware that you are training for a perfect front at the same time that you are working on attention.

If you are using a leash, it may be helpful to put your foot on it, as this leaves your hands free but keeps the dog close to you. Watch him and, the instant he looks at your face, use your CR and give him a piece of food. He may stare at your hands, but be patient and wait until he glances at your face. If he stares at one hand or noses at it, give him food from the other hand the moment he makes eye contact. This teaches him that his actions bring the food, but not always from where he expects it! You will add a command later.

You may need to do one or two exercises from the following list to jump-start your dog to look up, but don't do any of them more than a few times.

- Hold your hands behind your back to keep them out of your dog's sight.

- Let your dog sniff a piece of food. Slowly bring it up toward your face, and CR when your dog makes eye contact. Give your dog the food by lowering it directly from your face to his mouth.

- Accept upward glances, even if you are not getting actual eye contact. You can refine this later. Be aware that some dogs are very uncomfortable making eye contact.

As your dog figures out that eye contact brings food, gradually lengthen the time he must maintain that contact before you reinforce him. If he looks away before you can reinforce, simply start again and reinforce sooner the next time.

Remember, the food can come anytime, but the CR (conditioned reinforcer) must come the instant your dog does what it is you want him to do.

Next, begin to work on attention with your dog sitting in heel position (see *Heeling* chapter for a definition) or as close to that position as he is able to stay right now. Don't spend too long working on front attention before starting attention in heel position. Otherwise, it may be hard for your dog to learn to stay in heel position when he thinks he has to look into your eyes.

If your dog insists on moving away from your left side, position him with his left side against a wall. You should work on "sit in heel position" first, separately from your attention work. Hold a handful of food in your left hand. CR and feed rapidly, every one second, then two, then three, etc. This will build his desire to stay at your left side.

Focal Point

At this point, we teach a *focal point* for heeling. When we heel with our dogs, we want the dog to maintain a consistent head position with his attention focused on us. Choose a place on the left side of your body where your dog can focus comfortably without having to maintain an extreme position of his head and neck. It is difficult for many dogs to move with their heads cranked way up and to the right. Dogs have very good peripheral vision and can see your body cues well. If you insist on face attention during heeling, it will be nearly impossible for your dog to maintain correct heel position.

If your dog is small, you might use your knee as the focal point (Fig. 6.14). For an average to tall dog, use any point from your left hip to your left shoulder (Fig. 6.15). Many trainers use the point of their elbow, as it is in the correct place when the hand is held at the waist during off-leash heeling. You can teach your dog to look at this point the same way you taught him face attention. If your focal point is very low, you may want to put some cheese or peanut butter on a dowel. Hold the dowel so the food is at your focal point. When your dog looks at the food, use your CR and let him take the food. Gradually fade the dowel from the sight picture, but bring it back to reward your dog when he looks at his focal point. Using a dowel for a small dog helps you avoid the habit of bending over. For taller dogs, hold a piece of food or a toy at the point you have chosen. When the dog looks there, give him his CR and feed or release to the toy. You can use food on a dowel for any dog, but it is just one more piece of equipment to fade once the dog has learned the exercise.

Figure 6.14 If your dog is small, you might use your knee as a focal point.

Figure 6.15 For the average to tall dog, choose a spot between your left hip and your shoulder as a focal point.

It is imperative at this point for you to begin watching your dog with your head and shoulders straight, your chin down and by looking at him with your peripheral vision (Fig. 6.16). If you pull your left shoulder back and turn your head to see your dog, he will probably forge when you resume proper ring position. Remember to keep your food or toy at the focal point and bring it straight down to the dog when rewarding. This makes it easier for you to remember not to twist your head and shoulders.

Figure 6.16 Keep your head and shoulders straight, your chin down, and look at your dog with your peripheral vision.

Adding a Command

Once your dog is able to maintain eye contact for five seconds, add a command to the action. We use the word WATCH. When you are reasonably sure your dog is about to look at you, say WATCH. CR the instant he looks at his focal point and feed. When you first start adding the command, do not require long attention. Reinforce very brief looks, gradually increasing the length of time your dog watches before he gets a treat.

When he can watch for fifteen seconds, do not forget to reinforce the shorter periods of attention. This is another example of the variable reinforcement schedule that is so important for ring preparation.

Adding Distractions

Next, add mild distractions to your attention work. Sit your dog in front of you. Hold a few small treats in each hand and command WATCH. Move one of your hands slightly away from your side. This will probably cause your dog to look at your hand. Wait until he looks back to your face, use your CR and feed. Distract with the same hand again. It may take only a finger wiggle distraction at first to get him to look away! If, after four or five repetitions, you still haven't been able to keep his attention when you move your hand, reinforce him for his attention without the distraction. Your goal is to maintain his interest so he keeps trying. Add the finger wiggle again. If he cannot maintain face attention during the distraction, keep distracting, albeit mildly, and wait for him to glance at your face. Make sure you are ready for the return of attention, CR the instant it happens, and then feed him from the other hand. Once he figures out that looking back at you is earning the reinforcement, he should be able to maintain the desired eye contact. These exercises are fairly advanced and you may not be successful using them with puppies. If your puppy is too wiggly or distracted to learn this now, wait a month or two and try again.

Adding Verbal Corrections

The next step is to add a voice correction when the dog looks away. When is the right time to do this? For many dogs, it is appropriate after a week or two of consistent training. Other dogs may need a month or longer. If you're not sure, train another week or two before adding a verbal correction. **Your dog will tell you when he understands the basics of the exercise by how consistently he does the work.**

Once you decide the time is right, do the following: Command WATCH. If your dog looks away, use a verbal correction, such as AH-AH. You may, instead, use a neutral phrase such as WRONG or TOO BAD, said in a flat tone of voice. This indicates no reinforcement is coming for the action of looking away. Release and play the moment he returns his attention to you. Repeat the WATCH command and reinforce success with both your CR and a treat. If you find you are using corrections more often than reinforcement, make it easier for him. Move away from whatever is distracting him and use your CR and food sooner the next time.

Adding Physical Corrections

When your dog loses attention after the teaching and verbal correction phases of this exercise, it may be time to introduce a physical correction. There are dogs for whom this is not appropriate. *Dogs who are worried about their surroundings, rather than curious, often react poorly to physical corrections.* This is especially true in the early stages of training. It often makes the "swivel neck" problem worse. You can usually help this type of dog by being patient and using interesting food when he returns his focus to you.

If you are uncertain about whether to add a physical correction, review the earlier discussion of corrections in the *Methods* chapter. If you are not sure, your dog probably is not ready for a physical correction. If you decide he needs a correction, proceed.

When working with your dog in heel position, we recommend that you use a leash pop straight up toward your face as your physical correction. Use a buckle collar and keep your leash short with very little slack. Some dogs respond better to a tap on the head, a tweak of an ear, or a gentle lifting of the head back into position. If your correction is not causing your dog to focus better, make the task easier. We recommend the following sequence:

- Command WATCH.
- Your dog looks at you.
- You look at your dog and start counting in your head.
- Your dog gets distracted and looks away.
- Say WATCH and pop the leash up toward your face. *Use your WATCH command just before the pop of the lead so your dog knows what the pop is for.*
- Your dog looks back at you.
- Use your CR, but since you corrected, do not give him food.
- Release and play briefly.
- Set up again, repeat WATCH, count again (perhaps for a shorter period of time), CR and feed when your dog successfully maintains attention.

The goal is for your dog to succeed, because success builds confidence! Do you have to correct your dog for inattention more than half the time? If so, you are trying to advance too fast. *We generally don't give food after a correction. We repeat the exercise or portion of the exercise, giving the dog a chance to do the work correctly, then CR and treat.* You may want to review the *Methods* chapter section on corrections.

The "Leaving Town" Correction

In some cases, a very effective loss-of-attention correction for heel position attention is for you to walk away the instant your dog loses focus. If he is on leash, he will receive a mild correction. You may need to wait for this step until you have trained *find heel* (next section). Once he realizes you have left and makes an effort to catch up with you, CR and give him a treat. Again, it is very important for you to reinforce him for maintaining attention. Lower the distraction level until your dog is successful most of the time. Gradually increase the distractions as he maintains his attention longer.

More Attention Distractions

If your dog is paying reasonable attention, use additional distractions. Start with simple ones, gradually moving to harder ones. Start these distractions with your dog in either a stationary front or stationary heel position. It is usually much harder for him to watch and heel than watch while sitting still.

Here are some suggestions for distractions. Ask a friend to:

- Stand next to you and your dog.
- Talk to your dog and/or pet him.
- Pat her leg.
- Pat the floor.
- Offer your dog a treat or a toy.
- "Sweet talk" your dog.
- Walk in increasingly smaller circles around you and your dog.
- Open and close a door.
- Rustle papers.
- Rustle plastic bags (they usually contain food, you know!).
- Scrape a chair along the floor, first quietly and then gradually increasing the volume.
- Hold a toy near your dog.
- Drop a toy near your dog.
- Drop boards from a jump.
- Throw a dumbbell which hits the floor or wall. Start this quietly, at a distance, and with a small dumbbell. Work first with the dumbbell in front of the dog, gradually increasing the volume, proximity, and size of dumbbell.

- Open a bag of scent articles and rattle them as they are dumped on the floor.

Some other suggestions for distractions:

- Stand near a group of talking people.
- Shuffle or tap your foot on the floor.
- Wiggle the fingers of your right hand, first at your side, then in arcs around you.
- Have another dog going in and out of a crate.

Let your dog succeed most of the time. Too many corrections lead to stress, which negates your training.

Advanced Attention Proofing

Find a helper and give her a supply of items to drop or toss on the floor, such as dumbbells, articles, and toys. Have her stand about 40 feet away while you and your dog work on heel position attention. Your helper should drop the items one by one. When your dog has watched successfully through these distractions two times in a row, take a couple of steps toward your helper and begin again. Repeat until you and your dog can stand next to your helper with no loss of attention from the dog when he is in either heel or front position. As your dog gains confidence and competence, your helper can toss the items in the air, providing a visual distraction as well as an audible one.

Find Heel

Find heel is the initial stage of heeling. When we teach *find heel*, the goal is for the dog to learn that heel position is a great place to get to and the best place to be! We introduce distractions during *find heel* training as well.

To set up for *find heel*, hold a handful of treats in your right hand which will "feed" your left hand as needed. The food should be readily available for your dog the second he gets to heel position and immediately after you have used your CR.

Work off-leash if you are in a low distraction area and it is safe to do so. If you are somewhere unfenced or you try working off-leash and your dog keeps getting distracted, use a retractable leash held in your right hand and use more interesting food.

Lure your dog to your left side, using a piece of food in your left hand. The *moment* he hits heel position, use your CR, and give him the treat from your left hand. Don't reach out to feed him. Instead, make him come to the food in your hand, which you should hold by your left side. When first teaching this exercise, "hits heel position" has a much more relaxed meaning. Reinforce with your CR and food when your dog gets some part of his body close to your left hip. The first stage goal is to get your dog's nose close to your targeting left hand. Some dogs will be accurate very quickly; others will take a while to figure this out. Make sure you are reinforcing as often as necessary to keep your dog interested in the exercise.

Put another piece of food in your left hand. Walk away from your dog and turn slightly to your right. This causes your dog to be behind you (Fig. 6.17). If needed, use your left hand holding the treat and finger wiggling as a lure, then CR the *instant* he hits heel position. Repeat this sequence until you use up a handful of food. If your dog zooms past you, turn away to your right and head in the other direction. You may use your dog's name to get his attention just before you turn away. As soon as possible, stop using any verbal cue.

Do not wait for your dog, nor turn to look back over your shoulder to see what he is doing. Walk briskly around your training area, ignoring him until he is where you want him.

Next, tighten your heel position requirements. In addition to having your dog come to your left side, he should look up when he gets there (Fig. 6.18). This may mean you don't reinforce each time he gets to your

Figure 6.17 Walk away from your dog and turn slightly to your right. This causes him to be behind you.

Find Heel

Figure 6.18 Your dog should look up just before he gets to heel position.

left side anymore. That's okay! Just step off to the right again and wait for the next chance. If he fails to look up more than a couple of times in a row, help him the next time, perhaps using a wiggling finger or a larger piece of food. If you don't get the desired behavior after two to three attempts, back up and reteach the previous steps.

At times, your dog will come up on your right side. This usually happens when you turn too far to the right when stepping away from him. Reduce the sharpness of your turn. Check to see that your right hand is out of the way and your left hand is down, showing the dog where he should be. If necessary, reach behind you with your left hand (Fig. 6.19). As your dog gains understanding, he'll drive harder to catch up. You can then increase the angle of your turn.

As soon as possible, reduce the amount of luring you do. Move your food to your focal point as soon as he understands the game. Your dog needs to figure out that getting himself to your left side earns the CR and a treat. As usual, your timing is important. *Be sure to give your CR before moving your hand to give the food. The CR must come when the dog is in the correct place. The food should be delayed or else you will still be luring your dog.*

The most important step is for you to tell your dog that he is correct the instant he is in heel position. This is done with your CR, not with your food.

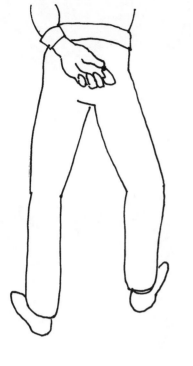

Figure 6.19 If your dog approaches on your right side, reach behind you with your left hand to lure him into place.

Once your dog is quickly finding heel position, begin to delay giving the food. Use your CR the instant he hits heel position, but don't give him the food. Heel for a few steps, repeat your CR, give him the food, and release him.

We like to teach the dog that we will turn in front of him for the release so he can jump on us and push for another treat (Fig. 6.20). This helps him move forward for the food and the release. It is a motivating and fun game. Variably reinforce how often your dog gets the CR and food. Sometimes it is just for hitting heel position, sometimes for heeling two steps, sometimes five steps. Keep stretching the upper limit, but don't neglect reinforcing fewer steps. This builds variability into your heeling from the beginning and is a valuable step toward the goal of doing an entire heeling pattern with no food. Longer heeling is covered in the *Heeling* chapter.

Figure 6.20 Turn in front of your dog to release him.

Adding Distractions to Find Heel

When your dog can quickly get to your left side with his head up, it is time to add distractions. Have someone walk around your training area. This person's job is to try to make your dog look away from you. The instant he looks at your helper, she should become very boring by crossing her arms and breaking eye contact with your dog. It doesn't take much to distract most dogs, especially young, social puppies, so use simple distractions in the beginning. Here is a list of distractions we use and the approximate order in which your helper should try them:

- Stand or walk nearby.
- Bend over and pat her leg.
- Bend over and clap her hands.
- Clap her hands and talk to your dog.
- Squat down and pat the floor.
- Move a chair a couple of inches across the floor.
- Move a chair a foot across the floor.
- Hold a toy.
- Wave a toy.
- Hold food.
- Wave food.
- Follow behind you and your dog.

- Follow along, waving food or toy — start with the less enticing distraction. We are trying to build on success.

- Follow along, petting your dog (Fig. 6.21).

- Follow along, touching your dog with a toy — use a squeaky toy as well as a ball.

- Toss a ball or toy on the floor.

- Drop jump boards an inch or two to the floor.

- Drop jump boards four to six inches onto the floor (when dropping boards, start in front of the dog so he has a chance to see the motion of the boards before he hears the noise).

- Open a crate door.

Most dogs quickly figure out that your helper isn't going to provide anything fun, so they hustle back to you for their reinforcement. Your dog can learn to ignore remarkably difficult distractions without the need for corrections. Since you haven't given him a command to heel, he is not wrong when he gets distracted; he simply misses any reinforcement from you.

Figure 6.21 Judy and Alec are ignoring Adele's petting in an advanced *find heel* distraction.

Sniffing

Some dogs really like to sniff! With this type of dog, it can help to have your helper stamp her feet near the dog or go to the dog and do some "pounding" — rough petting and poking — that the dog wants to avoid. It takes his mind off sniffing. You, the handler, should walk in circles nearby and entice the dog with an interesting treat. For the determined sniffer, find some place where there are fewer interesting things to sniff when you work on this exercise. You might also use your LEAVE IT command. In addition, use more interesting food as your reward and make sure your dog is really hungry before you start to work. You also might need to put him back on lead.

Freezing

If you have a dog who freezes at the sound of a scary noise (the definition of scary depends on the dog), *find heel* is an excellent way to help him figure out that the scary noises aren't going to hurt him. He learns that catching up to you makes good things happen; he gets good food and your approval. Make sure your helper starts out quietly so your dog doesn't get so stressed that he gives up. You may need to walk very close to your dog and do some luring to "jump start" him into motion if some noise has caused him to stop. Gradually have your distracter escalate the noise level.

Mark

Teaching your dog to *mark* is an extremely useful and important exercise. It is how we show the dog a given point, some distance away and in front of him. He learns to look in this direction when you give a signal or a verbal command. The signal is generally given with your left hand along the right side of your dog's head (Fig. 6.22). You will need the *mark* to teach the Utility glove exercise (the *Directed Retrieve*), the *go-out* (part of *Directed Jumping*), and to some extent, the *Retrieve on the Flat* in Open.

You may wish to use a leash. If your dog is young and not under good verbal control, you should probably use a leash to keep him near you. A leash may also be necessary if you are working in a group of other dogs. However, we prefer to work off-leash whenever possible.

Restrain your dog with your right hand by his leash or in his collar. Eventually, you will want your dog sitting in heel position, but he can stand now if it is easier for both of you. Hold a piece of food in your left hand. Throw it about six feet in front of your dog and, as it hits the floor, command MARK. Leave your left hand along the right side of his face

Figure 6.22 Hold your left hand along the right side of your dog's head.

pointing to the food. Use the broadest part of your left hand adjacent to the right side of your dog's eyes to block his vision to the right. When he is staring intently at the food, use your CR, and tell him to GET IT. The CR rewards your dog the instant he looks at the food. The command to GET IT lets him go out and eat his reward. ***This is a delayed reinforcer and it is extremely important that you give him verbal feedback for LOOKING in the right direction.*** Use food that is big enough for the dog to see, like large slices of hot dog or other training meat. Cubes of cheese or cooked macaroni are also easy for your dog to see. Again, the most important part of teaching the *mark* is to use the CR the instant your dog's eyes make contact with the food. If he looks back up at you when you use your CR, command MARK again and send him to the food as soon as his head drops. You are only teaching your dog to look where you are pointing.

A COME command should help speed up your dog's return to you after he gets his treat. Give the command as soon as he finishes the treat; reinforce faster returns with your CR and another treat. This helps your dog form the habit of returning quickly and will help later when there are multiple gloves, as in the *Directed Retrieve* exercise (see *Directed Retrieve* chapter).

Begin to lengthen the amount of time your dog *holds the mark*. This is the length of time he can stare at the food. CR and send him for his reward after varying lengths of time. When you see him begin to respond to your hand signal alone (i.e., his head drops as you place your hand beside it and he stares at the food), begin to randomly use your verbal MARK command. The *Directed Retrieve* is a signal exercise, so you should begin to fade the verbal MARK command as soon as your dog understands what your hand next to his head means.

Foot Touching a Target

Teaching your dog to touch a target with a front paw is both fun and useful. Once he understands the concept of "touch," you can use the target in different places you might want him to go, such as away from you on a *go-out* or past you to jump a *Broad Jump*. It is much easier than constantly putting food out for the dog to go to and it transfers responsibility to the dog sooner.

To teach the foot touch, start with a target like a paper plate or large plastic coffee can lid. Place it on the floor and have treats ready. Dogs who use their feet in play learn this quickly. You eventually want to reinforce for a front foot touching the lid, but start by rewarding any response, even looking in the direction of the target. You may find it easier to see what your dog is doing if you sit on the floor or in a chair.

Some dogs actively avoid stepping on the lid, which is comical to watch. Put a treat on the target and CR as he approaches to eat the food. After he has eaten the food from the target, toss another behind him and slip another treat onto the target without him seeing you do so. When your dog runs back to check the lid for a treat, he is ready to work without food on the lid. If you have done enough repetitions, he will return to the lid. Give your CR as he approaches and give him a treat.

Remember to be patient! Wait for the dog to figure out what is causing you to use your CR. If he is simply walking up and staring at the target or touching it with his nose, wait. Many dogs try digging at it when they get frustrated. This is very close to what you are looking for, so wait and reinforce it. If he wanders away, slip another treat onto the lid, and when he returns and dives for the treat, CR just before he eats it. If he starts offering other behaviors you have shaped, such as lying down or staring at you, wait again! He will eventually do some action more closely related to your goal (foot on the target), such as looking at the target or stepping toward it. Reward *any* small increment of behavior resembling your goal behavior.

The goal is for your dog to stand with a foot on the target, not just slap it and return to you. Once you see him touching rapidly, wait for a second touch before reinforcing. Go for doubles, then triples. You should gradually see some longer touches, which is what you should reinforce. This is *selective* reinforcement.

Gradually build distance between you and the target. Build this distance to at least ten feet before adding a verbal cue. At this point, your dog should be able to leave your side, go to the target to touch, get his CR from you, and return to you for his treat. When going for doubles and triples at a distance, your dog might start back to you after one touch, but should rapidly return to the target for another touch when he realizes you haven't used your CR. If he is coming back toward you between touches that haven't been reinforced, you may be moving too far away too fast. Stay a little closer to the target for a while.

When you add a verbal cue, move back to the target again so rapid repetitions are possible. What cue should you use? Many people use TOUCH. Adele started with GO-OUT, because she taught Treasure the "foot-on-the-lid" routine to use for *go-outs* for Utility. She has since thought of other uses for the touch, such as the *Broad Jump* and teaching a stop for the *Drop on Recall*, so she recommends using a more generic cue such as TOUCH.

Nose Touches

Another targeting exercise is a *nose touch*. Start with something small like a clothespin. Shape the dog to touch the non-clipping end. Present the clothespin in front of your dog's nose. Most dogs will sniff at it. If by luck he touches it, use your CR instantly and give him a treat. Any motion of the dog toward the pin should be rewarded. If necessary, touch it to his nose, CR and treat a few times. Most dogs catch on quickly. As he shows you he understands, move the clothespin farther away from his nose and to either side. Once he touches it in various places, wait for him to touch it two or three times — doubles and triples.

Once your dog understands how to touch the clothespin in your hand, clip it on various places you want the dog to go. A common use is for *go-outs* in Utility. You might want to use it when you teach *fronts* and it is also a preliminary exercise for teaching your dog to retrieve.

Once your dog will move away from you to touch the clothespin, add a command.

The *Fundamental Words* are the basis for all of your obedience work: Novice through Utility. Teach them thoroughly to give your dog the best start to a high scoring and confident obedience career.

Power Steering

I n this chapter, we explain what we call the *Power Steering* exercises. By using these words, you can steer your dog into either front or heel position without any ballet twirls or other fancy gymnastics. The four words we use for the four directions are BACK, CLOSE, OFF, and HEEL (Fig. 7.1). You may choose to use other words just as long as your dog understands what you want him to do. You will use them when he makes position errors, both during *Heeling* and *Recalls*.

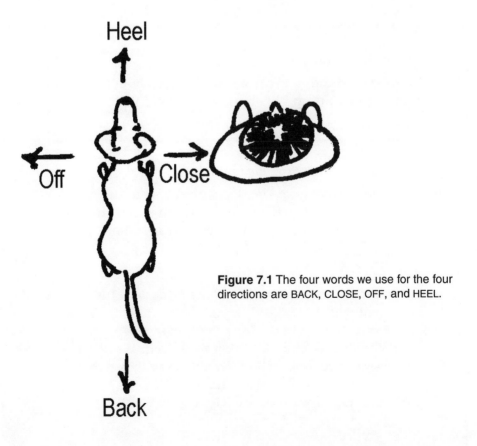

Figure 7.1 The four words we use for the four directions are BACK, CLOSE, OFF, and HEEL.

How These Words Are Applied

When we begin to put the parts of a heeling pattern together, we give the dog verbal commands for all moves until he has mastered the body cues. We then fade the verbal commands.

If a correction is needed, we precede the correction with the appropriate verbal cue to help the dog understand how he is wrong. We then repeat the same piece of the exercise with a verbal cue; CR and feed when the dog does the exercise properly without a correction.

The Exercises

The *Power Steering* exercises include:

- *Back:* Move straight backwards.
- *Close:* Side step to the right.
- *In:* Pivot counterclockwise around the front feet, the rear end making an arc to the right.
- *Off:* Side step to the left.
- *Heel start:* One step forward.
- *Right turn start:* One step right turn.
- *Hurry:* Speed up.
- *Dizzy spin:* Handler turns clockwise quickly in place. The dog wraps tightly around his handler, maintaining heel position.

Typical heeling position errors include (Fig. 7.2):

- *Forging:* The dog is too far forward.
- *Lagging:* The dog is too far behind.
- *Bumping* or *crowding:* The dog is too close to the handler. Bumping is more likely to happen when either the dog or handler weaves (i.e., doesn't walk a straight line).
- *Heeling wide:* There is too much space between the dog and handler.
- *Side-winding* or *crabbing:* The dog moves with his rear out of alignment with his front. It is more common for the dog to move with his rear to the left of his front, but he can also move with his shoulders farther to the left. We often see the latter with small dogs who lean out to try to see their handler's face or with a dog who paces (moves both legs on the same side forward at the same time).

Figure 7.2 Counterclockwise from upper left: forging, lagging, bumping or crowding, heeling wide, and side-winding.

Set-ups

We use the term *set-up* to mean getting the dog into heel position. **Heel position is when the area between the dog's nose and shoulders is in line with your left hip.** As a general rule, if you have your dog's right eye or ear in line with the left seam of your pants, assuming he holds his head up attentively, he will be in heel position. He should be neither touching you nor too far away. In the *Jumping* chapter, we refer to a *set-up distance*. This is the distance away from the jumps where you place your dog before a jumping exercise; it is not what we are referring to here.

It is extremely important for you to understand exactly where you want your dog to be when he is in heel position. It may be even more important for your dog to understand where heel position is! We often see people correcting a dog for improper heel position when the dog really hasn't a clue where he should be.

Once your *set-up* point is determined, it is important to teach your dog how to get there by himself and to pair a command with it. The *Power Steering* words in this chapter will help you do just that. You may have seen dogs who are very stressed as their handlers try to get them into heel position to begin an exercise. The handler twirls around, backs up, moves forward, and the dog hasn't a clue where he is supposed to be. This type of maneuvering can cause the dog to give up before he even begins!

We put our dogs in a sit and move ourselves into heel position to begin to teach the *set-up*. We then use the various words to help him when we step slightly to either side, forward or backward. Once the dog knows the *Power Steering* words well, we pair a command such as PLACE with the *set-up* exercise. We may say something like BACK-PLACE or CLOSE–PLACE. Some trainers tell their dogs to SIT in heel position and expect them to set up perfectly. We like the word PLACE and practice it as a separate exercise, helping the dog with the steering words when he has trouble. Many dogs are stressed when told to HEEL. If they are conversant with a *set-up* word, it makes for a smoother transition from *set-up* to heel position.

Back

You will find BACK useful when you want to do one of the following:

- Position your dog in heel position when getting ready to begin an exercise.

- Correct a dog who is forging.

- Do left turn pivots.
- Move from fast to normal pace or normal to slow pace.
- Move your dog away from you when he is facing you (you stand still while he backs up).
- Do distance work in Utility on SIT, DOWN, and STAND.
- Teach the *Drop on Recall.*
- Teach the *signal drop.*

There are three positions from which we suggest you teach your dog to BACK:

- With you facing your dog's right side.
- With him standing, facing you.
- With him in heel position.

We each teach the phases in a different order. Judy starts facing the dog's right side, while Adele starts with the dog facing her. As usual, we don't add a command until the dog shows an elementary understanding of the exercise.

Many dogs get stuck in a *sit* when learning BACK. When first teaching it, make it easier for your dog by starting him in a *stand.*

To start as Judy does, position your dog with his left side against a wall. This keeps him from moving to his left. Position yourself facing his right side, standing by his ribs (Fig. 7.3). Your legs will block his movement to the right. Hold the food in your right hand in front of, and just above, his nose. Take a small step to your left, using the leash and buckle collar to gently guide your dog backwards. You may also do this without a leash and merely lure him with the food. If need be, use your left foot to gently tap your dog's back toes and CR the instant he moves backwards, even slightly! Remember, reward *increments* and *effort.*

If your dog tries to sit, don't hold the food as high over his head. Instead, hold it just under his chin near his chest or push it gently into and just above his nose. Point the toe of your left foot upward so your dog will come down on it if he sits. He will quickly learn that this is not comfortable. Short dogs are often easier to train for this exercise as they hit your toe sooner!

To teach your dog to step back when facing you:

- Stand your dog facing you.
- Move slowly toward him. CR and treat any movement backwards.

Figure 7.3 Position your dog with his left side against a wall. Position yourself facing your dog, standing by his ribs.

If he side steps or sits, and a few attempts are not successful, try the following:

- Hold a piece of food under his chin near his chest. The position of the food is important — if it is too low, many dogs try to lie down; if too high, they will sit.

- Move toward him slightly, and when he backs up, even one step, reinforce with your CR and treat.

Once he is able to back confidently with you facing his side and with you in front of him, go to the next stage.

Stand your dog in *heel position*, with his left side against a wall and work on BACK from this position. It may be more difficult at first, so be sure he understands how to *back up* from both of the first two starting positions before moving to this new one. Gradually move away from the wall when your dog understands the concept. You may find it helpful to use a long, low barrier, such as an extension ladder or a curb, as you move away from the wall. This will help him move back in a straight line. You may also use a dowel held against your dog's left hip to remind him to stay straight. If you introduced him to a dowel in puppy training (see *Puppy* chapter), he should not mind your using it here. If you haven't used one before, you might want to introduce a dowel now.

The final phase is teaching your dog to start in a sit, back two or three inches without completely standing, and then sit again. Split this exercise into two phases:

- Start in a sit and back into a stand.

- Start in a stand and back into a sit (command SIT as needed). If your dog tends to do rock sits, delay this exercise until his *tuck sit* is well established.

Combine the two phases when your dog has mastered each combination separately.

Try a dance step with COME and BACK. This may be the first time you have asked your dog to be aware of his hind quarters. *Teaching a dog to control his rear is an extremely important part of good heeling.* In the *come and back* exercise, stand your dog facing you. Command COME, walk backwards six to eight steps, then command BACK, and walk forward six to eight steps. Don't forget to CR and feed for the effort when he is first learning this combination. If he has trouble, take fewer steps.

Close

We use the CLOSE command to move the dog to his right. The dog steps sideways perpendicular to the direction he is facing (Fig. 7.4). Some dogs cross the left legs in front of or behind the right legs. We use the CLOSE command during heel position *set-ups* and to correct a dog who is heeling too wide. It is also important for fine tuning fronts (i.e., teaching the dog to move to his right in the front position).

To teach CLOSE (Fig. 7.4):

- Stand your dog in heel position.

- If you are using a choke collar, attach the leash to the dead ring (the non-choking one); if you are using a pinch collar, to both rings. We prefer that you teach this using a buckle collar, but some dogs lean so heavily in their collar that the buckle collar may not be sufficient.

- Hold the leash behind you in your right hand, parallel to the floor, with tension on the leash. The leash will help get your dog moving. Your right hand position depends on the size of your dog; trainers with small dogs must bend over to keep the leash parallel to the floor (Fig. 7.5).

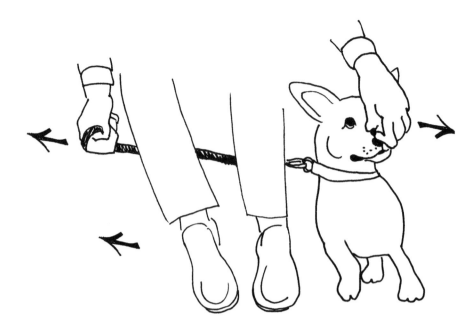

Figure 7.4 We use the CLOSE command to move the dog to his right, the dog stepping sideways perpendicular to the direction he is facing.

Figure 7.5 Set up for the *close* exercise this way.

- Hold food in your left hand, in front of and slightly to the left of your dog's nose. Don't hold the food too high — almost straight ahead works better. The food is used to steer your dog's head, and this, in turn, steers the rest of his body.

- Use the food to guide your dog's head to the left (Figs. 7.4-7.5). As his head moves to the left, his rear moves to the right.

- While pulling steadily on the leash, take small sideways steps to your right, starting on your right foot.

If you have a full-length mirror, now is a good time to use it. Watch your dog to make sure he is moving his body perpendicular to the direction in which you are moving (Fig. 7.5), as opposed to leading with his head or his rear. If his head is moving to the right sooner than his rear, position your left hand farther to the left (Fig. 7.6). If his rear is moving sooner than his head, position your left hand more to the right (i.e., closer to you [Fig. 7.7]). You might also need to keep the leash tighter. Reinforce correct action with your CR and a treat.

Add the CLOSE command when your dog is responding to your cues (the leash pressure and the steering motion). Fade the left hand motion first, then the leash pressure.

Figure 7.6 If his head is moving to the right sooner than his rear, position your left hand farther to the left.

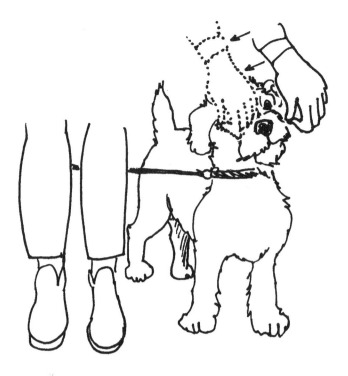

Figure 7.7 If his rear is moving sooner than his head, position your left hand more to the right.

In

We use the command IN to teach the dog to move his rear to the right, pivoting counterclockwise around his front legs. Horse trainers call this a "turn on the forehand." If you were looking down at the dog from above, he would make two arcs, one very small one with his front feet, one larger one with his rear (Fig. 7.8). *This rear control is extremely important for correct left turn and left circle training and is vital to fine-tuning his fronts and finishes.* We sometimes call this a *left quarter-turn.*

The starting position for this exercise is the same as for CLOSE (Fig. 7.4):

- Stand your dog in heel position.

- Hold your leash tightly behind your body and in your right hand. This helps hold your dog in heel position. Your right hand position depends on the size of your dog. Hold the leash parallel to the floor, attached to a buckle collar or the dead ring of a choke collar. The dog's right shoulder is bound to your left leg. Within reason, tighter is better, since your dog's front legs are the center of his pivot.

Figure 7.8 If you were looking down at the dog from above when he does *in* correctly, he would make two arcs, one very small one with his front feet, one larger one with his rear.

- Hold food in your left hand, in front of and slightly above your dog's nose.

Once you are ready, do the following, all at the same time:

- Move your left hand with the food in an arc slowly to the left of the dog's nose (remember, the food is used like a magnet). This should move your dog's head to the left, which should move his rear to the right. This is your desired goal. When he is first learning this movement, your dog may need to move his head close to his rib cage before he thinks to move his hind feet. This bending will fade as he learns to move his rear toward you.

- Take a step forward and around to your left (a left quarter-turn) with your right foot. Place your foot eight to ten inches in front of your dog's front feet (Fig. 7.9).

- Bring your left foot even with the right. If needed, take more quarter-turn steps to make sure your dog pivots around his front legs, instead of walking forward.

- Keep tension on the leash as you move; this helps keep your dog's front legs in place. You have to pull very hard with some dogs! When taking your first step on your right foot, the leash should tighten against the back of your left leg. If it doesn't, you probably aren't keeping the leash tight enough.

If you are still having trouble, study each part listed above and make sure you are not leaving out a step.

Figure 7.9 Take a step forward and around to your left (a left quarter turn) with your right foot. Plant it eight to ten inches in front of your dog's front feet. Complete the turn by bringing your left foot up next to your right foot.

Once you and your dog understand the mechanics and he is consistently moving his rear in toward you, add the cue word IN just before you start moving your hands and feet.

Some dogs, especially small ones, get pulled behind you when you apply the leash pressure. If this happens, don't pull as hard. If that doesn't solve the problem, hold the leash in front of your legs rather than behind them.

The first physical cue to fade is the left-hand motion. Keep the leash tight in your right hand. Once you no longer need your left hand with the food, begin to fade the leash pull, and eventually return the leash to your left hand. Some dogs take a long time to learn the left quarter-turn. Take your time and do not be discouraged by slow progress.

Once your dog moves his rear legs consistently, start with him in a *sit* instead of a *stand*. Work separately on having him *sit* after the left quarter-turn; start with him in a *stand*, do a quarter-turn, and tell him to SIT. Once he is doing each part well, combine the parts by starting and ending with a *sit*.

For a dog who swings his rear out on halts while heeling (crabbing or side-winding), this exercise is imperative. Straight sits during heeling are very important and IN gives you a way to help your dog correct flared-out sits. It is also useful for set-ups at the start of an exercise. Once the dog has mastered moving his rear when you move, use the command IN when you pivot counterclockwise in place. Your dog should now be able to move his rear and maintain heel position.

Off

OFF is the command to move your dog to his left. You will use it during heel position set-ups and any time your dog is heeling too close to you. Both of us use it for positioning our dogs in front position as well by giving the dog a word to move to his left during heeling.

To teach OFF:

- Face your dog's right side, with him in a *stand.*
- Stand with your left leg next to your dog's right hip and hold a piece of food in your right hand, just to the left of his nose (Fig. 7.10). If your dog is too long to allow this positioning, the hand by his nose is slightly more important, so use your left hand by his hip instead of your left leg. Just reach back as far on his body as you can.
- Nudge your dog's right hip slightly with your left leg or hand as you guide his head away from you to the left, using the food in your right hand.
- Reinforce the slightest sideways motion with your CR and food.

Position your right hand, which is holding the food, so your dog moves his whole body to his left. As with CLOSE and IN, this will take some experimentation. Long-legged dogs often cross their legs when side-stepping; short-legged dogs are less likely to do so.

Once you see the desired sideways movement by your dog, add your OFF command just before you nudge him. Do not forget to reinforce each effort early in this training.

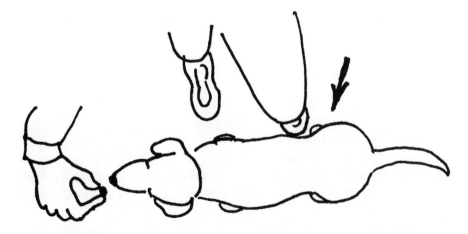

Figure 7.10 To teach *off,* face your dog's right side, with him in a stand, with your left leg by his right hip. Hold a piece of food in your right hand, just to the left of his nose.

When he side-steps with very little nudging, turn so you are facing the same direction as your dog. Hold food in your left hand, but instead of standing with him in heel position, stand so you are even with his rib cage (Fig. 7.11). This allows gentle nudges to help your dog move as you steer his head to the left with your left hand. Sometimes it is easier for him to understand this movement if you switch quickly from facing his side to this modified heel position while he is in the OFF mind-set.

As you see your dog beginning to understand this motion, do less head guiding, and eventually fade the leg nudge. Finally, move forward so you are standing in correct heel position.

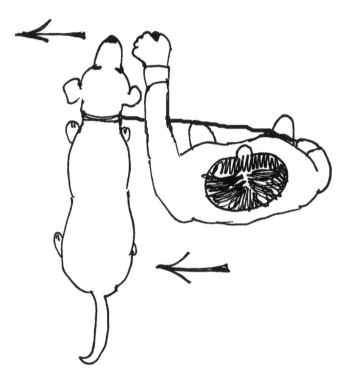

Figure 7.11 When he side-steps to the left with very little nudging, turn so you are facing the same direction as your dog. Hold food in your left hand, but instead of standing with him in heel position, stand so you are even with his rib cage.

Heel Starts

The purpose of a *heel start* is to get your dog moving forward quickly when you give a HEEL command. You will move only one step to begin this exercise. Have your dog *sit*, then step into heel position yourself. Use food over his nose, as needed, to keep him from moving as you adjust your position. You may want to use a *set-up* command when you do this.

Hold food in your left hand and show it to your dog. Slowly step forward with your left foot; your right foot remains in place (Fig. 7.12). Reinforce with your CR and food the instant your dog moves forward and release him. *Wait to add your HEEL command until your dog has some idea of what he is doing, which is to get up and move forward with you. After the CR and food, release your dog. Do not sit him!* Concentrate on moving, not stopping. You are looking for enthusiasm here!

Your ultimate goal is for your dog to maintain attention as you both take that first step. This is a very difficult phase for many dogs, so concentrate on keeping your dog's head up, even if it means moving forward only an inch or two.

This is a good place to add some games, especially if your dog is not enjoying *heel starts.* Stand your dog at your left side; precise heel position is not critical. Prime him — get him excited — with "Ready?, set?, go!" or something similar. While you are verbally priming, also excite him physically with body movements, such as rocking back and forth a few times before stepping out with your left foot. We like to see the dog jump forward for the food or toy immediately following the command to HEEL.

If your dog is not enjoying *heel starts,* you need to ask yourself "why?" and remedy the situation as soon as possible. A dog who does not start immediately on command will probably lag throughout the entire

Figure 7.12 To teach a *heel start,* hold food in your left hand and show it to your dog. Slowly step forward with your left foot only; your right foot remains in place.

heeling pattern. Adding the command too early can be detrimental as it may sound harsh to your dog. Make this fun and your dog will repay you with attentive heeling.

Be sure you are not reaching out of heel position when you give your dog his treat. Trainers with small dogs often make this mistake. Concentrate on keeping your left wrist against your left hip, thigh, knee, or whatever part of your body is just above your dog's head when you give the treat. If necessary, slide your hand down your left side to his mouth until he can reach the food. The goal is for your dog to want to be next to your leg!

Before all heel starts, shift your weight to your right foot before your first step. This makes it easier for you to step out on your left foot on the Judge's "Forward" command. Some handlers rock back onto their heels before stepping forward. Shifting your weight to your right foot will help eliminate this common handler error.

Adding Corrections to Heel Starts

We add a correction to *heel starts* to produce a hard-driving start. It is also a way to introduce a dog to heeling corrections. Adele prefers to hold most of the leash in her right hand, with her left thumb and forefinger encircling the leash close to the collar. Judy prefers to hold all of the leash gathered in her left hand with just a small amount of slack. We make the correction by popping straight forward on the leash, *keeping the leash parallel to the floor.* Use a buckle collar to put the pressure from the correction on the back of his neck. If you are training a short dog, you must bend over to correct properly.

Sit your dog in heel position. Prepare yourself for the correction by holding the leash in one of the ways discussed above and shifting your weight to your right foot. Command heel, step out on your left foot, give a quick pop forward on the leash, and immediately praise and release your dog. This is the *escape* phase. We release the dog by backing up. This causes him to turn and come back. **It is vital that you praise and release immediately!** Try another *heel start* without the correction and use your CR and a treat for reasonable effort. This is the *avoidance* phase.

We do not usually add corrections to *heel starts* until we have added them to the *come, sit, down,* and *attention* exercises. If your dog is confused by your *heel start* correction, review the corrections for these other exercises. Also, make sure that you start with a mild correction. Think of it as a "beat the pop" game.

Right Turn Starts

Once your dog understands *heel starts*, add a *right turn start*. This teaches him to bend around you for his first attempt at a right turn.

Use the same starting position as for a *heel start*, with your dog in heel position and your weight on your right foot, but instead of your right foot pointing straight forward, angle it to your right. Command HEEL and step across to your right with your left foot (Fig. 7.13). Move slowly enough so your dog can keep up with the new direction. Use your CR and feed. Move faster as he learns the turn. You might experiment with holding your food in your right hand.

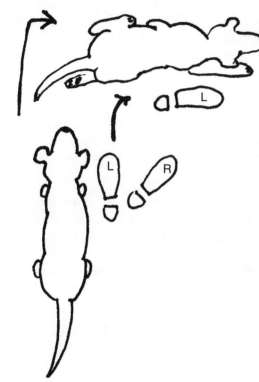

Figure 7.13 When doing a *right turn start,* use the same starting position as for a *heel start.* Your dog is in heel position and your weight is on your right foot. Instead of your right foot pointing straight ahead, angle it to your right. Command HEEL and step across to your right with your left foot.

Play Running

Play running is an exercise which teaches your dog how to run smoothly with you. It is a predecessor of the *Fast* needed in the heeling pattern, *when you must run and your dog must move fast enough to maintain proper heel position.* Play running also introduces your dog to the command HURRY, which means *speed up.* It should be a fun race for both of you.

Start with your dog standing at your left side. Prompt him with an excited "READY? SET? HURRY!" and burst into a run for a short distance. This is a good place to use a toy to reward your dog: say OKAY (or your release command) and throw the toy forward after a short spurt of running. If toys don't inspire him, try a piece of food. Be careful that your throw doesn't cause your dog to cut in front of you. If he barks and races ahead of you, that's fine when you first introduce *play running.* If he hangs back, encourage him to move out ahead of you. If your dog is naturally exuberant, get him used to running under control in heel position by keeping him in position with food in your left hand.

When you first introduce *play running*, ask for only an initial burst of speed. Gradually run farther until your dog will stay with you for 50 or 60 feet. It is best to master this exercise outside where you have plenty of room. Keep it fun! Precise heel position isn't the goal right now. We are looking for willingness and enough speed to stay with you when you run.

Dizzy Spins

The *dizzy spin* teaches your dog to wrap around you in a tight clockwise circle. It is an important prelude to successful tight *about turns.* Don't do more than a few revolutions in a row, especially with a small dog. The "head rush" feeling is what earned the exercise its name.

Stand your dog in heel position, with your weight on your right foot. You may hold the food in either hand. Experiment to find which works best for you and your dog. Keep your hand holding the food tight against your body or leg to keep your dog wrapped closely around you (Fig. 7.14). Turn *in place* to your right. Move slowly enough for your dog to keep up. He should be pushing his nose into the food in your hand. As he gets the idea, add a HURRY command before you start to move. When your dog has the idea of the spin, move faster. If you have a reluctant dog, you may need to throw a toy or food ahead of you as you come out of the spin to motivate him to spin faster.

Make sure you are turning in place, rather than making a small circle. Imagine trying to keep your feet on a paper plate.

Figure 7.14 Keep your hand holding the food tight against your body or leg to keep your dog wrapped closely around you. Turn *in place* to your right.

❖ ❖ ❖ ❖ ❖ ❖ ❖ ❖ ❖ ❖

The exercises you have learned in this chapter are important when teaching your dog how to *heel* and how to do accurate *fronts* and *finishes*. They help him understand how to fix heeling mistakes and help make corrections more informative. They allow you to efficiently position your dog in heel position (*set-up*) before starting any exercise. Work hard on them!

Stays

O
ur definition of STAY is that when told to do so, the dog remains
in the place and the position in which we left him, whether a *sit*,
a *down*, or a *stand*. We are particular about this because of the
requirements of the obedience ring. If the dog changes positions, say
switching from a *sit* to a *down*, he fails the exercise. We also don't want
him to move his front feet during the *Sit-stay*, or to shift from one hip to
the other during the *Down-stay*, nor do we want him to whine or bark.
We like to see a dog alert, yet relaxed and confident, while staying.

The Exercises

There are three different *stay* exercises and assorted *waits* used in
the formal obedience ring. We use the command STAY when we want the
dog to maintain a particular position — either *sit, down,* or *stand* —
when we go away from him for a period of time and then return to him.
We use WAIT when we want the dog to remain in a certain position until
we give him a command to do something else *without* returning to him.
An example of the latter is the *Sit-stay* before a *Recall*.

In the Novice class, your dog must be able to do a one-minute *Sit-stay* and a three minute *Down-stay* in a group of six to twelve dogs, with
you facing him from across the ring (twenty-five to thirty feet away). In
the Open class, the *Sit-stay* exercise lasts for three minutes and the
Down-stay for five minutes, both done with the handlers out of sight of
their dogs. Both types of formal stays are done with the dogs lined up,
side by side, with commands from the judge to "Sit (or down) your dogs,"
"Leave your dogs," "Return to your dogs," and "Exercise finished." In a
group of twelve dogs, there may not be much space between each dog
during the stay exercises, so be sure to practice stays with other dogs
fairly close to yours (Fig. 8.1).

Figure 8.1 There is not always much space between dogs during the group exercises.

We introduce the concept of *Stay* early in a dog's training. He needs enough physical control of his legs and body to maintain a position for a short time and enough mental control to handle the stress of this somewhat demotivating exercise. Somewhere between four and six months of age is probably a reasonable time to start. We occasionally start very brief, three-to-five-second stays with a two-to-four-month-old puppy.

Sit-Stay

We begin with the *Sit-stay* because it is usually the easiest for the dog to learn. It is very easy for a dog to move his feet during a *Stand-stay*, and the down position can be difficult for some dogs to maintain due to dominance issues. Also, adding any type of correction to the *Down-stay* or *Stand-stay* is almost impossible.

Begin your training of the *Sit-stay* with the dog wearing a buckle collar and a short leash.

During any stay exercise, the dog may only move his head and tail. Timing is very important during this exercise. You must make it very clear that remaining motionless gets positively reinforced, while movement does not.

The dog should sit squarely on his bottom with his weight shifted forward onto his front legs, rather than slouched back on his rear in a puppy sit (Fig. 8.2). The dog will generally balance himself more securely in a square sit if he sits with his tail extended straight out behind him. We prefer a straight sit because the "slouched-on-a-hip" sit often leads to the dog lying down during the *Sit-stay*. If your dog constantly flops over on one hip, reinforce the sit *before* the flop occurs. Some dogs and puppies may need separate work to build the hip muscles in order to sit

Figure 8.2 This puppy is sitting slouched over on a hip in an undesirable puppy sit.

straight. For a dog who slouches on one hip, you may want to add another command when working on it such as "sit up" or "sit straight." Teach *scoot fronts* (see *Combination Words* chapter) in order to get your dog to sit squarely on his bottom. *Scoot fronts* are an excellent way to build the intrinsic muscle strength that the dog needs for a correct, tight sit.

Begin the *Sit-stay* with the dog sitting squarely in heel position. Hold the leash so there is some upward tension on it (see Fig. 8.3). We do not want the dog to move any part of his body except his head and eyes, although tail wags are legal. *Demand immediately that the dog remain absolutely motionless,* as that will become the ultimate meaning of the word STAY.

Traditionally, dog trainers use a hand signal in front of the dog's face to accompany their verbal STAY command. This is usually a pushing motion of one hand with the palm moving toward the dog's face (Fig. 8.4).

Figure 8.3 Begin with the dog sitting squarely in heel position. Hold the leash so there is some upward tension on it.

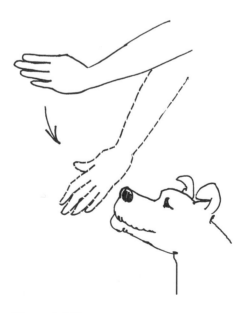

Figure 8.4 The most common way to give a signal to stay is a pushing motion of one hand with the palm moving toward the dog's face.

We use the left hand to signal STAY and the right hand to mean STAND. Any time you give a STAY command in the ring, you may also use a hand signal.

We want the dog to be successful immediately, so the initial stays are short in duration, perhaps three to five seconds total. When Adele first introduces the stay exercise, she stands in heel position. Until the dog can sit still for about five seconds, she doesn't move away from the dog. Judy takes one step forward with her right foot and pivots directly in front of the dog (Fig. 8.5).

Use your STAY command and, at the same time, signal with the palm of your left hand in front of your dog's face. If you want to pivot in front, as Judy does, do so. Count in your head to three or four, and if your dog has not moved, use your CR, and treat. After you give your dog a treat, immediately use your OKAY release command. Note the order: CR, treat, release. Make sure you give your CR and food for sitting and staying and not for the release. You may either pivot back into heel position or stay in front for the CR, treat, and release.

We want the dog to learn that he should not move until he hears his release command, so after three or four successful brief stays, give him a treat after the CR, but do not use your release command. Instead, pause

Figure 8.5 Judy immediately takes one step forward with her right foot and pivots directly in front of the dog.

a second or two, restraining him with your leash if needed, then repeat your CR, give him another treat, and then release him. You may also reinforce with food while still in front of him. This important concept of waiting for a release command is one that we want the dog to grasp early in his training. He must also get used to your returning and leaving again without releasing him. Feeding him treats repeatedly will help your dog build stamina for a single stay.

If your dog moves, a verbal AH-AH correction and snugging up the leash should stop the fidgeting long enough to allow you to use your CR and food for correct behavior. We use a mild correction (snugging up the leash) to give the dog information. When he is wrong, he gets a snug leash; when he is right, he gets a CR and a cookie. We do keep the corrections to a minimum at this stage. If your dog seems too immature to handle this exercise, wait a week or two and then try again.

Do not continuously repeat the STAY command when the dog is staying; instead, reinforce the good efforts with your CR and food. Another STAY command after an AH-AH may be necessary to tell the dog what he needs to do in order to be right. Watch your dog carefully to prevent the actual breaking of the stay and to be able to reinforce the desired stay. The dog must shift his weight to lie down or stand up and this weight shift often causes the dog to bob his head. It is at that moment when the AH-AH and the leash tightening should occur. If the dog breaks the stay, begin again.

Eye Contact

We do not require eye contact during the stays. You will be leaving the dog to go out of sight someday, and if he becomes dependent on the eye contact, it will be harder for him to tolerate your absence. Also, eye contact is intimidating for some dogs. When you are training, encompass the whole dog with your eyes or zero in on whatever part(s) he has a tendency to move. Do not take your eyes off your dog until his *stay* is reliable.

Building Time

The next goal is to build the amount of time that your dog does a *Sit-stay*. Add time slowly to get the most confident stays. Begin with just a few seconds if you have a very tense or wiggly dog. Do not add time until you notice your dog beginning to relax. Use a lot of food in the beginning, and always precede it with your CR. Food tends to have a relaxing effect!

Work toward a four-minute sit while still directly in front of him. Some dogs will do this in a matter of weeks, while others will take months. Don't panic — there's no hurry! This is a *confidence* exercise and your dog needs to be comfortable and relaxed about it. You are working toward a minimum three-minute *Sit-stay* and a five-minute *Down-stay* with you out of sight, so it is better to build this foundation now than to try to fix it later. Fixing an out-of-sight *Sit-stay* and *Down-stay* problem is one of the most difficult remedial training problems in obedience.

Building Distance

In keeping with the "train one thing at a time" rule, we build *distance* separately from *time* when teaching stays. When you start adding distance, reduce the elapsed time.

When your dog shows you that he is ready for you to go farther away, begin to walk away from him, *adding one step at a time*. Command STAY, walk away two steps, and turn to face your dog. We want to see a dog look confident on his stays: alert expression with his "ears up and eyes bright" and a relaxed body posture without being sloppy. Notice whether your dog looks relaxed. If he does, use your CR and food. If not, work closer to him until you see him begin to relax. If your dog tries to get up or lie down, he is telling you that he is not ready for you to leave him just yet.

Some dogs worry when their handlers leave them for *any* reason. If yours is one of these, practice leaving your dog with a friend who will feed him while you move around your training area. Your dog should not be in a formal stay. He should just be "hanging out" with your friend. While you are at a distance, your friend should use *your* CR and feed your dog periodically until she has used up a handful of food. You should then return to your dog, use your CR and feed him. Repeat this until he is more relaxed without you beside him. Then add the formal stay itself.

If you go too fast and notice your dog's stress level building, back up in your training to the point at which your dog is more relaxed. How far you back up will vary with different dogs. *Back up far enough to allow for success most of the time.* The occasional mistake is fine; it helps your dog better understand the exercise. Frequent mistakes show lack of understanding or training. It is important to take these first steps slowly in order to produce a dog who stays confidently.

The Return

When you return to your dog after a stay exercise in the obedience ring, you must walk around your dog, keeping him on your left as you step into heel position. Your dog should maintain his position until you release him, and in the ring, you release him when the judge tells you "Exercise finished."

One of the easiest ways to get your dog used to your walking behind him is to place your left hand on his head as you return (Fig. 8.6). You pass left shoulder to left shoulder and walk behind your dog on your way to heel position. Use your CR when you are behind him. If he stays, CR and give him a treat when you get back to heel position. You may even want to feed your dog following a CR when you are behind him or even as you approach from the front. Very excited or very worried dogs do better with more food and more frequent use of your CR. **Remember, when your dog is right, he is building confidence.**

Many dogs like to physically turn and follow you as you walk around them, thereby breaking the *stay*. A minor shift of a paw in your direction can escalate to the dog standing up and turning in a circle. The former

Figure 8.6 One of the easiest ways to get your dog used to your walking behind him is to place your left hand on his head as you return.

might cause a minor point loss; the latter results in a zero for the exercise. If your dog is having trouble sitting still when you walk in a circle around him, you may need to break this part of the exercise down even further. Once you are able to move a few steps out in front of your dog, start taking steps to either side. Work in an arc that gradually moves you further around behind your dog. Stop before he moves, step back to the front, CR and give a treat.

At this point, make sure you are using a random reinforcement schedule with your CR and food. Sometimes the dog gets a CR and no food, sometimes the dog gets both, and sometimes you ask for two or three repetitions before you use your CR and feed the dog. **Notice there is never a time when the dog gets food without the CR, but there are times when he will get the CR without food.** Throughout all of your *stay* training, it is important to remember that you should return to the dog often enough to reinforce and remind him of what he is doing. To reinforce, use your CR and food. To remind, as well as reinforce, use your hand on the dog — either a tap on the chest for the *Sit-stay* or on the shoulders for the *Down-stay*. These taps are essentially mild corrections, although when combined with the CR and food, most dogs will not be upset by them. **When we use corrections, we precede them with a verbal cue which tells the dog what he is supposed to do. We do not use corrections until we are positive the dog understands the exercise.**

When you can consistently walk to the end of your six-foot leash, turn and face your dog, and see a relaxed, confident, happy-looking dog, you are ready to introduce proofing to the *Sit-stay* exercise.

Proofing the Sit-Stay

How much proofing you must do when teaching your stays will depend on what sort of dog you are training. Dogs at the extremes of the temperament range usually require more proofing than an average dog. Social butterflies — Adele's Treasure fits this category! — and fearful dogs require more. The social dog must learn to restrain himself from "schmoozing" with the judge who is attempting to do an examination. In addition, he must refrain from playing with neighbor dogs and handlers during the group stays. Fearful dogs must learn to stay when what they would probably like best to do is run away and hide.

The first level of proofing is to add pressure to the leash. Dogs have strong "opposition reflexes," which means they pull or brace against pressure. This reflex makes leash pressure helpful in expanding the dog's understanding of the STAY command. If your dog can brace against these pulls, he shows that he understands he must not move.

This leash pressure is best done using a buckle collar. Use slight pulls forward (not jerks), slight pulls to both sides, and slight pulls from behind the dog. Some dogs move toward the pressure in response to even gentle pulls. A verbal correction and snugging up of the leash should stop this movement. When he is successful, CR and give him a treat. You should be able to use fairly strong pulls in a short period of time.

Next, add hand pressure to all parts of the dog's body, particularly his front legs. He should learn to push back against your pressure, maintaining the stay as you gently push him in one direction and then another. If your dog moves a foot when you touch it, use your other hand to put pressure downward on his shoulders. This settles his weight more evenly over both front legs. Keep your hand on his shoulders while you lightly touch his leg again (Fig. 8.7), using your CR and food when he is successful.

The next step is to change your body posture as you stand in front of the dog. Stoop down, jump up, hop from foot to foot, or run around him. All of these motions may excite him and cause him to move. You

Figure 8.7 Keep your hand on your dog's shoulders while you lightly touch his leg.

should gently and firmly correct any movement, verbally and then physically, if necessary. The physical correction, if needed, can be a slight upward pop on the buckle collar immediately after the STAY command.

Next, have a friend approach your dog and pat her leg or the floor a few times, as if calling the dog to her. Instruct this person to stop eight to ten feet away the first few times, as most dogs can stay successfully at this distance. Use your CR and feed immediately for success. **Remember, your dog needs immediate feedback every time he is right when he is learning something new.** The food can be delayed slightly, as long as the dog hears your CR. The CR and the food refocus the dog on you and helps him be successful. Your friend should start further away if your dog is especially nervous or extremely social. Gradually decrease the distance until he can successfully ignore someone close to him. Your friend should also walk close to your dog from various directions, as well as walk a very small circle around both of you. If this is difficult for your dog, ask your friend to avoid making eye contact with him initially, since many dogs view this as an invitation to visit.

Some more advanced forms of proofing include:

- Toys thrown or squeaked nearby.
- A dog or dogs moving around and behind your staying dog.
- Another dog jumping behind your dog.
- A dumbbell thrown nearby.
- A set of Utility scent articles dumped on the floor.
- A dog doing a *Recall* or a *Drop on Recall* with a verbal DOWN command while your dog does a *Sit-stay*.
- Applause.
- A friendly dog approaching and sniffing your dog. Do this very carefully with an insecure or dominant dog!
- Another dog visiting you, while you face your dog.

The Obedience Stands

Four different stands are needed for AKC obedience:

- The Novice *Stand for Examination*: The handler is six feet from the dog, who is off-leash. The judge approaches and examines the dog by touching him gently on the top of the head, the top of the shoulders, and the rear.

- The Utility *Signal Stand*: The judge gives the command to "Stand your dog." The handler and dog stop together as the handler gives a stand signal to the dog. The dog must maintain heel position. The handler does not move away from the dog until told to by the judge.

- The Utility *Moving Stand for Examination:* The judge gives the same command as in the *Signal Stand*, but in this case you must not stop or even hesitate as you signal and/or command your dog to stand. The handler continues to walk ten to twelve feet forward from the dog and then turns and faces him. The judge approaches and does a thorough examination, typically starting with his hand held out for a quick sniff by the dog, then both hands starting at the dog's ears, running down his neck, shoulders, front legs, back up to the shoulders, along the rib cage, and finally down the back legs. A few judges flip ears or tail, though this is not common. This exercise shows that your dog tolerates handling by a stranger.

- The Open and Utility *stand for measurement* by the judge: While this used to be required at the start of everyone's Open and Utility routines, it is now optional. Some judges still measure every dog, while others measure occasionally to check for the correct jump height. This is not a formal stand but sets the tone for the entire performance, so your dog must be able to handle it confidently. He must tolerate a stranger bending over him and touching his body with a ruler. This can be frightening for some dogs so should be taught and proofed before your first Open trial.

Adding an Exam

A dog who will stand still while being touched and petted by people, both familiar and unfamiliar, is a joy to live with and an easier animal to train. For the purpose of earning obedience titles, your dog must tolerate a relatively simple exam in Novice and a more thorough exam in Utility, as explained in the previous section.

When your dog can consistently *sit* and *stay* for about ten seconds while you walk around him, apply leash pressure to his collar, and squat down near him, he is ready for you to add an exam while he is sitting. Examine your dog by petting him on the head, his back, his front legs, and his ears. Make sure he is secure with *your* exam before having another person examine him. Do this from the front, sides, and back of your dog, and insist on a solid *Sit-stay* throughout the examination.

Next, have someone the dog knows well examine him. Even young puppies can successfully *stay* during an exam if you follow a few rules. Stand or kneel close to your dog, with the clip of the leash in one hand and some very interesting food in the other. Sit your dog and command STAY. Immediately use your CR and let your dog nibble on the food (Fig. 8.8). As long as the food is more interesting to your dog than the approaching person, he will continue to nibble and ignore the examiner. If you have a very social dog, you will need to use *especially* interesting food. Stay close to your dog and use a frequent CR and food for relaxation. Instruct your helper to touch your dog *only* if he stays.

Next, ask a person who is familiar with dogs to help you, but is not known to your own dog. If your dog is fearful, have the person offer your dog a treat and withdraw. Repeat until the dog seems more relaxed, and then have the person touch the dog under the chin. Some dogs may be frightened when a person reaches over the top of his head. This varies from dog to dog, of course, but with a fearful dog, you must practice each

Figure 8.8 Stand or kneel close to your dog, with the clip of the leash in one hand and some very interesting food in the other. Sit the dog and command STAY. Immediately start using your CR and let your dog nibble on the food.

step longer and more slowly than with one who is confident. The same may be true for the "social butterfly." Build on the initial touch by asking the examining person to pet the dog with both hands from ears to tail.

Finally, use an examiner who may be a little cautious with your dog. She will approach very carefully, and this puts some dogs on guard. Unfortunately, a few judges tend to be wary of some dogs, so this should be part of your proofing. If you have a toy dog, occasionally have the examiner be overly gentle with the exam. For some reason, many judges think toy dogs will break if examined with a firm hand!

More Proofing Ideas

The possibilities for proofing are nearly endless.

- Have a stranger wear a coat, hat, or carry an umbrella.
- Have the person stoop over and shuffle up to the dog.
- Have the person carry a clipboard.

Your goal is to train a dog who takes all of this in stride and is happy, confident, and relaxed during the stay. We recommend that you stay close to your dog to offer your CR and food quickly, until you see him begin to relax. You may then move farther away, but perhaps attach a long line in case your dog bolts. When you begin to move farther away, use your CR often but feed only when you return. **The dog has learned that your CR means he is right and the food is coming!** You should have built the confidence slowly enough so that your dog won't feel the need to bolt, but some dogs are afraid or have excitable personalities, and need the extra help that a long line can provide.

We have shown you, step-by-step, how to carefully shape the dog to do a *Sit-stay* and accept an examination by a stranger. This exercise should duplicate elements of the Novice and Utility stands for exam while the dog is doing a *Sit-stay*.

Taking the Stay on the Road

The next level of proofing requires you to change the location of your *stay* training. Until now, your dog has probably been learning this new exercise in a familiar environment, such as your backyard, your living room, or a familiar training facility. Now it is time to move to a new place and see if your dog can maintain his *Sit-stay* at the end of a six-foot leash. As you move to six feet and farther, use your CR randomly, and don't feed him until you return. If your dog cannot maintain his *Sit-stay* at six feet, move closer until he can consistently and confidently hold his *stay*. Keep working in the new location.

When he is doing solid *stays* in the front yard, you might move your proofing to the street or driveway. As your dog shows you he's comfortable, progress to a neighbor's yard, a park, or a school yard. Make sure he is comfortable and relaxed in each new location. Each time you move to a new location, you will probably need to back up a step or two to maintain confidence. As you can see, you can do a lot of training in new locations without actually leaving your neighborhood.

Slowly add outside distractions like other dogs and children. At this point, we take our dogs to a match or a training class and practice *Sit-stays* around other dogs, but not necessarily in the ring. Some dogs feel threatened in a line of strange dogs or are excessively excited to greet a new person or animal. We also do some attention work and other training at the match but do not yet enter as an exhibitor.

You must also get your dog used to a line of people walking toward him when they return to their dogs. Some dogs get intimidated by so many people coming at them. This can only be done with the help of other trainers and their dogs. It can be imitated with a line of people and no other dogs if absolutely necessary.

You want your dog to be successful. Success builds confidence.

We hope that you now have a secure dog that you can take anywhere, under any circumstances, and do a successful *Sit-stay*, either with or without an examination.

Shifting Front Feet

Adele has had trouble with both of her Flat Coated Retrievers shifting their front feet during a *Sit-stay*. For some dogs, this is a stress reaction, and corrections tend to make the shifting worse. For others, it may simply be a matter of comfort. It is physically difficult for some dogs to maintain that position for the three or more minutes needed during an Open *Sit-stay*. These dogs may be unaware that shifting their feet is wrong.

A device you may wish to make for a shifty-footed dog is shown in Figure 8.8. This is simply a small bell, available at craft stores, tied or sewn on to something like ponytail elastic or rubber bands and placed around each front leg. Put these on your dog when you train the *Sit-stay*. The bells alert you to any front foot movement by your dog and keep *you* honest about movement occurring when you have your back turned. They also serve as a reminder to your dog to think about what he does with his front feet.

Figure 8.9 You can put these bells on ponytail holders on your dog to alert you to any front foot movement, and to keep *you* honest about movement occurring when you have your back turned. They also serve as a reminder to your dog to think about what he does with his front feet.

When your dog moves enough to cause a bell to ring, we suggest that you correct him in some way. We use an immediate verbal reprimand, followed by either a thump on the chest or a collar correction.

Handling During Stays

The obedience rules and regulations do not mention how you should stand while your dog is doing a group *Stay*. During a *Recall*, we stand with our feet close together, and our arms hanging at our sides. To differentiate a stay from a recall, we cross our arms in front as we leave the dog for any *Stay*. We stand with feet apart, often with our weight shifted more onto one leg (Fig. 8.10). This helps us remain comfortable for the three-minute Novice *Down-stay* — it's not easy to stand still for that long! This position can also clarify the difference between the *wait* and *stay* exercises for many dogs. Both of us keep our arms crossed until we have returned to heel position and the judge has said "Exercise finished." We don't like to change arm position during the exercise. We use a wristwatch with a stopwatch that is set just after the STAY command and just before crossing our arms; with arms folded, it is easy to glance at the elapsed time. If you have conditioned your dog to this sight picture from the beginning, he has had an opportunity to understand it clearly throughout his Novice stays.

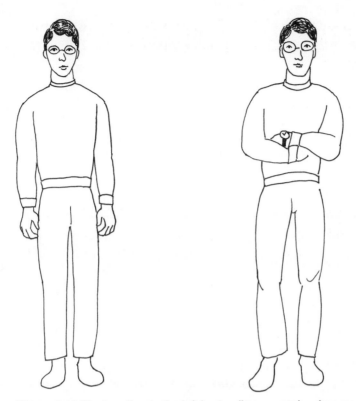

Figure 8.10 The handler on the left is standing as we do when we do a *Recall*. His feet are close together and his arms are hanging at his sides. The handler on the right has his arms crossed and feet apart, which is how we stand during any *Stay* exercise.

Down-Stay

The next type of stay your dog must do in the obedience ring is a *Down-stay*. In Novice, a group of six to twelve dogs do their *Down-stays* together side by side while the handlers stand across the ring. In Open, the handlers leave and go out of sight of the dogs for five minutes.

We like to wait several months after teaching the *sphinx down* and the *Sit-stay* before we introduce the *Down-stay*. We wait because we want the *sphinx down* solidly learned before teaching the down at the side for the *Down-stay*. We ask our dogs to roll onto a hip for the *Down-stay* and do not want to confuse that with the *sphinx down*. It is our opinion that the dog needs to be more settled in the down position for a three-to-five-minute long down than he is when he does an Open *Drop on Recall* or a Utility *Signal Drop*. The latter two exercises require the dog to perform another movement soon after the drop, so we prefer to see the *sphinx down* for these, since the dog can get up faster than if he is rolled onto one hip.

We add a command such as ROLL or SIDE to the *sphinx down* so the dog rolls onto one hip. We prefer the right hip, which puts the dog slightly behind us, although still in heel position. If your dog rolls onto his left hip, he is putting himself closer to the handler and dog on your left. In a close line of dogs, the other handler might have to step over your dog when returning to her dog.

Some dogs resist this rolling action, but you can shape this exercise by pushing on the left hip as you give the command ROLL, giving the CR when the dog rolls, and then feeding. If your dog resists the push on the hip, work first to get him to turn his head back slightly toward his hip as you lure him into position with a treat (Fig. 8.11). Keep the other hand gently on his shoulders to keep him lying down. Gradually increase how far you ask him to turn his head. Most dogs eventually shift onto their hip to continue following the food.

Practice on a comfortable surface such as carpeting before trying it on a hard surface like linoleum or training mats. Try rolling your dog onto his right hip. If he resists, use his left hip. Some dogs find one position more comfortable than another, and since they have to stay this way for five minutes or more, you should consider your dog's comfort

Figure 8.11 If your dog resists a push on the hip, work first to get him to turn his head back slightly toward his hip as you lure him into position with a treat.

Down-Stay

when teaching the exercise. We do encourage the hip roll, as most dogs seem genuinely more comfortable in this position. It is also harder for them to get up if they have to go back into the sphinx position first.

Observe how your dog relaxes at home. This may tell you which hip is more comfortable for him to lie on.

Some dogs shift from one hip to the other and you should discourage this early in his training. You might lose points for the shift and if he shifts repeatedly, you will not pass the *Down-stay.*

Some owners also teach their dogs to fold or tuck one paw during the *Down-stay.* Add the command TUCK. You can place the paw in a folded position and use your CR and food. Folding the paw is merely the act of bending the lower front leg at the first joint, thereby causing the paw to be tucked under (Fig. 8.12). This helps some dogs remember that they are to stay until released. Many dogs resist folding, and it is certainly your choice whether to train this or not. It may be physically uncomfortable for your dog to tuck a paw.

Figure 8.12 Tucking the paw is merely the act of bending the lower front leg at the first joint, thereby causing the foot to be tucked under.

Proofing the Down-Stay

The proofing for the *Down-stay* should proceed much as we described in the section on the *Sit-stay,* although it should go much faster since your dog has already been through all the proofing stages. Many dogs consider the down position a threatening one. If your dog is very dominant or very submissive, he may have more of a problem with the *Down-stay* than the *Sit-stay* in a line of unknown dogs. You should train more slowly as you introduce your dog to the *Down-stay* with other dogs beside him. Also stay close and reinforce often with your CR and food. This helps him relax. Use familiar, friendly, and nonthreatening dogs in your initial lineups, gradually adding dogs who are strangers to your dog. Keep the other dogs a little farther away from your dog in the beginning, gradually moving them closer as he becomes more confident. Again, reinforce intermittently with your CR, food, and a tap on the shoulders, as needed. As your dog relaxes, you should begin to move away until you are at the requisite twenty five to thirty feet from him.

Sniffing

Another problem in the *Down Stay* is sniffing the ground or the mats. The dog who does this needs a full understanding of the command LEAVE IT (see *Fundamental Words* chapter). You may pair another command such as NO SNIFF when you are teaching this.

Begin by placing obvious pieces of food in front of your dog while you stay close to correct or reinforce after you give your command. Then use more appetizing food. Try putting a little bacon grease or gravy in some water in a squirt bottle and sprinkling it on the ground outside. Have your dog do a long down on or near this delightful new smell. If there is a bitch in season in your class, have your dog do a *Down-stay* where she has been sitting. You never know what good smells are on some mats, and it is better to be prepared. In the ring, Judy often tells her dog DOWN, ROLL, NO SNIFF. All of this is allowable, as long as you can say it before the judge tells you to leave your dog.

Stand-Stay

In order to do any of the stand exercises that we discussed earlier, your dog must learn a solid *Stand-stay*. Before you start to teach the *Stand-stay*, we suggest that you teach the *kick-back stand* so your dog is comfortable in that position. He should also have a reliable *Sit-stay* and *sit for exam*. The progression of *Stand-stay* teaching is similar to the other stays except that the position is more vulnerable to foot movement.

Shape the *Stand-stay* slowly. Make sure your dog's feet are square when he does his *kick-back stand*. If they aren't square (i.e., one or more feet are out of position) place the misplaced foot parallel to the other foot while telling the dog FOOT. Taking a lesson from the conformation ring, it is best to adjust a front leg by grasping it at the elbow, lifting, and placing the foot (Fig. 8.13), and a rear leg by lifting by the hock (Fig. 8.14).

This controls the shoulders and hips and usually works better than grabbing the dog closer to his foot. Some dogs really object to having their feet adjusted. If yours does, you have two choices: either shape the adjustment of his feet until your dog is more comfortable with it, or teach him how to get up squarely into a stand without your help.

Notice how your dog is most comfortable when standing. Although stacking or positioning the dog for the Novice *Stand For Exam* is allowed, it is often not his most comfortable position.

Figure 8.13 Adjust a front leg by grasping it at the elbow, lifting and placing the foot.

Figure 8.14 Adjust a rear leg by lifting it by the hock.

If you have taught the *kick-back stand* properly, your dog should stand squarely. If you have neglected this part of your training or have never trained a dog to stand this way, go back and retrain the stand (see *Fundamental Words* chapter). You will be glad you did once you get to Utility training, where the dog is required to "freeze in the stand" two times, once for the *Signal Stand* and once for the *Moving Stand for Examination.*

We like to add pressure to the dog's head, shoulders, and rump to make sure he is standing solidly (Fig. 8.15). If he shifts when you do this, he will surely shift when someone else does it. Use your hand signal in front of his face as you command STAY, and pivot in front of your dog. Again, you might wish to begin by giving the STAY command and standing by your dog's side. Once he is able to remain stationary for five seconds, add your pivot to face him. If he holds the stay, give the CR and food. If he doesn't, go back to your *Sit-stay,* as your dog clearly does not yet understand that he may not move. There is no good correction for a dog in the *Stand-stay.*

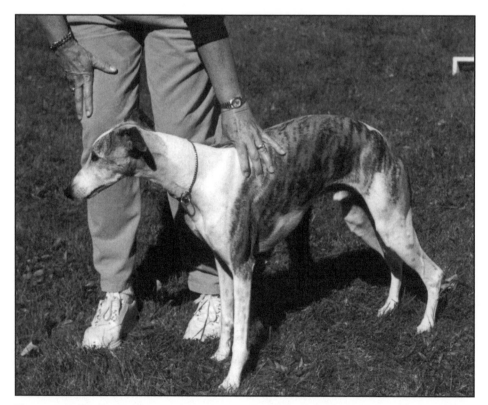

Figure 8.15 We like to add pressure to his head, shoulders, and rump to make sure the dog is standing solidly.

Your dog can learn to *Stand-stay* with leash pressure just as he did in the *Sit-stay*. This is an important part of the *Stand-stay* proofing.

Begin the examination yourself, running your hand down your dog's back, touching him lightly on his head, middle of the back and rear, and eventually going down all four legs, touching the ears and tail, if he has one. You should also do a rough exam similar to the way some judges do one, as well as a light or "tickle" exam, which many smooth-coated dogs and toy dogs object to.

Have friends examine your dog first, followed by friendly strangers. Do not forget to have them wear strange articles of clothing that a judge might wear when judging in the rain, for example. If your dog is leery, have the person offer him food and then back away. Continue to offer food to your dog as the person approaches until he is eagerly awaiting the approach of any stranger who may also feed him.

The Novice Stand for Examination

On the judge's order, the handler should stand her dog. She may leave the dog when she is ready without further orders from the judge and go about six feet away, turn, and face her dog. The handler should leave from heel position and she should not have her hands on the dog when she gives the STAY command. The judge then approaches from the front and touches the dog on the head, the body, and the hindquarters. The handler is then told to return to her dog. She must return to heel position by circling behind the dog as for the *Sit-stay*.

Errors on the Stand for Exam

- Dog will not stand without rough handling by the handler (NQ).
- Handler doesn't leave from heel position (points off).
- Handler touches the dog when she gives the STAY signal or has a hand on the dog when she commands him to STAY (points off or NQ, depending on the severity).
- Handler goes farther than six feet away or not far enough (points off).
- Dog moves his feet during the exam (points off).
- Dog moves from the place where he was standing during the exam (NQ).
- Dog sits during the exam (NQ).
- Handler does not return to heel position (points off).
- Dog growls or snaps (NQ).

Combining the Stand and Moving Exercises

Whenever your dog does a stand in obedience, he is required to do a moving exercise following the stand. For example, in Novice he must move from the *Stand for Examination* to the *Heel Free* exercise. It is important for your dog to learn to release enthusiastically from all stands so he is ready to go confidently to the next exercise.

Under the newest regulations, measuring of the dog is optional, but you should prepare your dog for those judges who continue to measure dogs. In Open and Utility, the dog and handler often have to cross the ring to set-up for the *Heel Free* exercise (as opposed to setting up near the gate). If your dog is stressed by measuring, shape this exercise carefully so he focuses on you as you cross the ring and is ready to heel when commanded.

We suggest that you practice the release from the stand by first drawing a series of numbers on the floor of your training area (Fig. 8.16). Move from one number to the next, and either sit or stand the dog in heel position and then release. You can add someone at one or two of the numbers who will measure your dog and then move quickly to the next number. Shape it further by taking a step or two of heeling, followed by a release. This is also an excellent exercise to work on set-ups. Work to have your dog sit in heel position with as few adjustments as possible.

Draw the numbers in different directions, as shown in Fig. 8.16. You must turn in various directions so the number is right side up when you set up. When in class, use as many numbers on the floor as there are trainers in the class.

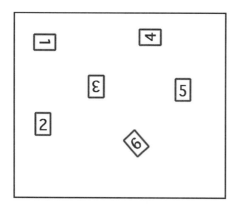

Figure 8.16 Draw a series of numbers on the floor of your training area. Move from one number to the next and either sit or stand the dog in heel position and then release.

Out-of-Sight-Stays

Leaving the dog and going out of sight demands that your dog thoroughly understands the STAY command and is confident that you will return. Practice first putting the dog on a *Sit-* or a *Down-stay* while you set up your ring or move equipment around your training area. This gets the dog used to your being in a different position than when you are directly in front, facing and focusing on him. When you do this, remember that you have given a STAY command and should never take your attention off your dog. You must verbally correct any mistakes as they occur, not after the fact! Initially you might only move a few feet from the dog in a different direction. Be alert for any signs of stress. Return often from your new and unusual positions, and use your CR and food. You may also use your CR from across the room to tell your dog that he is right and that food is forthcoming. This reinforcement schedule is one we use throughout all our training.

Judy does not like to do Open stays until after the dog is trained and shown in Novice. She believes relaxation is crucial to the exercise and does not want to introduce anything as stressful and time consuming as the out-of-sight stays. Once you have begun teaching this exercise, you should work on it every day, slowly extending the time you are away from the dog as he continues to show he is ready and confident.

Some dogs worry when their handlers leave them for any reason. If yours is one of these, practice leaving your dog with a friend who will feed him while you are gone. The dog does not need to be in any kind of stay, just standing around. While you are out of sight, your friend should use your CR and feed your dog periodically until she has used up a handful of food. She should then signal you to come back. When you return, use your CR and feed. Repeat this until your dog is more relaxed with you out of sight. Then add the formal *stay* itself.

We start with the out-of-sight *Sit-stay*. You may want to have another person stand right beside your dog. This person will feed your dog, more or less continuously, as you go out of sight. You will initially disappear for about one second and immediately return, CR and feed your dog. If your dog is relaxed when you walk out of sight for one second, you can probably train without the extra person. If your dog is highly stressed, you need to find a friend to help you. Your helper remains close to your dog until he begins to relax. She then leaves your dog and moves around the area, randomly returning and feeding him. Gradually extend the time you are away while your friend is randomly feeding your dog. This relaxes him and gives him something to focus on other than the fact that you are gone. You can start this process of having other people give a treat to your dog when you are still in sight. It transfers well to out-of-sight stays. It not only reinforces the dog for staying, but makes all judges and ring stewards look like prospective food dispensers!

We recommend that you find a hiding place from which you can see your dog continuously. If your dog is outside, use a back door window or garage window to see him. Indoors, set up some sort of barrier, such as a large cardboard box with a small hole to peek through. A high jump with a pen stuck between two boards near the top of the jump is useful. A strategically placed mirror can work well. Some dogs may figure out how to watch you in the mirror, but most do not.

Shape the out-of-sight stays slowly and carefully. Be sure your dog always trusts that you will come back and knows he must not move until you release him. It can be helpful to use your CR from the out-of-sight position, especially if you have an assistant who can feed your dog following your CR. Continue to extend the time you are away. Begin also to use a variable schedule of food, CR, and reminders as quickly as possible.

Problems With the Stays

The most common and obvious problem with stays is the dog moving from the position in which he was left. Lying down during the *Sit-stay* and getting up and moving around or sitting up during the *Down-stay* are common ways the dog may break the stay. Either the dog does not understand the STAY command or he is insecure in performing the exercise. In either case, go back and help him relax and retrain the exercise. Use more food, and set the dog up in a place where he is apt to make mistakes, such as on a bed or favorite chair. Set him up near a major distraction, such as another dog playing with a toy or a person eating. Work through the distractions with a combination of help and corrections, as described earlier in the teaching phase.

In practicing these remedial exercises, it is important for the dog to be relaxed. If he is tense, he cannot learn and work properly. Back up and help him. It may take a few weeks or months, but it will be worth it in the long run.

The dog who follows his owner away from the line of dogs is usually stressed. The owner hasn't proofed the dog properly. Proofing teaches the dog to be relaxed in a line of dogs, in a strange location, and to think about what he is supposed to be doing. It is often helpful to go back and use a constant feeding program with these dogs. Feed many times, stepping away a short distance. Have someone else feed your dog as you step away. Return often to use your CR, and feed him yourself. Build your dog's confidence. Again, many weeks of training may be necessary in order to make your dog secure. Whining or barking is usually the same problem. Again, go back and retrain for a confident stay.

For the confident dog who has been thoroughly proofed but is still breaking a stay, you may wish to use a correction. We use a pop up on the collar or a pat on the chest for breaking a *Sit-stay*, and a pop down on the collar or a pat on the shoulders for breaking a *Down-stay*. There are dogs who will take advantage of you when you are out of sight! Often, these dogs have not received the proper foundation to make them feel secure and comfortable during the *Stay* exercise.

Adele's first Flat-Coat, Tramp, had a severe problem with lying down on the *Sit-stay* throughout much of her career. It was not something she did very often in practice, but mainly in trials where Adele couldn't do anything about it. During the final year she competed, Adele practiced two *Sit-stay*s in a row when training at home and in matches, so during other dogs' *Down-stay*, Tramp had to do a second *Sit-stay*. It was at these times in practice that she would typically lie down from the *Sit-stay* if she was going to. A correction when this happened helped her understand that she was wrong. Adele also used jackpots extensively to keep Tramp relaxed. This demonstrates the proper balance between helping and correcting to produce a dog who clearly understands his responsibility in the ring.

More Proofing

Proofing for the ring is often difficult, as distractions do occur for which a dog has not been prepared. Some examples include:

- Someone in the ring behind the dog calling (in a loud voice) a DOWN command (as though they were doing a *Drop on Recall*) or SIT command (as though they were doing the *go-out* portion of *Directed Jumping*).
- Someone dropping a board while changing jumps in the next ring.
- Other dogs getting up or lying down beside your dog.
- Another dog in line leaving the line and going to his handler.
- Applause in or around an adjacent ring.
- A dumbbell landing behind the staying dogs, possibly hitting the wall or gate.

By giving your dog a firm, confident foundation in the *Stay* exercises, you should be able to meet these situations without fear of failure. If you have a high-stress dog who notices and reacts strongly to everything strange and different, you will need to take extra time proofing for these eventualities. It is important that these stressful situations occur first at a distance. Help your dog build confidence and then, as he relaxes, gradually move the distractions closer to him.

Once you have trained your dog to do reliable *Sit-stays* and *Down-stays*, it is important to practice these exercises as frequently as you do the moving exercises. Although they are somewhat boring for both the handler and the dog, there is no substitute for training! We generally practice stays several times a week, with the number of *Sit-stays* outnumbering the number of *Down-stays*.

Practice *stays* in a row of dogs with every other dog doing a *sit* and every other dog doing a *down*. This proofs the dog who thinks he should be in the same position as his neighbor. Practice the *Sit-stay* with the dog in various locations, such as on a bed or a couch. This can reveal some interesting behaviors. Practicing stays just before mealtime is another excellent way to proof them. Remember, once you give the STAY command, you also have to give the release command. This type of training can take some of the boredom out of training these static exercises. When practicing, don't forget to continue to use a random and selective reinforcement schedule.

Developing a Trial Routine

You should develop a routine for getting your dog ready for sits and downs at a trial. This preparation will begin with matches and run-throughs after you have completed the work of teaching and proofing. We like to use our vocabulary words and perhaps add a few, so the dog understands what is going to happen. Judy carries on a conversation with her dog as she is lining up, something like, "Now we are going to do the *Sit-stay*. You are going to sit and stay, and I will be right back." He understands what this phrase means as she uses it around the house when she moves from one room to another and does not want him to follow her. Judy might also tell him for the *out-of-sight stays* that she is "going to the store." She uses this phrase when she leaves the house for any reason. The dog knows she will return. Judy also sets the dog up and repeats the command to SIT and STAY several times while the other dogs are getting lined up and while she is putting her leash behind her dog. She has the same conversation that she just had outside the ring. The exercise does not begin until the judge tells you to "Leave your dogs." You do have to *sit* your dog and *down* your dog when the judge tells you to, but you may already have the dog sitting when he tells you to "Sit your dog." In this case, it is a good reminder for the dog. You may start the exercise from a stand and sit the dog on the judge's command if you so choose.

In hopes of preventing the dog from going *down* on the *sit*, Judy has the dog *stand* after the long *sit* and go into the *down* from a *stand*. The dog never does a *down* from a *sit*! This is allowed under the regulations, but not all judges are aware of this. If a judge asks you to *sit* your dog for the long *down*, you certainly would do so and then perhaps speak to the judge after the class to help enlighten him or her! But do *not* argue with a judge.

Adele releases her dogs between the *sit* and the *down* to accomplish the same thing — communicating to the dog that he should never go *down* directly from a *Sit-stay*. Another release exercise is to have the dog take a slight hop back between the *sit* and the *down*. This breaks up the exercises, and the dog should still be in good position to do the *Down-stay* properly. Beware, however, that a smart dog may release himself, scoot backwards, or stand up as you are returning in preparation for the next part of the exercise. This is not so different from the dog who lies down when anticipating the *Down-stay*.

Never be afraid to take *stays* "back to kindergarten." Adele did that many times with Tramp. Even though you are showing in Open, your dog may need some reminding that moving his feet is not okay or that sniffing is unacceptable. It is best to do this while you are close to your dog. It is also important to do shorter *stays* at times. Reinforce with your CR and food for the entire show career of your dog's Novice and Open *stays*. In our opinion, this exercise is *never* in the dog's long-term memory. Train and reinforce. If a problem occurs but your dog has the proper foundation, you should be able to fix it in a short time.

Combination Words

In this chapter, we discuss *Combination Words.* These words build on the foundation started in the *Fundamental Words* and *Power Steering* chapters. The combinations include:

- *Scoot Front:* Do a series of tuck sits while in the front position.
- *Pivots:* Turn to the right, the left, and about-turn in place.
- *Call to Heel:* Get to heel position quickly on command.
- *Scoot Heel:* Do a series of tuck sits in heel position.

Scoot Front

As soon as your dog has learned the word COME, is able to do tuck sits, and is comfortable with both, begin teaching *scoot fronts.* Have your dog sitting in front of and facing you. Hold a piece of food in both hands just above his nose to help keep his head raised. We introduce the FRONT command at this point. It may help to combine the new command FRONT with the familiar command COME. Take a four-to-six-inch step backwards as you command FRONT, COME, SIT.

Ultimately, the dog should bunny hop into a sit in front. This consists of his hopping his rear forward to his front, but without completely standing up. If he stands up, you are probably holding the food too far in front of his nose or backing up too far. *Hold the food against your body and do not reach out to give it to the dog. If you do, he may begin to sit farther away each time. Make him come to the food and do his tuck sit for his reward.* Some larger dogs may need you to move farther than four-to-six inches when you first start; otherwise they don't understand that they are to move forward. It may take some practice, but this is one of the best ways to get your dog to sit close. This exercise also strengthens some small muscles in the hip area which help the dog have a more compact and tighter sit.

Gradually add repetitions. Have your dog do one to six *scoot fronts* for one piece of food. Remember, you can use your CR more often than you give food.

Pivots

You will need pivots in Utility for the *Scent Discrimination* exercise and the *Directed Retrieve*. To do a correct pivot, *you* must turn in place, while your dog maintains heel position. Your dog should start in a sit, move with you as you turn, and then sit as you stop.

During our initial left quarter-turn training, we asked the dog to pivot around his front legs as we turned in a small circle around him. Now we want the dog to move while we pivot in place.

We use different commands for each turn. We say HEEL when we turn 90° to the right, TURN when we make a 180° pivot to the right, and IN or BACK when we turn 90° to the left.

We want the dog to keep his attention on us as we turn. Use food in your left hand to help him keep his head up while you teach him the pivots.

Initially work on the turning and sitting actions separately and then combine them. If your dog has a good understanding of the *Power Steering* words, he should soon be able to do the turn and sit together.

The footwork we use for each pivot is similar to the turn footwork we discuss in the *Heeling* chapter. To do a turn to the left (Fig. 9.1):

- Start the turn with your right foot, making a "T" with the arch of your right foot against the toes of your left foot.
- Turn your left foot so your toes face the new direction, while keeping the heel close to or against your right foot.
- Bring your right foot even with your left foot, if needed. This last step usually isn't needed during a 90° turn.

To do a turn to the right (Fig. 9.2):

- Start the turn with your left foot, making a "T" with the arch of your left foot against the toes of your right foot.
- Turn your right foot so your toes face the new direction, while keeping the heel close to or against your left foot.
- If needed, bring your left foot even with your right foot. Again, this last step usually isn't needed during a 90° turn.

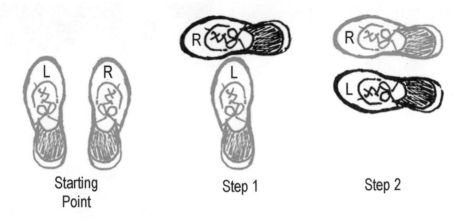

Figure 9.1 We use variations of this footwork for any pivots to the left. NOTE: In each step, the black shoe has just moved, while the grey shoe has not.

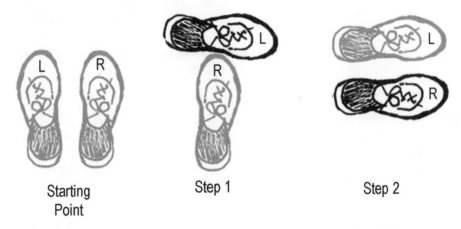

Figure 9.2 We use variations of this footwork for any pivots to the right. NOTE: In each step, the black shoe has just moved, while the grey shoe has not.

Call to Heel

The *call to heel* exercise adds a command to the *find heel* exercise. Leave your dog in a *Sit–stay*. We use the WAIT command for this. Walk forward to the end of your four-to-six-foot leash and continue to face away from your dog (Fig. 9.3). As you reach the end of your leash, call your dog to heel using your HEEL command. You may wish to use your dog's name before the HEEL command — Adele does, Judy does not.

Figure 9.3 To do the *call to heel* exercise, leave your dog in a *Sit-stay*. Walk forward to the end of your four- to six-foot leash and continue to face the same direction as your dog

Guide with your leash and have food ready in your left hand. The food is not used as a lure but as a reward. Reinforce with your CR and feed as soon as your dog arrives in heel position (Fig. 9.4), then release.

Work this exercise off-leash whenever it is safe to do so. This allows you to put more distance between you and your dog before commanding HEEL.

We have never worked with a dog who did not break the WAIT during *call to heel*. Occasionally step back and reinforce the WAIT with a treat. If your dog has a poor understanding of WAIT, have a person restrain your dog while you walk away. If your dog is good at *find heel*, you may find it hard to get very far away. Go back and reinforce the WAIT command to solve this problem.

A useful variation is to change directions as you walk away (i.e., turning either left or right before commanding HEEL). Turning to the right is typically harder for most dogs because it is so tempting to come up on your right side. Use food in your left hand, reach back, and lure him to your left side (Fig. 9.5). Make him go behind you rather than in front. The dog who really understands HEEL can get there no matter which direction you are facing. Again, the *find heel* foundation should be helpful here.

Figure 9.4 Reinforce with your CR and a treat as soon as your dog comes up into heel position.

Figure 9.5 A useful variation to the *call to heel* exercise is to change directions as you walk away. Use food in your left hand, reach back, and lure him around to your left side. Make him go behind you rather than in front.

Practice with your dog in front of you, to your right, and when you are facing in the opposite direction (Fig. 9.6). This simulates his getting distracted or lost before an *about turn*. This may happen on an *about turn* after a *slow* when your dog fails to go into a corner.

Train your dog to get to heel position while you are running away from him. This simulates losing him on the *fast*. Vary the timing of your reward once your dog has found heel position. He can and should hear his CR the moment he gets to heel position, but you can take a few steps before feeding.

There are times when *call to heel* can save a qualifying score in the ring. It is sometimes worth the substantial deduction to give an extra HEEL command, though more than one extra command may result in failing the *Heeling* exercise. There are times during heeling when it isn't an extra command. If your dog is not in heel position when you halt, you would give your HEEL command after the judge's next "Forward" command and your dog would — you hope! — catch up and continue to heel with you. We sincerely hope you will never have to use *call to heel* this way, but it pays to be prepared.

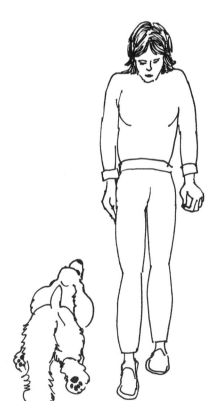

Figure 9.6 Practice *call to heel* with the dog in front of you and to your right. This teaches him to find heel when he is out of position after an about turn.

Adding a Sit

Once your dog has mastered the moving *call to heel*, introduce a *sit* at the end of the exercise. Walk about six feet away from your dog and stop. Stand with your back to him and call him to heel. Give a SIT command as soon as he comes to heel position. You may want to stand facing a mirror as you call to heel. This allows you to time your SIT command better. Ask for a sit while you are facing the same direction as your dog, and then make it harder by turning to the left or right before asking for it.

Scoot Heel

Once your dog can do *find heel* and *call to heel*, start with *scoot heels*. This is similar to the *scoot front* exercise, but the dog is in heel position. The commands are HEEL just before you take a small step forward with your left foot and then SIT as you bring your right foot even with your left foot. Hold food in your left hand directly above the dog's nose, positioned so that the dog keeps his head and body aligned (Fig. 9.7). Do not move your hand! Keep it still to keep the dog's head up and

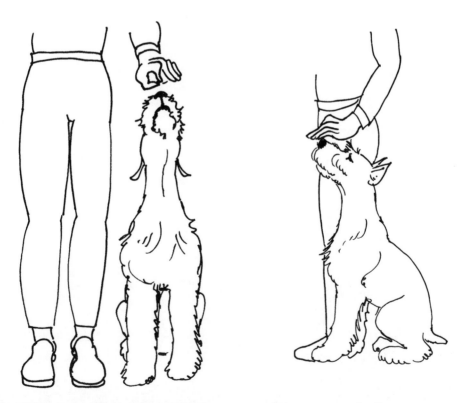

Figure 9.7 When you introduce the *scoot heel* exercise, hold food in your left hand directly above your dog's nose, positioned so that he keeps his head and body aligned.

his rear close to the floor. Take a small shuffle step forward. Make sure you move straight ahead, neither stepping into nor away from your dog. As with the *scoot front,* if your dog stands up, you are moving too far forward or holding the food too far in front of his nose.

This is a great attention exercise and is one of the foundation exercises for the automatic sit.

Heeling

eeling should be a dance between two partners perfectly attuned to one another. If one partner drags the other around, it detracts from the dance. Heeling is the obedience exercise in which the handler plays the most important role. A smooth dog and handler team provides a flowing picture. The good handler leads the dance, giving subtle cues that the well-trained dog instantly follows. Conversely, the poor handler weaves and jerks her way around the ring, steps into the dog on *halts*, steps away on *turns*, and pretends to do *pace changes*. This is hard for the dog to follow, not enjoyable to watch, and difficult to judge.

Elements of Heeling

Many ingredients are needed to produce a dog and handler team that heels to perfection:

- Attention
- Heel position
- Speed and gait
- Smooth handling
- Rhythm
- Attitude

Before teaching the mechanics of heeling, we will explore each of these elements further. We hope to provide you with a mental picture of what we consider the perfect heeling team.

Attention

Attention is not a requirement in that you don't lose points if your dog does not maintain a particular head or eye position. As you advance in your training, the exercises become more complicated, the dog is frequently working away from you and, after the Novice level, he is always off leash. An attentive dog learns better and works more confidently.

When you watch a dog and handler team that heels well together, they almost invariably have focused *attention.* They are completely attuned to each other. On the other hand, the dog who has not been taught *attention* usually makes position errors when he is looking elsewhere.

You should teach your dog where he should focus during heeling. We call this the *focal point.* Many people teach their dog an incorrect focal point by carrying food in their mouth which is periodically spit at the dog. This tends to teach the dog to forge and side-wind in his attempt to see the handler's face from *heel position.* Some dogs *can* heel and watch their handler's face, but it needs to be the side of the face, not the front. For the smaller dog, the focal point will probably be much lower; perhaps somewhere on your left leg. Adele is 5'10" tall and Rio was 11" at the shoulder. She decided she wanted him to look at her face, but this high focal point resulted in some position errors they had to overcome. The main problems were that he leaned his shoulders out and heeled wide, both errors that small dogs tend to make. Adele found it worth the effort to teach him to move and sit straight to gain the desired focal point. Judy, on the other hand, has medium-sized dogs and uses a focal point in the left hip area.

Heel Position

Heel position is the position of the dog on the handler's left side when sitting, standing, lying down, or moving with the handler. It means that the dog should be in a straight line with the direction the handler is facing. He should be at the handler's left side and as close as possible to the handler's left leg, allowing the handler to freely move forward without crowding or bumping. Some part of the dog's head, from the nose to the shoulders, should be in line with the handler's left hip. As a general rule, if your dog's right eye or ear is in line with the left seam of your pants, assuming he holds his head up attentively, he is in *heel position.*

To review the ways a dog can err during heeling (Fig. 10.1):

- *Forging:* The dog is too far ahead of handler.
- *Lagging:* The dog is too far behind the handler.
- *Bumping* or *crowding:* The dog is too close to the handler.
- *Heeling wide:* The dog is too far to the left of the handler.
- *Side-winding* or *crabbing*: The dog moves with his rear either to the left or the right of his front.

Figure 10.1 Counterclockwise from upper left: forging, lagging, bumping or crowding, heeling wide, and side-winding.

The dog who is just learning to heel may make any or all of these mistakes, simply because he hasn't learned how to maintain any position yet, let alone the correct one.

Speed and Gait

When heeling in Novice, the handler is expected to walk briskly and naturally with his dog on a loose leash. We want our dogs to move briskly and attentively with us when heeling at the *normal* speed, and we prefer that the dog move at a *trot*.

Trotting vs. Pacing

The *trot* is a diagonal gait in which the legs on the opposite corners move together (i.e., right front with left rear, left front with right rear) (Fig. 10.2). The *pace* is a lateral gait in which the legs on the same side move forward at the same time (Fig. 10.2). The pace produces a rolling motion that can cause bumping, even if the dog or handler aren't weaving. Dogs often pace because their handler does not or cannot go fast enough to allow the dog to *trot*. Some dogs naturally pace when moving around in everyday life. This is a structural problem and cannot be changed. Judy tried everything with Brig, who paced, and nothing worked. He was a structural pacer. He would sometimes *sit* crooked when a *halt* was called because he was off balance. Some dogs only pace in a training situation. If this is the case, the handler needs to speed up, if possible. If the problem is structural, you will have to learn to live with it and do everything you can to look smooth so your dog does, too.

To help a pacing dog learn to *trot*, work as follows: Heel in a large, clockwise circle with the dog on the outside. Walk at a brisk pace, even faster than you move for your usual *normal* pace. This helps force the dog to *trot* to keep up. Many dogs who pace try to extend or go faster in the pace but usually aren't successful, which causes them to lag. Sometimes it helps to get the dog to lift his head higher, which elevates his front. This elevation can produce a "strutting" gait, in which the dog throws his front legs higher than he does when he is not heeling. If you aren't sure what gait your dog normally uses, ask your instructor or another trainer to observe your dog.

Later in this chapter we discuss *pace changes*, which is the generic term for the changes of speed you are required to do within a heeling pattern. This is not the same thing as the dog who paces as a specific gait.

Figure 10.2 The dog on the left is trotting, while the dog on the right is pacing. The *trot* is a diagonal gait in which the legs at opposite corners move together (i.e., right front with left rear, left front with right rear). The *pace* is a lateral gait in which the legs on the same side move forward at the same time.

Smooth Handling

Heeling is the most important and active exercise for you, the handler. There is a greater potential for lost handler points, usually called *handler errors*, when you are heeling with your dog in a trial ring, than in any other obedience exercise.

The team who moves smoothly through turns, *halts*, and changes of speed is a pleasure to watch. At first, smooth handling requires hard work and concentration, but with practice, it can become automatic. By allowing muscle memory to take over, you can focus on listening and responding to the judge's commands. *Muscle memory develops when you repeat a move so many times you no longer need to think about it.*

Our suggestions for improving your handling are interspersed throughout this and other chapters.

Rhythm

A smooth dog and handler team needs good rhythm. This comes more naturally to some people than to others. You can learn to keep a consistent rhythm while you heel. Use a small pocket metronome (which you can buy at a store that sells musical instruments), or try heeling to music which has the "correct" number of beats per minute, usually somewhere between 120 and 138. These techniques may help you and your dog move more rhythmically. Heeling to music can really be fun! Make sure your walking style includes a solid heel–toe step to move as smoothly as possible. Also, choose a beat that causes you to move as fast as you can comfortably walk with your dog. It usually looks better. A good coach or observer can help you decide on the best rhythm.

You need to maintain a consistent rhythm during turns as well as during your *normal* heeling speed. This can be particularly hard for a new handler to do during *about turns* and the *Figure Eight*, so practice them slowly at first. Gradually speed up as you gain skill.

Attitude

Both the dog and handler should have fun during heeling, just as during all of their obedience work. We like to see a dog with focused *attention*, confidently trotting at his handler's side. Our image of a great heeling dog is one whose whole body posture says "This is fun!" We certainly understand that it is not always easy to achieve this image when trial nerves get in the way, but that is what we strive for. Having strangers come up to us at a trial to say how much they enjoyed our performance is one of the highest compliments we receive.

Before Heeling Your Dog

Before you start to teach your dog to heel, we suggest that you give some thought to your handling. This might save you some retraining in the future.

One of the concepts we suggest you think about is that of *lanes*. Imagine that you are driving a car on a multi-lane road. You are in one lane and another car is in the lane to your left, driving in the same direction at the same speed. If the other car starts to drift into your lane, it is disconcerting (to say the least!), and you tend to react by drifting away from the other car to your right. If the other car suddenly swerves into your lane, you react with a sudden swerve yourself. If you are the one doing the drifting, the other car usually drifts away from you.

When you are heeling with your dog, imagine that each of you is in your own lane, very much like when you are driving a car. It is important for both of you to stay in your own lane. Otherwise, you will collide and lose points from your score.

The next time you get the chance, watch someone heeling her dog. Position yourself so the team is either coming towards you or moving directly away from you. Does each member of the team stay in their proper lane? Or is one of them drifting or swerving into the other's lane? If the latter, how does the other teammate respond? Does the first drift cause another one? How many of the dog's errors are caused by a drifting handler? How many handler drifts are caused by a drifting dog?

To stay in your own lane, you must walk in a straight line. For many of us, this requires a lot of practice! Spend some time practicing without your dog. Concentrate on what you must do to keep yourself walking straight. Find places to practice that have long painted lines such as tennis courts, parking lots, or basketball courts. You might also train on sidewalks or mats, such as those usually found in obedience rings. Use the crack between the mats to keep yourself walking in a straight line. Think about where you will be looking when you heel with your dog and practice your straight lines using this head position.

Have a friend watch you walk. Do you swing your legs out to the side? If so, you are likely to cause your dog to heel farther away from you. Small dogs are typically very attuned to what you are doing from the knees down.

Normal Pace

Whenever a judge calls "Forward" during a heeling pattern, you should walk briskly and in a natural manner. This is the *normal* pace referred to in the regulations. The judge may deduct points if you are not walking briskly enough.

A good handler maintains the same *normal* rhythm throughout the heeling pattern. You will need to experiment with your dog to determine the best speed to walk when doing your *normal* pace. Use a metronome or heel to music to practice your rhythm.

The length of your stride is another component of handling. Taking very long steps with a small dog or baby steps with a big dog does not usually present a pleasant image. Many handlers adjust the length of their stride to the length of their dog's stride (Fig. 10.3). There are limits to this, such as the length of the handler's legs! Most people can match a medium-sized dog's stride length, and it looks smooth when it is achieved. A friend with a sharp eye or a video camera will be helpful in determining the "correct" stride length for you and your dog.

Which Leg?

Most good handlers start heeling on the same leg each time. We step out first on the left foot when heeling and the right foot for stays. Starting on the same leg cues your dog as to what you are doing and helps him respond faster.

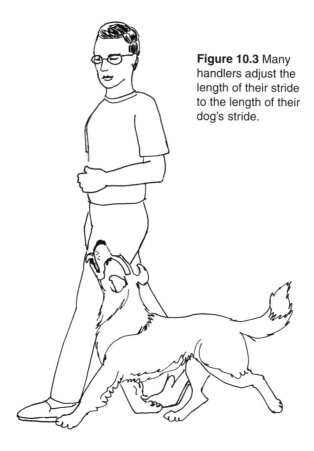

Figure 10.3 Many handlers adjust the length of their stride to the length of their dog's stride.

Handler Errors During Normal Heeling

There are many common errors a handler might make during a heeling pattern:

- Drifting into the dog's lane when heeling a straight line.
- Drifting away from the dog during straight heeling.
- Weaving in and out of the dog's lane.
- Adapting her pace to the dog's speed.
- Feeding the leash in and out, depending on where the dog happens to be at the moment.
- Holding her hand or arm improperly during heeling.
- Watching her dog too much, which puts her left shoulder too far back.

- Tugging constantly on or correcting her dog with the leash (the judge can fail the handler if this happens too much).

- Failing to walk at a brisk pace (this might be a minor deduction less than 3 points off, or a substantial one 3 or more points off, depending on the severity).

- Guiding occasionally with the leash (minor or substantial deduction, depending on the severity).

To Watch or Not to Watch Your Dog?

There is some debate about whether or not a handler should watch her dog during heeling. We like to be able to see the dog when we are heeling, but we are careful to maintain the same head position throughout the pattern. We don't swing our head to the left when we stop, nor do we twist at the waist. We look at the floor about six to eight feet in front of us, watching the dog with our peripheral vision. This is our formal heeling posture. When training the dog to heel, we watch more carefully to catch errors early, but without twisting at the waist or dropping the left shoulder back. If you twist too much or turn your head, you will teach your dog improper *heel position.*

Hand Positions On-Lead

As we discussed in the *Equipment* chapter, you should match the length and weight of your leash to the height and weight of your dog. When you show your dog in the Novice obedience ring, we recommend that you use a leash that is just long enough to allow the required slack. A leash that is 2 to 2.5 feet is long enough for most dogs. This gives you much less leash to hold in your hand. The leash should be neither too tight nor too loose. The clip of the leash should hang vertically. We often show a Novice dog on a lighter leash than we use for everyday training.

The leash may be held in either or both hands, as long as the position is natural. Both of us prefer to hold the excess leash gathered up in the left hand with the part of the leash towards the dog extending from the hand nearest the little finger (Fig. 10.4). We also hold the left hand near the hip, elbow in, which positions the leash as far back on the body as possible.

In Fig. 10.4, there are three handlers with three different sized dogs. Each handler is holding her left hand in a different place. This is a personal choice; all of these positions are legal. You should hold your hand in the position that keeps the leash out of your dog's way. A small dog is more likely to get his nose tangled in the leash when it is held more to

Figure 10.4 Each handler is holding her left hand in a different place. This is a personal choice; all of these positions are legal. You should hold your hand in the position that keeps the leash out of your dog's way.

the front of his handler's body. For this reason, we recommend that you hold your hand down at your side with a small dog, as the handler on the left is doing.

Handler Errors On-Lead

- Holding the leash too tightly.
- Varying the position of the hand(s).
- "Steering" on turns, *halts, pace changes* (i.e., moving the hand forward, backward, in, or out to guide the dog).
- Feeding the leash in and out or gathering it up during heeling.

Hand Positions Off-Lead

In the AKC obedience ring, you have two choices for how to hold your hands and arms when you heel your dog without a leash. The right arm and hand should always be down by your side, swinging naturally when you are in motion and hanging naturally at your side when you are stationary. The left arm may be down, also swinging or hanging naturally; or you may hold it with your left hand against your waist, centered on your body. If your left hand is over your belly-button, it is most likely in the right place. Your elbow must be against your body.

How do you determine which is the better hand position? Much of the decision rests with the size of your dog. If your dog's head or nose bumps your hand when it hangs down, or if the hand hanging down causes your dog to heel wide, you should hold your hand at your waist. Generally, it is better to let your hand hang down naturally at your side when working a small dog.

Handler Errors Off-Lead

- Inconsistent position of hands.
- Right and left arms not swinging the same amount.
- Not swinging arms at all.

Rhythm Heeling

Our definition of *rhythm heeling* is a dog and handler moving together at a *normal* heeling speed, the handler walking briskly and smoothly, and the dog trotting along in *heel position* with his *attention* focused on his handler. It is an excellent exercise to develop teamwork between the dog and the handler.

We want the combination of speed, position, and *attention* well established before adding *pace changes*, turns, and *halts*. These are harder for the dog to learn so we introduce them separately as stationary exercises before gradually adding them to *rhythm heeling* as the dog gains experience and confidence.

Rhythm heeling is a great way for you and your dog to warm up at a trial. It gives both of you a chance to get into the swing of heeling without as much precision as some of the more difficult parts of heeling. It also helps loosen muscles, both yours and the dog's.

Before starting *rhythm heeling*, your dog should have a solid foundation in the *attention* and *find heel* exercises as discussed in the *Fundamental Words* chapter. These exercises build the dog's understanding of *attention* and *position* before adding *rhythm*.

To Leash or Not To Leash?

We like to train off-leash as much as possible. It helps make the dog responsible for being in the correct position early in his training. If you are alone and somewhere safe for your dog to be off-leash, it may be easier to train this way. If your dog is very distracted by his surroundings, a leash is necessary. You may also need to keep a leash on your dog to keep him safe. Use a short (24" to 30") leash, rather than the retractable one you may have used during the *find heel* work.

Where's the Food?

We recommend that you use a bait bag, but make sure it does not interfere with the dog's focal point. It is best kept either behind you or on your right side. When you need many treats, hold most of the food in your right hand and one piece in your left. This allows you to hold one treat between your thumb and forefinger above the dog's nose. After giving the left-hand treat to the dog, transfer another one from the right hand to the left.

By keeping a handful of food ready, you avoid the inevitable delay that comes from digging in your pocket or bait bag. Keep moving until you have used up the supply in your hand. Release your dog while you reload your "food-holding" hand. The presence of the food in your left hand excites some dogs so much that they don't settle into a *trot*. They jump up and down as they move rather than using a smooth forward motion. Bigger dogs may poke your hand with their nose. Reinforce the dog only for a smooth *trot*. You can ignore the wrong behavior (bouncing rather than trotting) and let it extinguish. Sometimes it helps to have an observer click a clicker when your dog *trots* for a few steps. This tells you when to give your CR. Gradually extend the distance your dog must *trot* before you CR and treat. Begin early to vary the frequency of your CR.

Note that you still have the food in sight in the left hand. For many dogs, the rhythm is easier to maintain if the food is in sight. First, build your dog's endurance and ability to keep *attention* while maintaining his rhythm with the food in sight. Weaning from food in sight is discussed later in this chapter.

Commands

When first starting *rhythm heeling*, do not use a command. Once the dog is heeling attentively for 10-12 steps, add a HEEL command.

Straight Line Heeling

Lure your dog into *heel position* as you start to move. Do *not* start with your dog in a *sit*; instead, "fall into heeling" from a *stand*, as you've done with the *find heel* exercise. Keep his *attention* directed up towards his focal point. Start with short, straight lines of heeling. When you have progressed 10 feet (three or four steps) and, while your dog is still looking up at you, use your CR and stop to give a treat. If your dog cannot maintain his *attention* for three or four steps, go back and review *heel starts* in the *Fundamental Words* chapter. Pay attention to where your dog is looking. The first step is often the hardest, so don't neglect it. **Use your CR before the food and before you move your hand to give the food.** The latter point is not as important in the beginning because your hand is close to your dog's nose. As you progress in your heeling work, this timing becomes critical.

After giving the food, do not start moving until your next treat is ready in your left hand and your dog is looking at you. This is very important because you now want the dog's *attention* on you before you move. Vary the number of steps you take between treats. Start with one or two steps and gradually increase the maximum number of steps you take. Eventually, you need to be able to heel an entire heeling pattern without praise and food, a task that usually takes from 30-60 seconds.

If your dog's head drops, take fewer steps before the next treat. *Your dog should be rewarded for the correct position and attention.* If you push him too far and he is not getting reinforced often enough, you will lose his *attention* and enthusiasm.

This initial work gives your dog a chance to adjust to moving with his head up, which may be a new experience for him. The dog must trust that you won't run him into a barrier or a hole! If your dog has been trained to walk with you without *attention*, you must back up and retrain the "heads up" *attention* (see *Fundamental Words* chapter).

Our goal is to have the dog continue to move attentively while eating a treat. Not every dog is physically able to walk, eat, and keep his head up at the same time. If your dog cannot swallow with his head up when sitting still, it is unlikely that he'll be able to do so when he is in motion. This ability to swallow and keep his head up isn't a requirement, but if you wish to work on it, here are some steps to follow:

- Feed in a stationary position first. By giving multiple treats in very rapid succession, you can help your dog learn to maintain his *attention* and head position while swallowing.

- Use slippery food, such as small pieces of hot dogs or cooked macaroni. Do not overcook the macaroni or it will fall apart in your hands!

How Long?

How long should your dog be able to heel without a release to a toy, verbal praise, or a treat? In the obedience ring, you rarely heel without a break for more than 30-45 seconds! However, this should not be your dog's maximum, but instead an easy request. You should be able to heel for five to ten minutes with only occasional breaks. This endurance takes time to develop! Pay attention to how long you are *really* asking your dog to heel. With a novice dog, you will spend a lot of time working on heeling, both on-leash and off-leash. The training is done in short intervals because you haven't built endurance yet. As the dog's endurance builds, increase the amount of time in any given session that you ask him to work without reinforcement or play. In training the advanced dog, spend more time on refresher work, perhaps picking out a particular problem area on which to concentrate. Every dog has his own problem area!

Large Clockwise Circles

Once your dog can heel for 10-20 steps in a straight line, start doing large 20-30 foot circles. We start most dogs using large clockwise circles, so the dog has to drive harder. A young, inexperienced dog often moves with his rear out to the left (i.e., side-winding). We want the dog to move with his body in a straight line, the rear moving along the same line as the front. Clockwise circles are especially beneficial for this sort of dog. By walking briskly in a large arc, the dog must work hard to keep up. This takes up some of his momentum and helps prevent the side-winding.

Large Counter-clockwise Circles

Once your dog can move smoothly with you in large clockwise circles, begin some circles to the left, with your dog on the inside. He must slow down to stay back with you. If your dog has a tendency to pace, he is likely to do so here. Keep your speed brisk. He may also resume side-winding as he tries to figure out how to adjust to this new request. He needs to learn to curve his body gently to the inside and to use his rear with more control. Typically, the longer the dog, the harder this is to accomplish. Go back and review the stationary exercises that helped develop the dog's control of his rear, such as IN, BACK, and OFF in the *Power Steering* chapter.

Serpentines

The next exercise is a combination of big half circles, which we call *serpentines*. To help guide you, set up posts of some sort, such as garbage cans, traffic cones, chairs, or the uprights from the Utility bar jump. Place them 15-20 feet apart, in a staggered set-up (Fig. 10.5). Start at one end and make big loops around each post.

This introduces your dog to the posts. If your dog is a worrier, don't go too close to the posts when first beginning. Stay six to eight feet away and use them as guides. This is not a Nordic ski slalom where the fastest time wins! Your dog must make adjustments to your speed, slowing down when he is on the inside of the *serpentine* and speeding up on the outside. You should maintain the same cadence throughout.

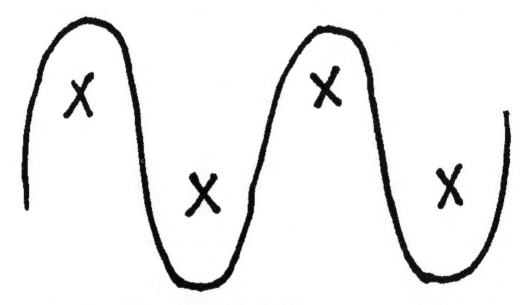

Figure 10.5 To help guide you when training *serpentines*, set up posts of some sort, such as garbage cans, traffic cones, or chairs. Place them 15-20 feet apart, in a staggered set-up. Start at one end and make big loops around each post.

Weaning From Food in Sight

It is imperative for you to complete the process of changing the food from a lure to a reinforcer to get a solid ring performance. **Changing the use of the food from a lure to a reinforcer is a process many people never fully make.** *Food used as a lure is very obvious to the dog; it is in sight. It helps and even sometimes causes the dog to perform. Food used as a reinforcer is given because the dog performs, not to prompt the perfor-*

mance. We don't want to lie to the dog and make him think we have food when we don't. Part of the difficulty of making this change is knowing *when* your dog is ready to make this transition. It is important to start hiding the food in your closed fist early in your training, even if just for a step or two. The food can disappear and reappear at varying intervals. Begin this as soon your dog is able to do 15-20 steps of heads-up *rhythm heeling* with food in sight. Hide the food in your left hand, but still have your hand in your target position. The dog doesn't see the food but still has a target on which to focus. He knows the food is there and is gaining understanding that the food does not have to be visible to be given as a reward.

Silence

Up until now, you have probably been talking to your dog a great deal to encourage him. Start heeling silently for brief periods, beginning with three or four steps and progressing slowly. Many people fall into the trap where their dog works well when given frequent verbal encouragement but falls apart when the handler is silent. You must practice silence during heeling for the dog to become comfortable with it.

Small Left Circles

The next goal is to teach your dog to heel in a five- to six-foot circle to the left. You will need this for the inside post of the *Figure Eight*. The dog must slow down and maintain *heel position* throughout and this requires good control of his hind quarters. Refer to IN in the *Power Steering* chapter. Your dog also needs to have a reasonable understanding of *rhythm heeling* (i.e., *attention*, *heel position*, and *rhythm*).

The end result is for your dog to keep his *attention* on you, keep his neck and shoulders in line with your left hip, and use his front legs as a pivot point. Each step he takes with his hind feet should follow the curve of the circle. Many dogs, especially long-bodied ones, cross the inside hind leg in front of the outside one, as they do during IN work. The dog's nose should be turned somewhat inwards, though his *attention* is still upwards. His body is gently curved around the circle. Often, bigger dogs slow from a *trot* to a *walk*.

Some common mistakes seen on the inside circle are:

- Dog does not maintain his focus on the handler.
- Dog bumps the handler (often due to lack of *attention*).
- Dog forges (moves too far ahead).
- Handler does not maintain a consistent circle size.

A well-executed inside circle involves both dog and handler constantly adjusting their direction. The dog that has hind quarter control will be better able to perform this difficult maneuver.

Set up one post. Start far enough back from the post to give you and your dog time to get into your rhythm before you get to the post. Typically, 10-12 feet from the post works well. Also start about three feet to the right of the post (Fig. 10.6), so you can make a fishhook or backwards letter J around the post. Hold your leash behind your back in your right hand, as you did when teaching the *left quarter turn* (IN). You don't need to start with your dog in a *sit.*

This may be the first use you make of one of your *steering* words when in motion. Hold a piece of food hidden in your left hand until you are almost even with the post. Start heeling towards the post and, as you get even with it (letter A in Fig. 10.6), command BACK or IN, show your dog the food, tighten your leash, and steer his head a bit to his left, towards the post. Keep his head up during this phase of teaching to maintain *attention.* After you have gone halfway around the post (letter B in Fig. 10.6), CR and treat. Release your dog and go back to your starting place. Vary the place in the circle where you reinforce him with your CR and treat.

After you are both comfortable with this phase, add one more piece. As you get half way around your circle (letter B in Fig. 10.6):

- Use your CR but no food (this tells the dog that the first half was good).

- Cue with HURRY.

- Break into a run towards letter C in Figure 10.6.

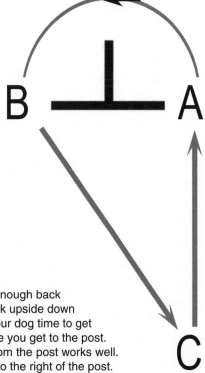

Figure 10.6 Start far enough back from the post (the black upside down "T") to give you and your dog time to get into your rhythm before you get to the post. Typically, 10-12 feet from the post works well. Start about three feet to the right of the post.

Your goal is to teach your dog to accelerate into a *trot* from the inside circle he has just completed to the straight line which follows. This acceleration must happen at letter B to be successful. If needed, toss food or a toy just after your HURRY cue to help your dog speed up. If he is slow to respond to this cue, review the *play running* exercise from the *Power Steering* chapter.

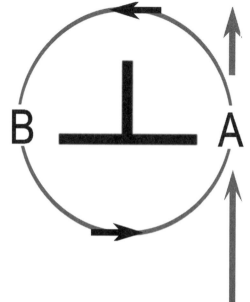

Figure 10.7 As you and your dog gain skill on the inside circle, sometimes do a complete circle around the post to continue in the same direction in which you started.

As you and your dog gain skill on the inside circle, sometimes do a complete circle around the post to continue in the same direction in which you started (Fig. 10.7). Make sure you are reinforcing at various points around the circle, not just before a HURRY cue.

Small Right Circles

Before starting this exercise, your dog should understand HURRY and the *dizzy spin* exercise. These lay the foundation for small right circles, which you need for the outside post of the *Figure Eight* exercise.

Most dogs need to *trot* to keep up with you when you are making a small five- to six-foot circle. Some mistakes commonly seen on a small right circle are:

- Dogs who don't accelerate soon enough, so they lag behind the handler.
- Dogs who go too wide.
- Dogs who flare their hind quarters out while keeping their front end in the correct position.
- Dogs who lose *attention*.

Set up your post. Begin about 10 to 12 feet back from the post to make sure your dog is trotting before you get to the post. Start about three feet to the left of the post (Fig. 10.8), so you can make a letter J around the post. As with the left circles, you don't need to start with your dog in a *sit*. Have food hidden in your left hand, which should be held against your body as in the *dizzy spin* exercise (i.e., slid around more to the front of your body).

Begin heeling towards the post. As you get even with it (letter A in Fig. 10.8), command HURRY, show the food, and make a half circle to your right. CR when the dog is correct, and reinforce with the food. If your dog tends to lag on this exercise, it is okay to repeat your HURRY command, but avoid repeating HURRY, HURRY, HURRY! You might want to start with a quarter circle and progress from there. As you come out of the circle (letter B in Figure 10.8), tell your dog BACK to get him into *normal* pace. It is often best to wait to add this command until the dog has a tendency to forge coming out of the turn. Most dogs can be moved back more easily than they can be hurried.

Judy adds another part for slower dogs or a dog who needs to be retrained following a long period of lagging on the outside turn. Follow the HURRY cue with a forward leash pop on a buckle collar. This works well, and your dog should not resent the pop due to the presence of the

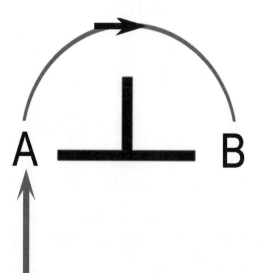

food. Hold the leash in your left hand and pop parallel to the ground. Have the food in sight in your right hand, using it as a lure. Next have the food hidden in your right hand as a target. Gradually fade the use of your target hand. This is an exception to the rule that we don't feed following a correction. *Do not* correct your dog for forging. This means he is thinking!

Figure 10.8 Begin about 10 to 12 feet back from the post to make sure your dog is trotting before you get to the post. Start about three feet to the left of the post.

As your dog improves, do a full circle, and continue in the direction in which you started. Again, remember to reinforce using your CR and food at various points in the circle.

In addition to the above, Judy starts with very large circle heeling (both directions), gradually making them smaller. At some point, when the dog loses focus or position, she returns to a larger circle. Work that distance for a few repetitions before returning to the smaller circle where the dog had the problem.

Figure Eight

When your dog can do both left and right circles, you are ready to combine all three phases — the left circle, the acceleration out of the left circle, and the right circle — into a *Figure Eight* (Fig. 10.9).

The *Figure Eight* exercise begins from a starting point equidistant between two people who serve as posts. The posts stand eight feet apart and the handler faces the judge. We like to start approximately three feet back from the imaginary line connecting the posts. The dog and handler walk briskly around the two posts two complete times, making two *Figure Eight*'s. The judge will call two *halts* during this exercise; one during the exercise and one at the end. The *Figure Eight* in the Novice class is done on-leash; the one in Open off-leash. The handler may go in either direction and there are no pace changes in the *Figure Eight*.

When you do the *Figure Eight* exercise in the ring, you must walk at the same speed around both posts and will be penalized if you vary your speed. It is the dog who must change speeds, slowing down when he is on the inside and speeding up when he is on the outside. In describing how we train the *Figure Eight* exercise, we have written about you, the handler, slowing down and speeding up, but this is for training purposes only!

Think of the *Figure Eight* as an "X" connected by two arcs that go around the outside of the posts. Set up two posts approximately eight feet apart, with small X's marked at about 33 inches from the center of each post. Use these X's when you practice the *Figure Eight* (with and without your dog). The X's help you maintain a consistent distance around each post. You may prefer to do larger circles, in which case, make the X's further from the post. If you have a big dog, you may want to start with the posts farther apart. Warm up with a few circles around each post, including your speed up command when completing the inside post and your slow down command when completing the outside post.

When we first start, we walk through "X1", then start the first circle. Adele goes to the left first, through "X2", while Judy goes to the right first, through "X5". Experiment to see which direction better suits you and your dog. The first time we start the circle (going from X1 to X2 or X1 to X5), we make an arc. This is the only time we make an arc between the posts and it is smoother than making an abrupt turn.

Once we get moving, the sequence looks like this: X2, X3, X4, X1, X5, X6, X7, X1, X2, etc. We make straight lines from X4 to X5 and from X7 to X2, going through X1 in both cases. The judge typically calls a *halt* somewhere near X1, so it is to your advantage to be on a straight line at that time.

The dog's speed should increase for the outside post just as you come out of the slow arc (letter X4 in Fig. 10.9). The speed decreases as you come out of the fast arc (letter X7 in Fig. 10.9). Once you start working the complete exercise, do *not* go around and around (and around and around) the posts endlessly. Work on perfecting and reinforcing different sections separately (i.e., the slow arc into the straightaway, the straight lines into each arc). Combine a few of them occasionally. Don't worry

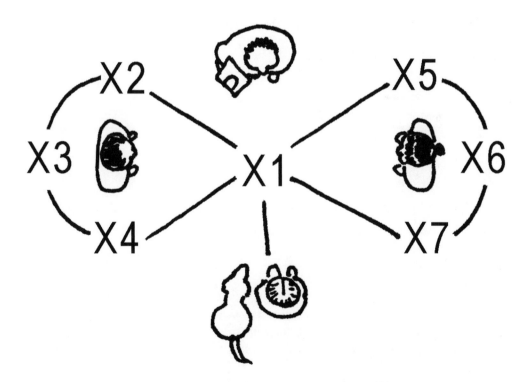

Figure 10.9 Once your dog can do both left and right circles, you are ready to combine all three phases — the left circle, the acceleration out of the left circle, and the right circle — into a *Figure Eight*.

about adding the *halt* until you and your dog have mastered sits while heeling in a straight line and until the rest of your *Figure Eight* is completely trained.

Judy deliberately uses exaggerated head cues when teaching the *Figure Eight*. The purpose of the head cue is to emphasize which direction she is moving. A head turn to the right brings the left shoulder forward and cues the dog to speed up. A head turn to the left brings the left shoulder back and cues the dog to slow down. Do not look at the dog when cueing him to speed up. Look at the posts while teaching and then refine the obvious head turns as the exercise becomes solid. The refinement comes in the form of looking at the steward's feet in the ring.

The *Figure Eight* combines the most complex combination of heeling parts in the obedience ring. The dog must heel in a straight line, do two curves (one in each direction), slow down, speed up, and *halt*. The small size of the *Figure Eight* requires constant adjustments by both handler and dog. A lot of the dog's skill has to do with muscle memory. In practice, do very slow inside curves, very fast outside curves, and no *halts*. The dog should have a fast, driving start. Do this until he shows that he understands the exercise by anticipating the changes he must make.

Handler Errors Made During Figure Eights

Typical errors include:

- Inconsistent size of *Figure Eight* loops (a loop is defined as half of a *Figure Eight*).
- Inconsistent distance from post on a loop.
- Leaning around arcs.
- Irregular pace on loops.
- Adapting your speed to the dog.
- Radically changing stride lengths on different parts of *Figure Eight*.

Serpentines Revisited

In addition to the *serpentine* we introduced earlier, we also work on a more difficult version. Set up five or six posts in a straight line, about eight feet apart (Fig. 10.10). Do a *serpentine* 10 feet in either direction, getting the dog to stay tight on both the left and right arcs into the next pass. You may also make loops that are closer to *Figure Eight*-sized loops, weaving your way through the whole line of posts.

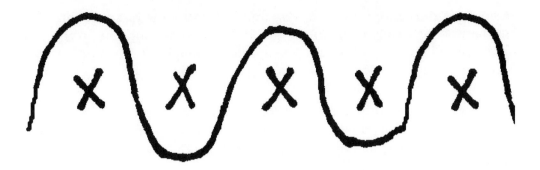

Figure 10.10 Set up five or six posts in a straight line, about eight feet apart. Do a serpentine 10 feet in either direction, getting the dog to stay tight on both the left and right arcs into the next pass.

Pace Changes

There are three different speeds at which you must move during a heeling pattern. These are *normal*, *slow*, and *fast*. The *normal* pace is the brisk pace you have been using during *rhythm heeling*. Develop a stride that fits the size of your dog. Generally speaking, your stride length is about the same length as the dog's trotting stride length, except for very small or very large dogs. *Fast* means that the handler must run, handler and dog moving forward at a noticeably accelerated speed. *Slow* means that the dog and handler must move forward noticeably slower than during the *normal*.

The goal when doing *pace changes* is for your dog to maintain *heel position* during each change.

During a *slow*, we typically walk about half as fast as we do during a *normal*, so we are walking at a rate of 60 to 70 beats per minute. We keep our stride length about the same as the one we use during a *normal*. It may help you to think about curling your toes into the mat when you walk in a *slow*. This can help you keep your balance better.

During the *fast, the handler must run and the dog must noticeably accelerate.* The small-to-medium-sized dog usually needs to canter to keep up. The canter is a three-beat gait. If your dog typically lags when you start the *fast*, have someone watch what gait the dog uses in trying to keep up. Is he trotting during the *normal* pace? If your dog doesn't have enough drive to keep up in an extended trot when you run, teach him to canter when you speed up (see *play running* in the *Power Steering* chapter). Some bigger dogs *pace* during the *normal* and *trot* during the *fast*. There isn't anything in the regulations about gait, but a few judges deduct for the dog who doesn't change gait. It can be harder to judge whether the dog has noticeably accelerated if the dog simply extends his *normal* gait during the *fast*. It is very important that the handler, with this sort of dog, really runs during the *fast* to leave no question in the judge's mind about whether the *fast* was fast enough. Teach your dog to maintain *heel position* when you run, and there will never be a question as to whether the *fast* was correct.

During a *fast*, RUN, using a stride length that is approximately the same length as your *normal* pace stride length. Many handlers don't run fast enough on their *fast* because their dog lags. Don't be guilty of this error!

A question we are frequently asked is, "How many steps should I take when making a pace change?" There is no written rule, but you should make the change within two to three steps, without being abrupt. If you take too many steps to make the change to the new speed, you put yourself at a disadvantage as you will usually run out of ring space. You also make the judge wonder if you have actually changed pace.

Remember that the judge must make rapid scoring decisions while he is calling a pattern for you. When you make good *pace changes*, you make the judge's job easier.

Handler Errors During Pace Changes

Common handler errors during *pace changes* include:

- Surging (i.e., not maintaining a consistent speed).
- Anticipating the judge's next command, most often returning to *normal* from the *fast* before the judge's command to do so.
- Taking too long to change to the new pace.
- Not returning to the same *normal* pace as before the *slow* or *fast*.
- *Pace changes* that are not different enough from the *normal* pace.

Teaching the Dog

When you want your dog to slow down (*normal* to *slow*, *fast* to *normal*), command BACK just before you slow down. When you want your dog to speed up (*slow* to *normal*, *normal* to *fast*), command HEEL or HURRY just before you speed up. Eventually, you must be silent during these changes. *It is important for you to give verbal cues to your dog during the learning stage or he will have no way of knowing you are about to change pace and will probably lag or forge.*

Your dog will eventually read pace change cues from your body (slight lean forward for the *fast* and slight lean backwards for the *slow*), but when he's just learning, you must give him extra help.

Make changes gradually using a few steps to change to the new pace. This gives your dog a chance to react smoothly, and also presents a better picture. Use slightly exaggerated body posture when teaching these cues. Lean forward for the *fast* and back for the *slow*. It is easy to fade the extra body motion as you smooth out your *pace changes*. To help your dog, hold food visible in your left hand for awhile. Make sure you use your CR when your dog is doing the new pace correctly and not just after you have completed the change back to *normal*. He needs to know the exact moment he is correct. After you hide the food, keep reinforcing each effort for a few more training sessions. Then move to variable, and finally to selective reinforcement.

Some typical errors you may see on the *fast* are:

- Handlers who do not run.

- Dogs who do not change pace when their handler does, causing an immediate lag.

- Dogs who do not accelerate enough, so they never catch up.

- Dogs who start the *fast* on the Judge's command, as opposed to their handler's cue, causing a forge.

- Dogs who go wide.

- Dogs who bounce up and down.

- Dogs and/or handlers who do not maintain the *fast* long enough.

Some of the typical errors you see on the *slow* are:

- Handlers who do not do a correct *slow* pace.

- Dogs who lose *attention* ("Gee, thanks for giving me the time to look around, Mom!").

- Dogs who try to *sit*.

- Dogs who don't slow down enough, causing a forge.

- Dogs and/or handlers who don't maintain the *slow* long enough.

- Dogs who side-wind during the *slow*; the front slows down but the rear doesn't match the slower speed.

- Dogs who surge, speeding up and slowing down multiple times during the *slow*.

Work on heeling long distances in the new pace to help your dog gain an understanding of how to move at this different speed. Many dogs rarely *walk* around the house or yard, so you may need to teach them how to do so. Lazier dogs don't speed up very well. You should do frequent *play running* with this type of dog to teach the transition to the *fast.* Don't forget that you can throw food or a toy ahead of you to help speed him up. Gradually ask him to run farther before giving him his CR and his toy or treat. The use of the CR during the *fast*, rather than after slowing to the *normal*, can be very reinforcing for the dog and keep him running with you as he knows his treat will follow soon.

Once you and your dog are comfortable about making *pace changes* in open spaces, both of you need to get used to working in a more confined area. In a 30-foot by 40-foot Novice ring, you often must do a *slow* along the 30-foot short end. Many dogs and/or handlers do not return to the *normal* pace from the *slow* when heading into a wall or other barrier. This can create substantial lagging errors, especially if an *about turn* follows. These may be so severe that the dog ends up on the wrong side of the handler after waiting for his handler to come out of the corner.

If you are having this type of problem, make sure both you and your dog are returning to *normal* rhythm after the *slow.* Check this without a confining barrier. If you are doing a good return to your *normal* pace, make sure you and your dog are maintaining a *normal* pace right up to barriers, such as walls, gates, ropes, bushes, tables and chairs, or gates and tables with people sitting nearby. If your dog is hanging back, figure out *when* this behavior occurs. An observer, watching from the side, can be useful in telling you the exact moment your dog starts to lag. Once you determine this distance, reinforce with your CR and food *just before* getting to that spot. Gradually reinforce as you move closer to the barrier, until your dog is comfortably heeling up to the barrier.

Another common problem is handling the *fast-normal-about turn* combination often called in the Novice and Open class heeling patterns. Many people have trouble slowing themselves down into their *normal* pace after the *fast* which may cause problems on the *about turn.* Some dogs swing their hind quarters out in anticipation of the turn after the *fast.* Do *halts* and/or *left turns* after the return to a *normal* pace to help solve this problem. Make sure you get back to your *normal* pace before the *about turn!*

About Turn Footwork

An *about turn* is one of the most challenging parts of heeling for both dogs and handlers to master. In AKC obedience, *about turn* means you turn 180° to the right, in place. A correctly performed *about turn* has you returning in the same lane you were in before the turn, without stepping out of your lane before, during, or after the turn. The *about turn* requires a lot of practice for most handlers.

We use the following footwork when we do *about turns* (Fig. 10.11):

- The right foot is planted at a slight angle, between one and two o'clock (Step 1).

- The left foot makes a "7" (or a "T") with the toes (or the ball) of the left foot touching the big toe of the right foot (Step 2).

- The right foot makes an "L" with the right heel against the left heel (Step 3).

- The left foot straightens out, taking a small step, the length of which depends on the size and speed of the dog (Step 4).

A useful prop to use when practicing *about turn* footwork is a small towel. If you use one, the first three steps should be on the towel. You may want to begin by practicing landing on the towel with your right foot from a variety of distances before you worry about adding the second, third, and fourth steps. It may be difficult to keep all of your steps on the towel, but do try to stay there as much possible.

Ultimately, you need to maintain the same rhythm throughout the *about turn* as you do during your *normal*, 120 to 138 beats per minute. This takes considerable practice so try to be patient.

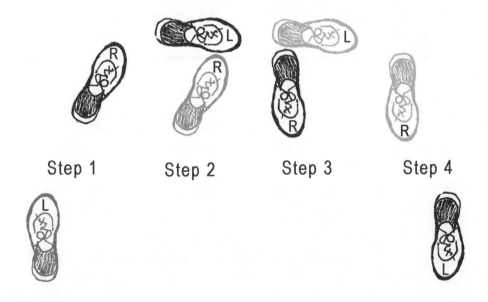

Step 1   Step 2   Step 3   Step 4

Figure 10.11 *About turn* footwork. Note that the black shoe is the one most recently moved, while the grey shoe did not just move. Also note that the turn must be made in place.

Remember: keep your feet under your hips and shoulders, maintain your rhythm, and make your first step out of the turn proportionate to the size of your dog. With enough practice, this footwork becomes part of your "muscle memory," so you don't have to concentrate on where you put each foot; you can rely on your body to do the right thing.

Handler Errors During About Turns

- Making P-shaped turns.
- Making U-turns.
- Not staying in the same lane before, during, and after the turn.
- Doing "cha-cha" *about turns* (i.e., taking a big step backwards on the third step, instead of keeping the feet close together).
- Pausing on the turn, usually to wait for the dog.
- Making the turn with the feet too far apart, which tends to cause the dog to lag.

Right Turn Footwork

We use this sequence when making a *right turn* (Fig. 10.12):

- Plant the right foot at an angle, between one and two o'clock (Step 1).
- Step smoothly with the left foot in the new direction to the right (Step 2).
- Step out on the right foot in the new direction (Step 3).

Left Turn Footwork

We use this sequence when making a *left turn* (Fig. 10.13):

- Plant the left foot at an angle, still in your "lane", between ten and eleven o'clock (Step 1).
- Step smoothly with your right foot in the new direction to the left (Step 2).
- Step out on your left foot in the new direction (Step 3).

Do not start turns with your dog until you are comfortable doing the turn footwork without him. If you have to stop and think where to place your feet during the turns, you will not be able to concentrate on your dog. Review the footwork until it does not require your full concentration.

Step 1

Figure 10.12 *Right turn* footwork.

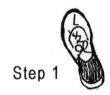

Figure 10.13 *Left turn* footwork.

Transition Turns

Before starting *moving turns*, in which we heel before and after the turn, we teach the dogs how to do *transition turns*. These are not quite as difficult as *moving turns*. We define a *transition turn* as doing a turn in place and then heeling out of it.

For the *transition left turn*, begin with a *left quarter turn* (IN) and, as the turn is completed, but before the dog has a chance to *sit*, give a HEEL command and heel forward in the new direction three to four steps. Use your CR and a treat for good efforts.

For the *transition right turn*, begin with your *right turn start* and add three or four more steps in the new direction before using your CR and giving a treat.

For the *transition about turn*, begin with a *dizzy spin*, probably no more than one complete circle and, when your dog is driving hard in position, heel out in a straight line. You may need an additional HEEL command when you change from spinning to heeling forward.

Moving Turns

The next goal is for your dog to maintain *heel position* during a *moving left turn* (90° to the left), a *moving right turn* (90° to the right), and a *moving about turn* (180° to the right, returning on the same track). We have laid the foundation for the *moving turns* with the work on turn footwork (Figs. 10.11–10.13) and various stationary exercises.

Start the *moving turns* in slow motion, gradually speeding up as you and your dog get more comfortable with the footwork. Make sure your dog is successfully doing the turn before going faster. When teaching turns, we use extreme head and body cues. This helps the dog focus and listen for the turn command. Later, your body follows your foot cues, and this subtle combination of cues tells your dog to turn. For the *left turn*, move your left shoulder back, bring your right shoulder forward, and turn your head to the left. For the *about* and *right turns*, turn your head to the right and pull your left shoulder forward while moving your right shoulder back.

In the following descriptions, we discuss using a snug leash to help hold your dog in position. If he is very good at following food, and you are a good "driver," you can teach the turns without a leash.

Left Turns

First, warm up with some *left quarter turns*, then some *transition left turns*. Set yourself up as follows (Fig. 10.14):

- Hold your leash snugly behind you in your right hand, with your right hand at your side, as you did when teaching the *left quarter turn* (IN).

- Hold a piece of food in your left hand.

- Slowly heel forward a few steps. Starting from a *sit* is optional.

- Cue your dog for the *left turn* with your IN command as you plant your left foot at a slight angle. Do not step into the dog. Turn your head to the left, pull your left shoulder back, and bring your right shoulder forward.

- Show him the food in *heel position*, moving your hand out to your left a short distance to guide his head in that direction, as you did when teaching IN.

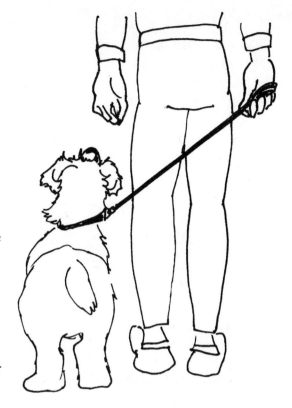

Figure 10.14 Starting position for the *moving left turn.*

- Complete the turn with your right foot turning in the new direction. CR, stop, and reinforce with the food.

Use constant reinforcement when first teaching the *moving left turn.* Not every repetition needs to be perfect, and your dog will be more likely to continue trying if he is rewarded frequently. Move to variable reinforcement and selective reinforcement as soon as he begins to show some understanding. Make sure you keep the food very close to your body to encourage your dog to stay close.

If your dog is having trouble maintaining attention, you will not be successful teaching the turn properly. Work first on the lack of attention before trying to teach the turn.

Right Turns

Warm up with some *heel starts* and then some *transition right turns*. Set yourself up as follows (see Fig. 10.15):

Figure 10.15 Starting position for the *moving right turn.*

- Keep your leash short to help keep your dog in *heel position.*

- Have a piece of food in the appropriate hand, as you did when you taught the *transition right turn.* The hand in which you hold your food will depend on your height as well as the height of your dog. If the hand you are using is not producing the desired results, try the other. Do not be afraid to experiment to see what works best for you and your dog.

- Heel forward for a few steps. Starting from a *sit*, once again, is optional.

- Cue your dog for the *right turn* with HEEL or HURRY as you plant your right foot at a slight angle to your right. Do not step into or away from your dog. Pull your right shoulder back and bring your left shoulder forward as you look to the right.

- Show your dog the food in *heel position* and move it across your body just above the level of his nose.

- Complete the turn with your left foot. CR, stop, and reinforce with the food. Make sure your CR is given as the dog "drives" or accelerates into the turn and not after it is completed.

Always remember to use your CR first to let the dog know he is correct. Using the CR rewards the dog's effort just as it occurs. Sometimes dogs do not do the whole turn correctly but still make an effort. This needs to be reinforced so the dog continues to try. **A CR and no food, means "good try." A CR and food means "you're right" or "you're close!"** Continue to use variable and finally selective reinforcement.

Once your dog has the idea of driving through the turn, don't move your hand as far across your body. Keep the food hidden in your hand until you cue your dog with HURRY. Then show him the food, CR, and reward. Do this until he has a clear understanding of the exercise. Make sure you keep the food close to your body to encourage your dog to stay close. This position reinforces the focal point for him.

About Turns

Work on the *about turn* without your dog if you need to review the footwork (Fig. 10.11). *About turns* are one of the most challenging heeling skills for your dog to perfect, so take the time to teach yourself how to do them well before introducing them to your dog.

Also review *dizzy spins* and *transition about turns*. These two exercises help your footwork and help teach your dog the needed skills.

Next, heel in a straight line into a *dizzy spin*. This is a good time to start using your more precise footwork. Be sure you are turning *in place* during the spin, rather than making a small circle. The dog should drive hard to keep up with you.

Once your dog is doing this well, you are ready for "real" *about turns*:

- Keep your leash short to keep your dog in *heel position*.
- Have a piece of food in your hand.
- Start in a *stand* and heel forward a few steps.
- Show him the food in your hand held in *heel position*.
- Cue your dog for the *about turn* with HURRY as you plant your right foot for the turn. Turn your head to the right, bring your left shoulder forward, and pull your right shoulder back.
- Slide the food across to the front of your leg or waist, just above the level of your dog's nose, and keep your wrist against your leg or waist.
- Make the "T" (or a "7") turn step with your left foot, instep (or toes) against the toes of your right foot.
- Repeat HURRY as your right foot turns and plants again.

- Take the final step with your left foot.
- CR and reinforce with the food.

You may want to reinforce using your CR and no food as the dog "drives" into the *about turn*. This gives him immediate information to keep on driving, as he is correct.

Once your dog has the idea of driving around the turn, don't move your hand as far across your body. Keep the food hidden in your hand until you give him the first HURRY cue; then show it to him. Make sure you keep the food close to your body to encourage your dog to stay close. It is especially important to have his *attention* before starting into the *about turn*. Work on *attention* separately if needed.

As with the *right turn*, the hand in which you hold your food will depend on your height as well as the height of your dog. If the hand you are using is not producing the desired results, try the other. Do not be afraid to experiment to see what works best for you and your dog.

Halts

When a judge calls "Halt" in the obedience ring, you are expected to stop promptly, though not abruptly. Your dog is expected to stop and *sit* in *heel position* at your left side with no additional commands or signals from you.

It is very important for you to be consistent with your footwork when you *halt*. You must non-verbally cue your dog that you are about to stop and give him enough time to react and *sit* smoothly. This non-verbal *halt* cue needs to be subtle, which is why reliable *attention* is so important.

Poor halts are often due to the dog's inattention and to the handler's inconsistent or nonexistent cues. Make sure to add steps slowly when shaping the *halt* to prevent one error from building on another.

Three steps to remember when halting are (Fig. 10.16):

- *Pre-plant step* subtly shift your weight back in preparation for the *plant step* as you take your last full-length step.
- *Plant step* take a half-length step on the other foot as you verbally tell your dog to SIT.
- *Closing step* bring your first foot up to the second foot as you complete the *halt*.

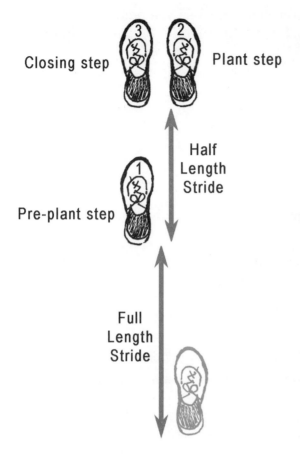

Closing step   Plant step

Pre-plant step

Half Length Stride

Full Length Stride

Figure 10.16 Three steps to remember when *halting* are the *pre-plant step*, the *plant step*, and the *closing step*.

You have the choice of taking an odd or an even number of steps. If you start heeling on your left foot and close with your left foot, you will take an odd number of steps. If you start with your left foot and close with your right foot, you will take an even number of steps. We recommend that you experiment to see which works best for you and your dog.

The SIT command, given with the *plant step*, will be gradually faded as your dog gains competence. Hold food in sight in your left hand as you did when you taught *scoot heel*. It is positioned over your dog's head. This will help keep his body straight in *heel position*. If possible, work in front of a mirror (store front windows make excellent mirrors) so you can determine the hand position that produces the straightest *sits*. If your dog sits with his shoulders leaning out, keep your hand closer to your body; if his rear is out, keep it farther away. If your dog is too far away, hold your leash snugly behind your back in your right hand.

Both of us start and stop on the left foot most of the time; the half-length *plant step* is done with the right foot and the *closing step* with the left (Fig. 10.16). There are times when it is best to do the opposite (i.e., the *plant step* done with the left foot and the *closing step* with the right). By practicing both ways, you will be more comfortable in the ring. You may also find one way may make your dog's *halts* better than the other. Experiment with both ways (with and without your dog) until you can stop smoothly.

Practice your *halt* footwork (without your dog) with someone calling commands for you. This is undoubtedly harder than doing it by yourself! Be sure to walk in a straight line. Use parking lot lines, tennis court lines, or mats to help you. Stay on that line when you *halt*, as this keeps you from stepping into the dog. If you step into him when you *halt*, he will learn to drift to the left.

We are often asked, "How many steps may I take before stopping?" There is no written rule about this, but if you take more than four, it is usually too many. There are times when it is really hard to stop! We suggest that you try to stop within two or three steps.

Handler Errors on Halts

The following common mistakes made during *halts*:

- Stepping into or away from the dog.
- Stopping too abruptly.
- Stopping without properly cuing the dog.
- Taking too many steps before halting.
- Taking baby steps before halting.
- Dipping the knees during the *halt*.
- Moving hand(s) during the *halt* to guide the dog.
- Twisting the upper body to the left in order to check the dog's *sit*.
- Turning the head to see the dog.

Teaching the Dog to Halt

Warm up with a series of *scoot heels*. We assume that you start and close on your left foot, but modify these directions as needed.

- Start with food in your left hand, held in a position which helps the dog keep his head straight.
- Say your HEEL command.
- Step out on your left foot (the *pre-plant step*).
- Take a half step with your right foot (the *plant step*) and say SIT as your right foot lands.
- Close (*halt*) with your left foot.

Initially, use your CR and a piece of food with each *halt*. Gradually become more selective. Different parts of a good automatic *sit* include *attention*, speed, and *heel position*. Focus on one of these elements during a given series of sits. You may use your CR and no food to tell your dog to keep trying, but save the food for the best efforts. For an outstanding effort, give multiple treats or a *jackpot*.

The goal is for your dog to sit during your closing step, not after you have completely stopped. This makes for a much smoother *halt* than when the dog reacts only after you have come to a *halt*.

As your dog learns to *sit* promptly after three steps, add two more. Be sure to hold your left hand close to your body as you do during *normal* heeling. Just before you give the SIT command, move your left hand out over your dog's head. This helps him remain in straight *heel position* for the *sit* (Fig. 10.17). The sit command is given with your *plant step* (the fourth step at this point), not the *closing step*. *Remember to use both verbal and foot cues to help your dog sit promptly and in the correct position.* Use your CR just as the dog sits and give him the food after you have come to a *halt*. Continue to add two steps at a time until both of you are stopping correctly after a total of nine to eleven steps.

This method of teaching the *halt* by counting steps helps you stay consistent. It keeps your body under control, which helps your footwork. Vary the number of steps you take, from three to your current maximum. As the number of steps increases, remember to keep your left hand close to your body, moving it out just before the *plant step* and SIT command. When you stop using the food in sight, continue to use the left hand movement to cue your dog, but gradually fade this as well. Continue to give your SIT command with your *plant step*. We use this for quite a few months, until the dog is sitting reliably in correct position. Fade the hand movement completely before eliminating the verbal *sit* cue.

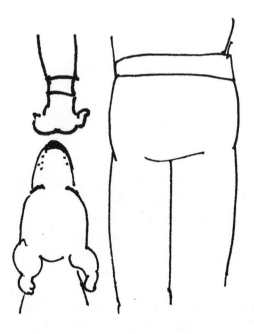

Figure 10.17 Just before you give the SIT command, move your left hand out over your dog's head. This helps him remain in straight heel position for the sit.

Use a verbal sit cue randomly throughout your dog's training. The *automatic sit* is often a stress point and the verbal reminder helps the dog.

Combining It All

Once your dog has learned the individual parts of heeling, begin to combine two parts of the heeling pattern, then three, continuing until you can do an entire pattern similar to what you might see in the ring. There is a fairly standard "L" pattern used in Novice and Open (Fig. 10.18), and a frequently seen modified "T" pattern (Fig. 10.19) in Utility. The typical patterns usually include a "*fast, normal, about turn*" and a "*slow, normal, about turn.*" A judge may also call a *right* or *left turn* following a *change of pace*. It is therefore important to practice various combinations of *turns* and *pace changes*, as well as *halts*, before putting them all together into a single pattern. We have seen Novice and Open patterns that were devilishly hard for a new team to negotiate, with many turns, using the center and all corners of the ring. We hope this is the exception rather than the rule, but we recommend practicing complicated patterns so the more standard ones will seem easy.

You will probably find that some individual elements, and certain combinations of elements, haunt you throughout your dog's career. No matter what you do, these mistakes crop up every so often. For Rio, the "*fast, normal, about turn*" often produced a wide *about turn*. Leaning out on *sits* was his other recurring problem. When Treasure is feeling insecure, she heels a bit too close. For Alec, wide *about turns* and crooked sits sometimes show up under ring stress.

When you first combine a few elements, you may discover unexpected weaknesses in your dog's skills. Work on these weaknesses individually to produce improved results.

A very common mistake we see on the *about turn* is the dog who flares his rear outwards as he comes out of the turn. If you have this problem, work on *left turn stars*, which is an *about turn* followed immediately by a *left turn* (Fig. 10.20). Start in the center of your training area. Heel forward four to six steps, do an *about turn*, and then as soon as you can, do a *left turn*. Start out with one combination of *about turn* and *left turn*. Then go to two: *about turn, left turn, about turn, left turn*. When you have done four combinations, you have made a star or a plus sign. These drills help the dog who flares his rear out after the *about turn*. This should help the dog understand that he needs to keep his rear straight coming out of the *about turn*. Judy fixed Alec's wide *about turns* by practicing an *about turn* followed immediately by her CLOSE command and a side step to the right.

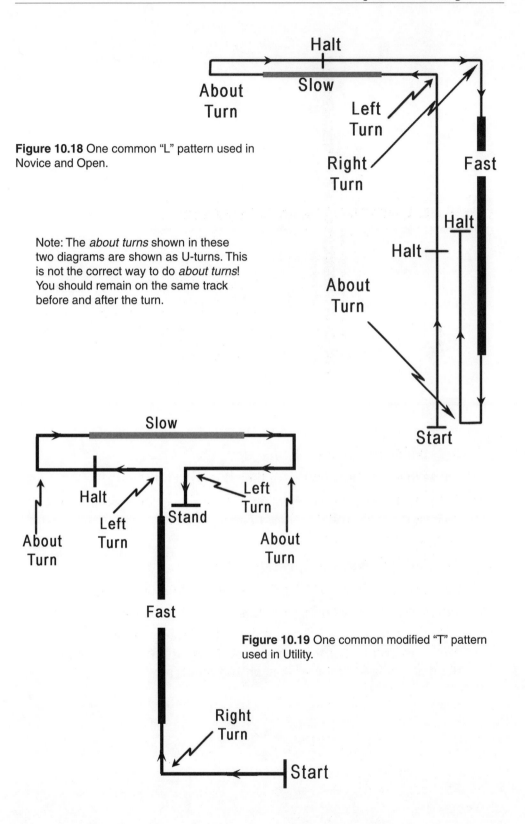

Figure 10.18 One common "L" pattern used in Novice and Open.

Note: The *about turns* shown in these two diagrams are shown as U-turns. This is not the correct way to do *about turns*! You should remain on the same track before and after the turn.

Figure 10.19 One common modified "T" pattern used in Utility.

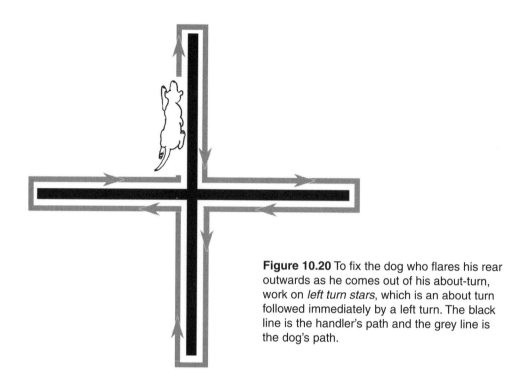

Figure 10.20 To fix the dog who flares his rear outwards as he comes out of his about-turn, work on *left turn stars*, which is an about turn followed immediately by a left turn. The black line is the handler's path and the grey line is the dog's path.

Other combinations to work on:

- *Turns* followed by a *halt* — makes the *halts* harder.
- *Turns* followed by *pace changes* — you almost always have to do a *turn* before and/or after a *pace change*.
- *Fast, normal, about turn, halt.*
- *Fast, normal, halt* — often seen in runoffs.
- *Turns* very close to barriers — critical for ring preparation.
- *Halts* very close to barriers — makes the *halts* harder.
- *Right turn stars* (Fig. 10.21). Follow the directions for the *left turn* stars, replacing the *left turns* with *right turns*. This helps the dog who goes wide or lags on the *about turn*.

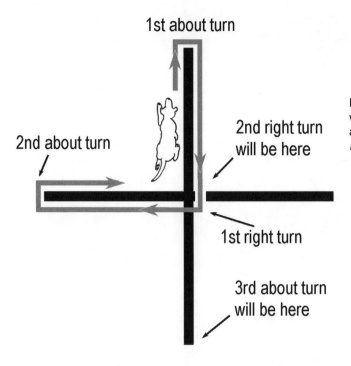

1st about turn

2nd about turn

2nd right turn
will be here

1st right turn

3rd about turn
will be here

Figure 10.21 Help the dog who goes wide or lags on the about turn by working on *right turn stars*.

- *About turn* drill — the dog is on the inside and you are moving counterclockwise. At each corner, instead of doing a *left turn*, do a 270° spin to the right, and head out in the *left turn* direction (see Fig. 10.22). This improves the dog's drive on *about turns* and helps prevent anticipated *left turns*.

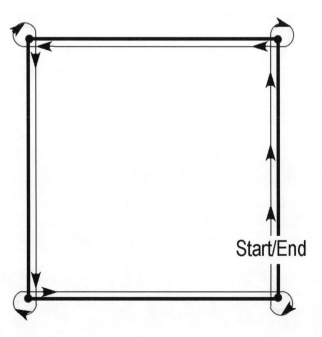

Start/End

Figure 10.22 An *about turn drill:* at each corner, instead of doing a *left turn*, do a 270° spin to the right and head out in the *left turn* direction. This improves the dog's drive on *about turns* and helps prevent anticipated *left turns*.

- *Stair steps* (Fig. 10.23). Start in one corner of your training area. We assume your first turn will be a *right turn*. Heel forward a few steps, make a *right turn*, heel a few more steps, make a *left turn*, heel a few more steps, make another *right turn*, then another *left turn*. Continue until you run out of space. This is a great *attention* exercise, and any errors your dog makes on the turns become exaggerated by the next turn. Some dogs go wide after a *left turn*, which causes a lag on the following *right turn*. As you begin to see what your dog's problem areas are, vary how many of each turn you do in a row and add *about turns* to the mix. You must have good footwork to be successful with this drill!

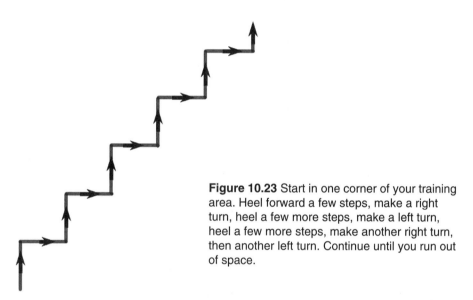

Figure 10.23 Start in one corner of your training area. Heel forward a few steps, make a right turn, heel a few more steps, make a left turn, heel a few more steps, make another right turn, then another left turn. Continue until you run out of space.

- *Random turns*. Make sure you and your dog are not dependent on having a barrier to help you make the turn. Practice turns down the center and/or in the middle of a straight heeling pattern.

- *Pace changes* at the barriers. Many dogs hang back as they get close to a barrier. Make sure your dog is comfortable running up to a wall or gate. Review the *Pace Changes* section.

- *Call to heel* with handler in many places, including the dog facing the opposite direction, to simulate recovering from an incorrect *about turn* (Fig. 10.24).

Figure 10.24 To simulate recovering from a poor *about turn,* practice the *call to heel* exercise with the dog facing the opposite direction.

- Figure L's and T's (4 posts) to help keep the *Figure Eight* fresh, occasionally use more than two posts. We like to set up four posts in an "L" shape or a "T" shape (Fig. 10.25). This keeps you and your dog alert and helps keep the exercise more interesting.

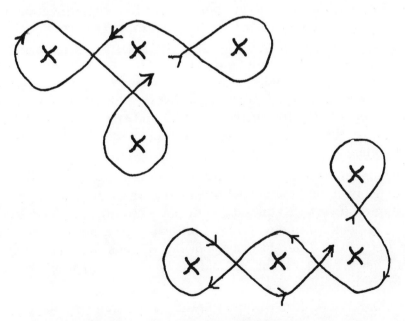

Figure 10.25 Figure L's and T's (4 posts) help keep the *Figure Eight* interesting. We like to set up four posts in an "L" shape or a "T" shape.

Proofing Heeling

Once your dog is heeling well in a quiet location, it is important to add distractions. Add the following one at a time:

- Have a person follow at a distance and then closely.
- Have someone call a heeling pattern for you.
- Pause a long time on *halts*. This simulates a judge taking many notes.
- Have someone walk around you and your dog on *halts*.
- Put chalk marks, duct tape, or sticky dots on the floor.
- Do *Figure Eight*'s around people who are of different sizes and genders. Do not forget to use children.
- Have your *Figure Eight* posts wear bait bags or hold food or a toy in their hand.
- Have people with different types of voices call heeling commands.

Off-Leash Heeling

We rarely have a problem heeling off-leash since we do most of our early training without a leash. If you must train in an area that requires you to keep your dog leashed, you need to be sure that your leash is loose at all times and that you are not using it to constantly guide your dog. You may use a six-foot leash with the extra length over your shoulder. Try to keep your hands off the leash. The purpose of the leash is strictly for safety, not for training. If you have trained for a long time with the leash as a guide, go back and teach or retrain your steering words (see *Power Steering* chapter). Show your dog that he must take the responsibility for being in the correct position and stop using the leash to control him. Do this by ignoring any incorrect position and rewarding the correct position.

If heeling off-leash is a problem because your dog would rather look elsewhere, go back and review the *attention* work in the *Fundamental Words* chapter. If you have proofed your dog's attention, and he still thinks he can look around when he is off-leash, an attention correction is in order. Use your left hand to give your dog a quick rap on the top or side of his head, tweak an ear, or hold his head up with your left hand around his muzzle.

You should have little trouble working off-leash if you make sure he fully understands and *likes* heel position.

Problem Solving

Lagging

There are different types of lagging problems. The chronic lagger is a dog who is behind his handler the majority of the time. Dogs who have been corrected frequently usually fall into this category. The occasional lagger drops back when he loses attention or at certain points in a heeling pattern. Typically, this happens when he is required to accelerate, such as during a change of pace or a turn.

If you have trained your dog for some time and he lags frequently during a heeling pattern, you should go back and reteach the *find heel* exercise in the *Fundamental Words* chapter. Build his heeling slowly and carefully using the *rhythm heeling* exercise and be sure that you have a well established CR. A dog who hates heeling is a real challenge as a rehabilitation project and you must take the time you need to make it more comfortable for him. Correcting this type of dog generally doesn't work and only makes him hate heeling more.

Dogs sometimes lag when they lose attention for a moment. If a dog loses attention frequently, he usually does not heel well. If you have not taught attention, go back and train it now (see *Fundamental Words* chapter). We train primarily off-lead so our dogs get their heeling direction from our words and body cues. We seldom use physical corrections for heeling mistakes except for loss of attention.

If your dog lacks drive and doesn't start with you when you take your first step, it is probably time to add a correction to his *heel starts* (see *Power Steering* chapter). When you have success with the correction on *heel starts,* you can use a similar correction if your dog lags instead of speeding up on *about turns, right turns,* the outside arc of a *Figure Eight,* and the *fast* pace. However, use caution when correcting a dog who lags on a transition from *normal* to *fast.* This type of correction can increase the lagging problem instead of solving it! First, review *play running* in the *Power Steering* chapter to make sure your dog can do a correct *fast.*

Forging

Most trainers who have worked a dog with a chronic lagging problem are thrilled with one who forges! It is generally easier to get a dog back into heel position than trying to convince him to come up into heel position as you must do if your dog lags.

To fix forging problems, reinforce your dog only when he is in the correct position. Ignore the forging and see if it extinguishes on its own. If not, attach a short leash to your dog's buckle collar, hold it tightly behind your legs with your right hand, and bind your dog in heel position. Reinforce often with your CR and a treat every time you feel slack in the leash. These are the times your dog is trying to stay back. Use your BACK command to give your dog some verbal feedback about what you are asking him to do. You might also stop when he forges, take a few steps backward using your BACK command, and then proceed forward a few steps. Do this slowly as forging dogs are often excitable dogs.

If your BACK command is not enough, you might also add a backwards leash correction immediately following the command.

If he has been forging for a long time, the problem will be much harder to solve since he thinks he is in the right place. As always, plan to take the time you need to retrain this problem.

Weaving, Drifting, Side Winding, Heeling Wide

When first learning to heel, dogs and handlers often make many errors. It is easiest to deal with these errors early before they become chronic.

If your dog tends to go wide on turns, or weaves or side-winds on the straight away, it may help to use barriers on the floor (Fig. 10.26). When your dog makes an error, he steps on or bumps into the barrier. He should work to avoid the barrier, which helps correct going wide. Possible barriers include broad jump boards standing upright, PVC poles laid in a straight line, curb stones in a parking lot, the bar from the Utility bar jump, a wall, or curbs along a street. When using a curb, you can heel either on top of the curb or down in the gutter. The dog falls off when you are "up" or bumps into the curb when you are "down."

Judy's Brig was a structural pacer, meaning he moved in a *pace* all the time. As a result, he was a side-winder (rear out). She walked many miles against a curb or on the edge of the street to get him to have "rump straight" muscle memory. If he went into side-winding mode, he would bump into the curb or fall into the street.

Handlers who weave can benefit from practicing with a barrier on their right. The barrier helps the handler the same way it helps the dog.

Rio's P-shaped *about turns* were effectively fixed by walking along a bar on the floor, starting with it to the right (Fig. 10.27). If he went too wide, he bumped into it. Typically, the dog with very focused *attention* doesn't even notice the barrier until he bumps it or steps on it. Expect some attention loss the next time you are near that barrier. It shows your dog is thinking about what he is doing with his feet and that the barrier is having an impact. Remind him to pay attention and perhaps help him with a verbal cue to speed up.

Figure 10.26 If your dog tends to go wide on turns, or weaves or side-winds on the straight away, it may help to use barriers on the ground.

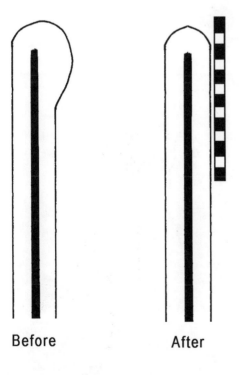

Figure 10.27 To fix P-shaped *about turns*, walk along a bar on the floor, starting with it to the right. Your dog will bump into the bar if he goes wide on his *about turn*.

Before   After

Drifting with a Purpose

If your dog consistently heels too wide or too close to you, we recommend that you drift on purpose for a while. If your dog is consistently too close, drift to the left; too wide, drift to the right.

For the crowder, start on the right side of your training area. You will drift left, but don't simply turn and heel diagonally across the floor. Instead, sidestep every two to four steps as you heel along (Fig. 10.28). You need to experiment with which foot you side-step, in order to see which is more effective in moving the dog off your leg. Cue your dog with OFF just before you step into him. You might bump into him at first, but that's okay. With enough repetition, you should see your dog starting to heel farther away from you. Do not correct him for this, but rather praise him. He will drift back into correct *heel position* when you have practiced enough.

If gentle nudges don't decrease the crowding, try raising your left knee as though marching. This is also helpful on the inside post of the *Figure Eight* and on *left turns*. Another useful variation is to swing your left foot out to the side, which will make the dog stumble if he is heeling

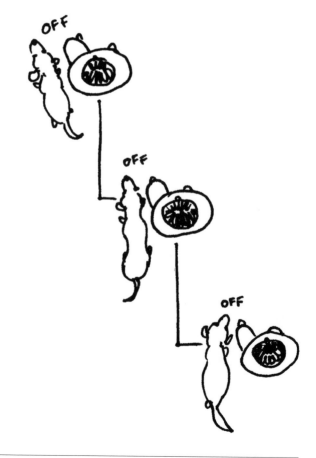

Figure 10.28 For the crowder, start on the right side of your training area. You will drift left, but don't simply turn and heel diagonally across the floor. Instead, side-step every two to four steps as you heel.

too close. When the dog collides with your knee or foot, you might say something like "Whoops, look what you did!" Don't feel sorry for your dog! When he heels into your lane, he will collide with you. It is his error and the bump is his fault.

For the dog who heels wide, start on the left side of your training area. You will end up farther to the right than when you started. Remember not to just turn and heel on a diagonal line, but side-step to your right (Fig. 10.29). Do this every two to four steps, cuing the dog with CLOSE just before you step away from him. With enough repetition, you should see your dog start to heel closer to you. Do this in combination with heeling the dog next to barriers.

Teach your dog to accept a long dowel rod made of either wood or plastic. He needs to be acquainted with this training tool before you use it for training (see *Puppy* chapter). You can use the dowel to teach him to keep his rear in by touching him lightly on his left hip. Hold the dowel in either your right or left hand. This takes coordination on your part, so do not be discouraged if you do not see immediate results. Any new tool takes time to work.

❖ ❖ ❖ ❖ ❖ ❖ ❖ ❖ ❖ ❖

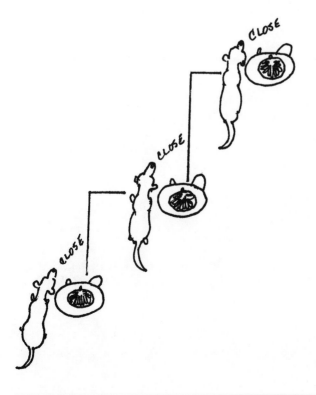

Figure 10.29 For the dog who heels wide, start on the left side of your training area. You will end up farther to the right than when you started. Remember not to just turn and heel on a diagonal line, but side-step to your right.

When done correctly, heeling is complicated! It is also beautiful! Many ingredients contribute to making a smooth heeling team. It may take a couple of years to feel synchronized with your dog, but when you reach that point, you will truly feel as if you are "dancing with your dog."

Recalls

The recall is a foundation exercise for many different formal obedience exercises, including the Novice *Recall*, the Open *Drop on Recall*, and all of the retrieve exercises. The basic purpose is for the dog to come directly to you at a brisk trot or gallop. The recall is also one of the most common reasons many dog owners sign up for an obedience class; they want their dog to come to them when he is called.

The Novice Recall

The Novice *Recall* appears to be a simple exercise. The handler leaves her dog in a *Sit-stay* at one end of an obedience ring, walks 35 feet away, turns to face the dog and, on the Judge's cue, commands or signals the dog to COME. He comes briskly and sits in front of her. On the Judge's command or signal, she cues her dog to move to a sit in heel position. Most dogs quickly learn to do a crude version of this. The problems come in perfecting the exercise!

There are several balance points in the Novice *Recall*. We teach each one separately and put them together only when the dog is securely doing each one. The balance points are:

- The *set-up:* Your dog moves to a sit in heel position.
- The *wait:* The dog sits at one end of the ring while you walk to the other end of the ring, about 35 feet away.
- The *recall:* Your dog comes briskly and directly to you at a trot or gallop.
- The *front:* He sits in front, centered and directly in front of you, but not touching your toes or between your feet.
- The *finish:* He moves rapidly from sitting in front to sitting in heel position.

The Wait

The wait or stay needs to be proofed separately from the recall. The recall should be so motivating for a beginning dog that he has a tendency to break the wait and come before he is called. **It is essential that you not punish the dog for breaking the wait when he anticipates the recall.** If you do, he will either not come at all or will come slowly. Anticipation usually means the dog is thinking about what he is supposed to do. Teach him to STAY (see *Stays* chapter) and, if you choose, transfer the command to the word WAIT. *STAY means you will return to the dog. WAIT means you want the dog to obey another command without your returning to him.* The word really doesn't matter as long as the dog understands what it means! Proof the WAIT or STAY apart from the recall and don't begin the formal recall until the dog has a solid *wait*.

Come

You started to teach the *Recall* when you first began training your puppy to COME. It was one of the first words he learned. A reliable response to your COME command is imperative as a potential life saving exercise, so you should teach this when your puppy is young. It is also an exercise where some degree of compulsion may be needed to make it reliable.

Let's review what you should have taught your dog to this point (from *Fundamental Words* chapter). He has learned the word COME which means "stop what you are doing and return to me." He has learned to do a *restrained recall* with someone else holding him, as well as a *food-toss recall* and a *chase recall*. He has learned that returning to you is always a pleasant experience and he is always rewarded for his return. The reward may be in the form of food, toys, play, or petting. The most important parts are:

- Your dog responds immediately to the command.
- You make it pleasant for your dog to come and stay near you.

During the teaching phase, ignore any wrong behavior. Do this by withholding the food for performances that are not up to your expectations. Stop the exercise when your dog makes a mistake. There is no anger, no harsh correction, just no reward. However, you must reward your dog for trying harder, especially if he is distracted or is trying to figure out what you want. In the early phases, reward the attempt even if it isn't perfect. Reward correct behavior on a variable schedule and continue to ask your dog for increased effort as soon as you think he is ready to assume responsibility for the exercise.

Motivational Recalls

A *motivational recall* combines a *wait* and *come*, but does not include a *front*. There is some formality involved. To do a *motivational recall*:

- Leave your dog in a sit, using your WAIT command.

- Face your dog in your "formal recall stance," with your hands at your sides and your feet close together. Call your dog as you would in the ring, "Fido, COME!" (or COME! if you don't use his name). Watch your body! Head-bobbing or other extra movements cause point deductions. A correct sight picture for your dog is very important.

- Release your dog when he is part way to you by tossing him a toy, tossing a toy or treat between your legs, or letting him jump on you. The distance at which you release him to the toy or food depends on your dog's level of training. With an inexperienced dog, we usually start to praise and use the CR as soon as he gets up.

At this time, we also introduce a *motivational recall* from a *down*. This allows you to work on the final portion of the *Drop on Recall* exercise. Put your dog in a *sphinx down*, tell him WAIT, walk 15 to 20 feet away, and call him to you. The instant he moves towards you, release him in the same way you did during the regular *motivational recall*. Some dogs may have some uncertainty about getting up quickly so encourage these early efforts enthusiastically.

Recall Problems

Some common problems with the recall:

- Not coming on the first command.
- Coming slowly.
- Anticipation.
- Arcing.

Not coming on the first command means either that your dog is unsure or he is used to you giving him two commands. **You must know "why" before you can figure out "how" to fix the problem.**

Any time your dog does not come on the first command, go to him and take his collar. Carefully walk backwards with the dog to the spot where you called him. Praise enthusiastically and return him to the starting point. Do not use a second command, since he has already refused one command. This exercise gets the point across very quickly to most dogs.

Another correction is to put him back on a leash and a buckle collar, command COME, and give a quick leash pop on his collar. Be sure the clip of the collar is under his chin, so that the correction is applied to the back of the dog's neck, causing him to come toward you. As soon as he gets up to come, praise enthusiastically and pet or play with him briefly when he gets to you. After the correction, sit your dog, leave him using your WAIT command, and command COME. If he comes even a short distance, immediately use your CR and feed him when he gets to you. He does not have to come all the way to be making an effort to be right. Remember, dogs only understand right or wrong! There is no need to "cheerlead" a dog on the recall. If he knows he is right the moment his bottom leaves the ground and you have an interesting reward at the other end, he should race to you. If your dog doesn't understand the COME command, go back to the *Fundamental Words* chapter and reteach it.

Dogs who are slow on the recall usually:

- Have been corrected for anticipating.
- Have not been reinforced for their first response or for completing the recall.

Anticipation is a wonderful thing. Remember, it means your dog is *thinking*. If he anticipates, keep a smile on your face, put him back where he was, correct him mildly with a tap on the chest, and leave again. Go a few steps away, turn, and before moving back to him, use your CR. Then go back to him and give him a treat. *Think about what you are trying to get your dog to do. His stay was broken, not his recall. Fix the broken part and forget the recall for a moment.* You may have to do this a lot with an enthusiastic dog! By not getting mad and not yelling at the dog, he won't be afraid to be wrong and will gladly do whatever you ask him to do. Some dogs and breeds learn faster than others. Some people learn faster than others. It's all right. This isn't a race!

Remember to reinforce the *first* move for a dog who is confused about responding immediately when called. This may be as small a move as shifting his weight as if to stand up. TELL him he's on the right track!

Arcing: Dogs who arc are not coming directly to you. If your dog arcs, sitting straight in front will be much harder for him. If he arcs too much, you may receive a failing score for the exercise. Some dogs always arc to the same side. Sometimes dogs arc away from a distraction. As they get used to the distraction, the recall straightens. Go back and work on shorter recalls. You may want to use a chute to get the dog accustomed to coming in a straight line (Fig. 11.1). Chutes are explained more thoroughly in the *Front and Finish* chapter.

Figure 11.1 If your dog arcs, sitting straight in front will be much harder for him. You may want to use a chute to get the dog accustomed to coming in a straight line.

Proofing the Recall

Some ideas for proofing the recall include:

- Practice the recall with a person standing behind your dog. If your dog is especially worried, have the person start farther away and gradually move closer. For any proofing you do with people distractions, it is a good idea to start with someone your dog knows.

- Practice the recall beside baby gates with people sitting or standing near the gates.

- Practice near an adjacent ring where another dog is working.

- Take a deep breath, but don't call your dog.

- Use nonsense words so your dog learns to listen for the command and not just words. We do not teach the commands using the dog's name. However, using the name in the ring is allowed and we implement this if the dog is not paying attention.

Return to your dog from time to time to reinforce the WAIT command. This is especially important for anxious, nervous, or excitable dogs.

The Handler

When we leave a dog to do a *Recall* of any sort, we step off on the right foot first as opposed to the left, which is the foot we use when we want the dog to heel. It may be superstitious, but we figure it can't hurt to be consistent!

When you turn to face your dog for a *Recall,* you must stand with your arms hanging naturally at your sides. They should not be crossed, nor should they be held on the front of your thighs or behind your back.

We recommend that you stand with your feet fairly close together. The dog will block your legs better when sitting straight in front if your feet are closer together. Why make it more obvious to the judge if your dog is slightly off center?

Judges vary in how they cue you to call your dog. Some use a signal only, some a verbal command (typically "Call your dog!"), and some a combination of the two. Most judges tell you before you leave your dog how they will cue you. You should watch exhibitors who show earlier in the class — unless of course you are first — to see where the judge stands and what cue he uses for the *Recall.* Most give an obvious signal, but occasionally it can be a subtle hand wave.

During the *front* balance point of the *Recall* — when your dog comes into the sit in front of you — you must be careful to avoid any movement that might be misconstrued as an extra signal to him. You may watch your dog as he is coming in, but don't make obvious head motions in an attempt to get him to straighten out. Even worse would be moving your hands or feet. Above all, stay relaxed; don't clench your hands into fists and don't grab your pant legs in nervousness!

As with the cue to call your dog, judges vary in how they cue you for the finish (when your dog goes from front position to heel position at your left side). Some give a verbal cue "Finish," some make a hand motion, some do both. If you are looking at your dog on his front, don't lift your head in a big motion to look at the judge; instead, lift your eyes. This again avoids the appearance of any extra cues to your dog. If the judge seems to be taking a long time to give a "Finish" command, it may be because he is using a signal. Be sure to get in the habit of looking up for the signal. You will need to proof this so your dog will not anticipate the *finish* if you shift your eyes upward.

Also, don't make a big motion and turn your head to look at your dog as he does his finish. A small turn of the head is okay, though we prefer to watch the dog with peripheral vision.

Handler errors seen during a Novice *Recall* include:

- Using an excessively loud voice during the command.
- Using improper arm positions.
- Bowing from the waist when giving the command.
- Bobbing your head when giving the command.

- Turning or dropping your head to watch the dog on the *front* or *finish*.
- Adapting your body to the dog's position on the *front*.
- Standing in an unnatural manner.

The Drop on Recall

The Open *Drop on Recall* exercise is made up of these balance points:

- *Set-up:* The dog moves to a sit in heel position.
- *Wait:* The same as the Novice *Recall.*
- *Come:* The same as the Novice *Recall.*
- *Drop:* On your command, the dog stops and *drops* promptly.
- *Come from drop:* The dog *comes* promptly from the *drop.*
- *Front:* The same as the Novice *Recall.*
- *Finish:* The same as the Novice *Recall.*

Your dog should have a solid *sphinx down* before you proceed with the *Drop on Recall.* Make sure he can drop in place when you stand in front of him and drop in place when you are a few feet away. He should also be able to drop promptly in place from about 15 to 20 feet away from you. If your dog cannot do that, go back and rework the *down in place* (*Fundamental Words* chapter). Once you have a solid *Recall* and *sphinx down* and have proofed it in many locations, you should have little trouble with the *Drop on Recall,* but *a dog who cannot do a fast sphinx down in place cannot be expected to do a drop while moving toward you.*

The dog must drop when commanded or signaled to do so and will be judged on the promptness of his response to the command.

If your dog tends to have trouble getting his elbows all the way to the floor, consider adding the chin-on-the-floor requirement to the drop. Review the *Splat Drop* section in the *Fundamental Words* chapter.

Teaching the Drop on Recall

We use a barrier, such as a bar, a dowel, or a broad jump board, to help the dog learn the exact place to drop. This gives him a point on which to focus. When the dog is taught to drop behind a barrier, it seems to clarify the exercise for him.

Begin with your dog in a *Stand-stay* behind the barrier. Give your DOWN command while you are directly in front of him, just on the other side of the barrier (Fig. 11.2). Progress to leaving the dog behind the

Figure 11.2 Give your DOWN command while you are directly in front of your dog, just on the other side of the barrier from him.

barrier while you gradually move back to about twenty feet from the barrier. Each time your dog drops successfully, CR and feed him at the barrier. Praise him while he is down, with big pats on his shoulders. This may be used later, if needed, as a correction.

Feed him after he drops, but remember to use your CR *before* you give your dog the food. Work up to doubles and triples, as you do with all exercises, to get your dog used to a variable reinforcement schedule early in the training of this exercise. Even as you move away from him, the CR allows you to give immediate feedback about the drop. The food can come a bit later when you return to your dog. This is a good example of a delayed reinforcer.

If your dog is making an effort, use your CR and treat. Begin early in this training to wait for faster drops before you reward. If he is going down slowly, go back to him and use your hand on his shoulders or in his collar to help him understand that you want a fast drop. Sometimes stamping your foot or dropping an object, like a set of keys, on the floor at your side will make an impression as well. By not rewarding the slower or incorrect drop, most dogs catch on and drop more quickly.

Teaching the Drop on Recall

If your dog is one who wants to creep or come to you when he is worried, try throwing your motivator, either food or a toy, behind him. Use a release command just before you throw the motivator. *Make sure you give your CR for the drop before you release the dog.* **The release is just a release, it is not a form of praise.**

Food-Toss Drops

Many dogs find the following exercise fun. It should be familiar since we taught it for the *food-toss recall* in the *Fundamental Words* chapter. Toss a visible treat four to six feet away from you and let your dog run out to it. As he finishes eating the treat, give your DOWN command. Step close and help him if necessary. At first, he might be distracted by sniffing for more food. That's okay, but be there to help him and give treats following your CR when he is down. Release him with another treat tossed out behind him. As your dog gets better, toss the treat further. This is an easy way to build more distance into your *drop* exercise.

If your dog loves toys, toss one to him after a good drop. Progress is slowed because of the time used to play with the toy, but he may give you better attention. Remember to use your CR *before* you throw the toy.

Figure 11.3 You may combine the barrier drop work discussed in the previous section with the *food-toss drop*. Stand near the barrier and toss a treat over it so the dog ends up on the other side of the barrier.

You may combine the barrier drop work discussed in the previous section with the *food-toss drop.* Stand near the barrier and toss a treat over it so your dog ends up on the other side of the barrier (Fig. 11.3). After he eats his treat, call him to you and have him drop at the barrier as usual.

Formalizing the Drop on Recall

Leave your dog in a sit using your WAIT command. He should be a few feet back from the barrier; you should be right next to the barrier but on the other side of it from your dog. Call him and drop him behind the barrier, reinforcing him for stopping and going *down.* You do not want him to come across the barrier when you give the DOWN command. If he does, use your BACK command and, when he is in the proper place, tell him DOWN again, CR, but do not give a treat. Save your treats for success on the first try. Begin to move your dog's starting place back from the barrier a few steps at a time.

Finally, as he gains confidence in the exercise, both of you should move further away from the barrier, a few steps at a time. Even dogs with good drop foundations have problems comprehending the "come to me," "don't come to me" sequence. We like to work through this potential confusion in as few sessions as possible, as long as the dog isn't too stressed. The sooner you can make the point of the exercise — *come, stop and drop, come* — the sooner the dog will be comfortable with the exercise. We have some Open training sessions where we train only the *Drop on Recall.*

Judy likes to do about five repetitions of a straight recall, followed by five drops. This teaches the dog to listen to which cue she is giving. She will often do a week of training *only* the *Drop on Recall* until it is clear to the dog what she expects from him. It is better for him to make his mistakes in training rather than in the ring. Corrections are not always possible, even at a practice match, so proof this work carefully.

Once your dog shows competence with one barrier, add a second one. Randomly drop him behind one of the two barriers. Sometimes, drop him behind both; sometimes neither. This will help your dog understand that the cue comes from you, not the barriers. Finally, add a third barrier. When he has mastered this, shrink the size of the barriers. Use thinner poles, then leashes, and finally string. Once your dog understands the exercise with string, he is ready to do the exercise without the barriers. You may wish to vary your drop work by sometimes using one or more barriers and sometimes not.

Anticipation

At this stage in your training, your dog may anticipate the drop. The barrier has become a cue to him to drop, so he starts going down before you give the command. *It is vital that you work through this cue confusion.* Sometimes you should call him to you over the barrier without dropping him. You should plan for what you will do when he drops without a command. Initially, we use a verbal reprimand and repeat the command such as AH-AH, COME. If this doesn't fix the problem, Adele puts a leash or retractable lead on the dog so she can use a pop correction when he starts to anticipate the drop. Judy goes to the dog and corrects as discussed in the *Recall Problems* section earlier. We also do many *motivational recalls* with the barrier in place.

If your dog is anticipating one part of the *Drop on Recall* or skipping one, it means your reinforcement is "out of balance;" you have been reinforcing one part — the anticipated one — too often. Skipping a part means you have given too little reinforcement for that part. Switch your focus to restore balance.

Using a Signal

You have a choice about how you cue your dog to drop during the *Drop on Recall*. You may use a verbal command, which can be preceded by the dog's name, or you may use a hand signal. Which cue you use depends largely on which one your dog responds to faster. We generally use a verbal command, but have both used a signal with certain dogs. Don't use both unless you are showing in a UKC Open class!

Experiment with your dog to see whether a verbal cue or hand signal works best for him. See the *Signals* chapter for suggested signals. As a rule, inexperienced Open dogs (i.e., those without much ring experience) do better with a verbal command. For a dog to drop promptly on a signal while moving toward you, he must be totally focused on you. When a dog is stressed, his brain may not be fully engaged. He may not be looking at you, but he should hear you loud and clear.

Problems with the Drop

The most obvious problem with the *Drop on Recall*, of course, is that the dog doesn't! This is probably the most common way for an Open A dog to earn a non-qualifying (NQ) score. Other problems include:

- A dog who doesn't start at all (NQ).
- A dog who comes before being called (NQ).
- A slow recall in anticipation of the drop (points off).

- An anticipated drop (NQ).
- A slow response to the command to drop; sometimes because of too much speed (points off).
- An elbows-not-quite-all-the-way-down drop (NQ).
- A dog who doesn't come after the drop (NQ) or comes slowly (points off).
- A dog who comes before you call him after the drop (NQ).

We have encountered these problems at one time or another with our dogs. To overcome most of the problems, you must make sure that all the balance points of the exercise are solid. Work each point separately and gradually put them together.

Proofing the Drop On Recall

Proofing the *Drop on Recall* is essential! Even a minor loss of attention can be enough for an inexperienced dog to forget to drop. When you start proofing, *expect* your dog to make errors. Don't get mad at him! When he makes a mistake, go to him and help him complete the *down* where he was when you gave him the command. Release him as soon as he's right, and try again.

Add the following distractions, one at a time, as the dog's confidence and skill improves:

- Do random drops at meal time.
- Drop the dog as he is returning to you after retrieving a toy.
- Have a person walk up behind the dropped dog or around to the side to check to make sure that the dog's elbows are all the way down.
- Down the dog near a standing person.
- Down the dog near a person holding either food or a toy.
- Down the dog near a person offering either food or a toy.
- Down the dog near a person waving either food or a toy.
- Do a straight recall while the distracter calls a drop.
- Have someone sit on the floor or in a chair nearby.
- Have someone sit and eat nearby.
- Have someone play with their dog nearby.
- Do recalls very close to the high jump. Some dogs will want to jump the jump, especially if you have proofed the dog for angle throws during the *Retrieve over the High Jump*.

- Have someone toss a dumbbell nearby. An excellent proof involves at least one other person. Leave your dog at one end of your training area. The other person is at the same end of the area as your dog, but some distance away to one side. A verbal "Call your dog" cue from this extra person (or a third person) is your cue to call your dog, and the other person's cue to throw her dumbbell. The dumbbell usually lands when your dog is halfway to you, so he will be distracted when you cue him to drop.

- Place dog hair, small scraps of paper or small colored labels (some judges use these as markers) on the mat near where you down the dog.

- Down the dog at varying distances from you. Most judges have you down your dog about half way to you, but some have you down him very early, as soon as he gets up to come, and others very late in the recall.

- Call the dog to you out of a down from ten feet or less. Many dogs will walk to you, which costs points. If your dog is slow, review the motivation ideas explained earlier in this chapter.

- Have someone play judge so you have to watch the judge for the signal to call and to drop. If you don't have a helper, simulate this by calling your dog, then watching an imaginary person, then looking back to your dog as you command down. Look back to the person for the recall signal or command once the dog has dropped. Your dog needs to know that you can always see him, even when you appear not to be looking!

- Do a series of recalls, perhaps several straight ones followed by a drop, or several drops followed by a straight one. When the dog hears the same command a few times in a row, he is apt not to obey the next one you give him. Your dog may need a correction or he may need gentle help. You must decide why he is not obeying before you can fix the problem.

Do command the dog to DOWN. **Don't** ask the question "down?" He won't!

Handling the Drop On Recall

The judge must give you a hand signal for when to drop your dog, so you must watch the judge to see his signal. Most often, the signal is the judge dropping his arm back to his side from a raised arm position.

These signals vary, and inexperienced handlers sometimes miss the signal. Unless you are first in the class, watch earlier exhibitors to see what signal a judge uses.

Handler errors:

- Shouting any command.
- Bowing during a command or signal.
- Holding the signal.
- Giving both a hand signal and verbal command on drop (you fail the exercise if you do this!). You are permitted to give both when showing in UKC trials in Open.

A dog who has a clear understanding of the *Drop on Recall* exercise is fun to train and show. He is ready for a fast recall, listens for your command without slowing, and responds immediately with a *sphinx down* to your command to drop. He watches intently for the recall command, comes in briskly, and sits in a straight front. Finally, his finish is snappy and straight. Fronts and finishes are explained in the following chapter.

Fronts & Finishes

A s we mentioned in the *Recalls* chapter, it is not hard to teach your dog the basic concept of sitting somewhere in front of you. Neither is getting him to move from sitting in front to somewhere at your left side. However, perfecting either of these is usually a long-term project. Most trainers find that *fronts* and *finishes* require frequent training throughout their dog's show career. A dog's precision can seem to come and go. Don't be surprised if your dog appears to understand how to do either perfectly one day and not the next day.

The Front

With the exception of the Utility *Moving Stand*, your dog must sit in front of you every time he comes to you in the obedience ring. This sitting in front of you is commonly called a *front*. To earn full points for the *front*, your dog must sit straight, centered in front of you, close enough for you to touch without stretching, but not so close as to be touching you (Fig. 12.1). He should not sit between your feet and his front feet should be about an inch or two from your toes.

In Novice, the dog is required to do one front. In Open, he must do four, and in Utility six. In Novice, you have every opportunity to stand directly in front of your dog at the far end of the ring, which gives him a fair chance to sit straight on his *front*, assuming he comes straight on his recall. When you get to Open and Utility, the chances of your dog always returning in a straight line decrease. This may be due to a poorly thrown or badly bouncing dumbbell, your dog's jumping style, or simply the increased difficulty of the exercises. We want the dog to start to adjust his front when he is still some distance away, not after he has arrived directly in front. The following exercises are designed to teach your dog how to do this adjusting himself, first with your help, then on his own.

Figure 12.1 These are perfect fronts.

Chair Fronts

The *chair front* exercise introduces your dog to the concept of coming close and sitting straight in front of you. *Chair fronts* also teach him about *chutes*. We use the word *chute* to mean a set of guides that help your dog sit or move straight.

Sit on the edge of a chair or stool with your feet and legs stretched out in front of you. Start with your feet fairly far apart and lure your dog between your feet and legs and have him sit (Fig. 12.2). CR and feed him as soon as he is sitting acceptably close to you. Toss a treat out about five feet behind your dog and release him to get it. As he finishes his treat, command COME and encourage him to come and sit between your legs again. Review *food-toss recalls* in the *Fundamental Words* chapter if he doesn't return to you quickly.

As your dog improves, gradually narrow your leg chute until his only choice is to sit straight. If he tries to sit on your feet, raise your toes to prevent him from doing so.

Next, toss your treat to one side rather than directly behind your dog. Do this at gradually increasing angles (Fig. 12.3). Have him do repetitions first to one side and then to the other. These angled food tosses introduce the dog to straightening himself *before* sitting. When

Figure 12.2 Lure the dog between your feet and legs and have him sit.

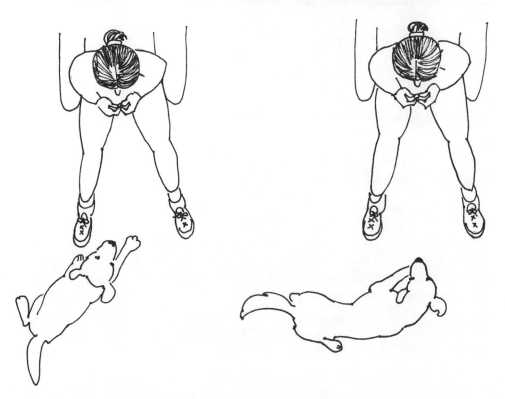

Figure 12.3 Throw food behind your dog and at gradually increasing angles.

you make the angles harder, you may need to return to a wider chute for a while. If your dog comes to you outside your leg chute, guide him around your leg as needed. Make the next try easier.

While you may start teaching this exercise with your hands "front and center," gradually move them until they are at your sides (Fig. 12.4).

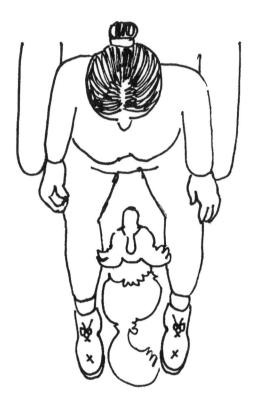

Figure 12.4 Gradually move your hands from in front of you to your sides.

Head Position and Attention

To do an accurate *front*, the dog should raise his head before he starts his sit. For many dogs, the "heads up" recall is a natural position. Other dogs prefer to run with their heads down. If your dog runs this way, he needs to learn to focus upward as he approaches. If you did your *front attention* work as we discussed in the *Fundamental Words* chapter, you used food in both hands held at your side and reinforced your dog when he focused on your face. Therefore, he should be comfortable in *front* position. If not, review the *front attention* exercise, including proofing (see *Adding Distractions* in *Fundamental Words* chapter).

Before doing a lot of *scoot front* work (explained in the next section), your dog should understand where he needs to look. Many trainers get stuck with *HIC* (hands in crotch) syndrome, where the dog only sits straight in front when the handler's hands are "front and center". To counter this tendency, train *moving front attention* as a separate exercise.

With your hands at your side, tell your dog COME and slowly back up. CR the instant you have head-up attention, even if he isn't perfectly straight. Stop, give a treat, then continue to back up. Shape this gradually so your dog can move with you, maintaining attention on your face while ignoring your hands. For small dogs, you may want to use your knees as your front focal point.

As we've said before, the dog's head position often determines the position of the rest of his body. Pay attention to where his head is and reinforce when it comes close to the center of your body.

Scoot Fronts

Scoot fronts were introduced in the *Combination Words* chapter. When working the *scoot front*, hold the food against your body. Make a chute with your knees or if you have a small dog, with your feet (Fig. 12.5). Do not reward rock sits. If the dog rocks back, his nose will not be near the food. If you hand him the food, even a few inches away from your body, he will learn to sit away from you. This starts as a luring exercise. Do not worry about the dog being too tight between your legs. Teaching him to back up is the easy part. Getting him to come in fast, straight, and tight is much harder.

Figure 12.5 Make a chute with your knees or your feet.

If you wish, this is the time to change your command from COME to FRONT. This command cues the dog to come in to a straight position, sitting in front of you rather than just coming to your immediate vicinity.

As your dog's *scoot fronts* and *moving front attention* improve when your hands are at your side, start to combine the two. Begin with *scoot fronts*, hands in front luring the dog, and then move your hands to your sides. Remind your dog to WATCH, if necessary. Continue to back up to see if your dog can do just one scoot front without a lure. Use your CR for any attempt on the dog's part to sit in front of you, even if he is not as straight as when you were guiding with your hands. Hold food in both hands, and vary which hand you feed with. We do not recommend spitting food, as it usually causes the dog to sit too far away.

Chutes

A *chute* is a guide that forces the dog to sit straight. You introduced him to a chute by using your legs when you taught *chair fronts*. Use two broad jump boards or two pieces of wood or PVC pipe to make a chute (Fig. 12.6). The separated parts of a metal extension ladder also make a good chute. They are extra long and most dogs work to avoid the annoying noise the ladder makes if they hit it with their paws. The sides of the chute need to be high enough so the dog can't sit crooked on top of the chute but instead has to sit straight between the sides.

Start with the chute extra wide, as you did with your legs on the *chair fronts*. Most dogs require some guiding when you first introduce a chute. Some dogs are merely suspicious, but others are afraid. Start by having him walk through the chute without asking for a sit. Continue this until your dog is comfortable.

Stand at one end of the chute and work *chute fronts* like *chair fronts*. Start by tossing the food directly behind the dog to get him to move away from you. Progress to tossing the food off to the side. If your dog wants to sit too far away, add a cross piece to the chute that he must go over before he sits (Fig. 12.7). Gradually reduce the width of the chute to match the width of your dog's rear.

Side-Passing

One of the most important parts of teaching the *front* is to make the dog responsible for knowing how to move his body in both directions. **Teaching the dog to move his whole body to the right or left is imperative if the dog is going to understand how to get himself into a straight front.** This is sometimes called *side-passing*. Go back to the

Figure 12.6 Proper fitting chutes.

Figure 12.7 Add a cross piece to your front chute.
Your dog must go over this before he sits.

Power Steering chapter and review CLOSE and OFF in heel position. If you prefer the words RIGHT and LEFT, by all means use them. The words don't matter as long as you are consistent and the dog knows what you want.

When your dog understands CLOSE and OFF in heel position, do a few repetitions in either direction with the dog at your side. Then quickly step in front of him to try to get him to move sideways in the same direction as he did at your side. It is much easier for the dog to move when he remains standing (as opposed to hopping sideways in a sit). This is a difficult maneuver for many dogs. Most dogs have a favorite direction to move, as if they are right- or left-pawed. Teach the direction he finds easiest first.

It may help to use an "arm-extender" — a PVC pole or dowel that you hold against your dog's ribs or hips — to help guide him in the correct direction. Use food in the hand that doesn't hold the pole to center your dog's head at the front of your body.

Remember to use the correct command! OFF means the dog moves to *his* left. When you face him, you must move to your right while he moves to his left. CLOSE means the dog moves to the right and, when you face him, you move left. If you have trouble remembering this, write a small command and paste it on your shoes!

Steering Fronts

Once the dog understands how to do *side-passes* and *scoot fronts,* begin to put the two together. Use food or a toy almost every time throughout this training, as it is very repetitive and can be boring for some dogs (as well as their trainers). We prefer to do these *steering fronts* up close and without a leash. Some dogs are intimidated by the close work if they are on a leash. Obviously, if you are working in an unsafe area, use one.

Work on *straight line fronts* first. Leave the dog in a sit, step two to three feet away from him, and turn to face him. Tell him FRONT and reinforce the straighter sits.

Once your dog is comfortable doing *straight line fronts*, start doing some angled or *steering fronts*. Choose the dog's easier side to work first. Begin with him sitting in a *wait*. Walk out about two feet from the dog and do either a *right or left quarter turn*. Put your foot that is closest to the dog out in front of you so he has to come around your foot and swing his rear in the opposite direction (Fig. 12.8) in order to get straight. Now call the dog to you with your FRONT command and say CLOSE or OFF to get the dog moving his rear in the correct direction (Fig. 12.9). Reward *any* movement of the dog's rear in the correct direction with your CR. He

Figure 12.8 Put your foot closest to the dog in front of you so your dog has to come around it.

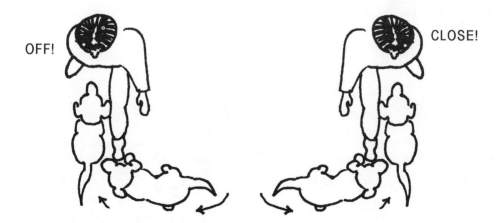

Figure 12.9 Use the correct verbal command to help your dog move his rear in the correct direction.

will not do this perfectly at first. He has to think FRONT, CLOSE or OFF, and SIT, all at the same time. You can lure your dog at first, but quickly go to random reinforcement, as he should be able to follow your word cues. If he can't, you have put the pieces together too soon. The word tells the dog which way to move his rear and takes a lot of pressure off him when he knows how to respond. A generic STRAIGHT command doesn't mean much to most dogs. On the other hand, the command CLOSE or OFF tells him to move to the right or left.

As the dog gains skill, move farther away before you call him to you. Do three to six fronts in one direction, then switch to the other direction. You don't always have to turn. Sometimes position yourself off-line to one side by three or four feet (Fig. 12.10). As you get farther from the dog, wait to put your foot out until he is almost to you. We actually prefer to step back on the other foot when the dog is almost to *front*. It is easier to balance this way. Don't forget to use your steering word! Gradually fade the foot guides, using only your steering words, and then finally fade the words as well.

Don't fall into the trap of adjusting your position to your dog's mistakes. If anything, step in the opposite direction to make him work harder to get into a correct front.

Fronts always need work. Many dogs don't really learn to think about doing a straight front until they are well into the advanced classes. This is a hard exercise and one where physical and mental maturity means a lot.

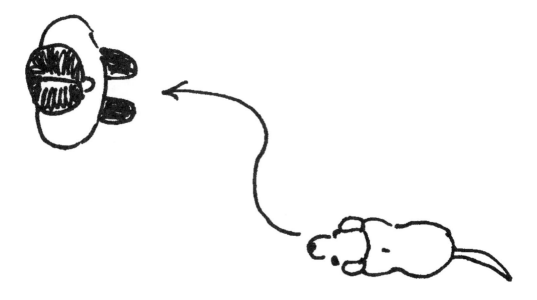

Figure 12.10 Position yourself off line about three or four feet.

Wagon Wheel Fronts

Wagon wheel fronts are an advanced exercise that we use when training for Open and Utility. In this exercise, the handler pivots in place while the dog adjusts his front to the handler's new position. When you first try this, make only a small pivot in place, gradually turning further before you stop. This is a great warm-up exercise to use at a trial since it requires little space (Fig. 12.11).

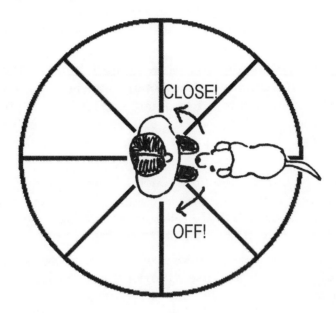

Figure 12.11 Wagon wheel fronts are a great warm-up exercise to use at a trial, since they require little space.

Front Problems

The most difficult thing for a dog to understand about fronts is that you not only want him to come in close, but to also sit straight in front.

Other problems you might encounter during *front* training:

- The dog sits too far away.
- The dog comes in too close, which results in the dog either bumping you or sitting with his feet between or on your feet.

Dogs may *sit too far away* because they have been asked for fronts too early in your teaching of the recall or precision has been demanded too soon and too often. Dropping or spitting food from your mouth may cause him to sit too far away. Rock sits may also be the cause of this problem. We spend a lot of time motivating the dog to come in close with his head up.

It may help fix the *too far away* problem if you take an extra step back away from your dog just before he starts to sit. You will need to do this for an extended period of time; don't expect it to fix the problem in only a few training sessions.

As we mentioned earlier, a chute with a cross piece added (Fig. 12.7), may also help fix or prevent the problem from developing in the first place.

One other suggestion is to teach your dog to touch a clothespin with his nose (see *Fundamental Words* chapter). Once he reliably touches the clothespin when you hold it in your hand, clip it to your clothes, wherever his nose should end up for a tight sit. He should touch the clothespin with his nose before he sits for the *front*. This should help get him closer to you.

If you teach your dog the nose touch for fronts, he may start poking you with his nose. While it shows he is getting close enough to you, the nose poke is not desirable! If you use this method, you will have to fade the nose touch when you have the desired straight *front*.

For a dog who *comes in too close*, use a SIT command when he is about six feet away. You may use a barrier like a broad jump board or a piece of chicken wire in front of your feet to keep your dog from bumping. Also, try bending your knees slightly just as he gets to the front position (Fig. 12.12). This helps to gently bump him off. A barrier or bent knees can also help if you have let him come between your feet when you taught *scoot fronts*. You do not want to discourage *close* and yet you do not want your dog to bump you. It's a fine line in the training of this exercise.

At some point, you may encounter the problem of your dog skipping the *front* altogether. This is usually an anticipation of the *finish* and is covered later in this chapter.

Figure 12.12 If your dog tends to come in too close on his front, bend your knees slightly as he gets to front position.

Proofing the Front

Once your dog understands that it is his responsibility to adjust himself to your position, you should introduce some proofing to test his knowledge of the *front*. Have another person off to one side, about four feet away from you. This person starts by simply standing nearby, escalating to squatting down, patting the floor, and tempting your dog with food or a toy. Sudden noises often distract a dog just when he needs to straighten himself. Help him to be correct when you first introduce a new proof, gradually shifting the responsibility of staying focussed to your dog. Keep expanding the difficulty of your proofing. Be sure to practice with another person walking up behind your dog as he does a *front*. Start gradually and eventually have the judge/person standing directly behind your dog.

The Finish

There are two acceptable *finishes* in competition obedience: the *around finish* and the *swing* or *side finish*. In either case, the dog should move promptly from sitting in front of you to sitting in heel position. In the *around finish*, the dog gets to heel position by going around to your right and behind you. We like to see the dog move with his head up as he goes around. In the *side finish*, the dog moves to your left, leaping or swinging himself into heel position.

We teach both finishes, but generally use the *around finish* because most dogs do it better, faster, and end up sitting straighter. The greatest disadvantage of the *around finish* is that the dog passes out of sight for a few seconds and many dogs take the opportunity to gawk at the crowd.

Judy teaches the *side finish* for use in the *Moving Stand* exercise in Utility, in which the dog goes directly to heel. This is the only exercise in which the dog does a Recall but doesn't sit in *front*. Adele has taught the *side finish* to all her dogs but uses it far less often in competition than the *around finish*. There may be a time when you want to use the *side finish* during the regular exercises. To avoid the confusion when you introduce the *Call Your Dog To Heel* part of the *Moving Stand*, you may want to use the finish that you don't use in the rest of the exercises.

Teaching the Around Finish

To help your dog learn this new exercise, work on *dizzy spins* (see *Power Steering* chapter) before starting the *around finish*.

With your dog in front of you, as if he has just done a perfect recall, start spinning slowly in a tight turn to your right. Spin in a complete circle while your dog does a U–turn around you. When you begin the spin, hold your motivator (food or a toy) close to and centered in front of your body, just above your dog's nose (Fig 12.13a). When you are about three-quarters of the way around your spin, shift the motivator to your left side (Fig. 12.13c). After you have completed the spin, your dog should

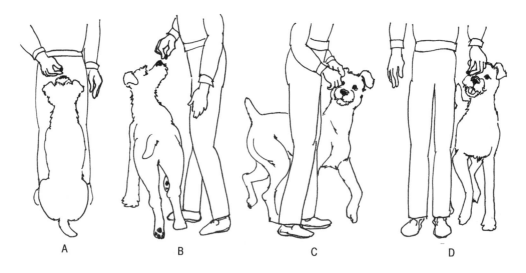

A   B   C   D

Figure 12.13 Spin in a complete circle while your dog does a U-turn around you. When you begin the spin, hold your motivator (food or a toy) close to and centered in front of your body, just above your dog's nose. When you are about three-quarters of the way around your spin, shift the motivator to your left side.

be facing in the opposite direction from where he started and be in approximate heel position. Use your CR as your dog follows the food and release him when you have completed the circle. Do not add the *sit in heel position* at this point, as it will slow your dog down.

Once your dog moves easily as you begin to spin, stop spinning and just lure him around you with the food or toy (Fig. 12.14). Hold a piece of food in each hand as you start your dog moving with the food in your right hand. Hold your left hand behind your back, ready to get his attention as he gets behind you. Instead of moving your right hand back to your side, slide it straight up your back out of the way (Fig. 12.15). This helps prevent your dog from following your right hand back to your side. Pass him off to the piece of food in your left hand behind your back. Then return your right hand to your side. While we use two pieces of food when teaching this, you may find that it works better for you to pass a treat from your right hand to your left as your dog moves behind you.

Don't add a command until your dog has some idea of what he is doing. It takes most dogs a long time to assume responsibility for doing the finish.

Figure 12.14 Lure your dog around you for the *around finish*.

Figure 12.15 Slide your right hand holding the food straight up your back to get it out of the way.

We like prompt finishes. Work on speed by using one of these suggestions:

- Throw a motivator forward when the dog is behind you and let him chase it.
- Release the dog upwards to his motivator when he gets to heel position.
- Run forward when the dog is behind you. This helps attention, too.

Do not introduce the *sit* at the end of the finish until your dog has good speed and focus.

Your dog begins to learn the hand signal to finish when you use your right hand with the food in it (see Figs. 13.10 and 13.11 in *Signals* chapter).

Adding a Command

As soon as your dog is moving quickly with the food lure, add your command *just before* you start your luring motion.

We have heard a greater variety of commands used on finishes than any other obedience exercises. Some suggestions:

- GET AROUND (Judy uses this), AROUND, or ROUND
- BY (Adele uses this) or BY ME
- CIRCLE
- HEEL
- PLACE
- SWING
- RELOAD
- PIVOT

We feel strongly that the dog should know a verbal finish command. If he isn't watching, he'll miss a hand signal. Teach a signal (you will need it later in Utility), but teach the verbal cue as well.

Teaching the Side Finish

We have found that the *side finish* takes longer to teach, but for many dogs it is more reliable. If you want to use it as your regular *finish*, you may want to use the *around finish* when you do the *Call To Heel* portion of the *Moving Stand*.

When doing a *side finish*, it is important for the dog to get far enough behind you so that when he makes his turn to come up into heel position, his body is straight. Many people skip or rush this step and end up with a dog who is crooked or forged because the dog pivots incompletely on his front feet instead of going back far enough to turn around.

Begin with your dog sitting in front of you. Lure him to your left with food in your left hand, stepping back as far as you can on your left foot as you turn your body to the left (Fig. 12.16). This gets your dog behind you and will later allow you to bring him up straight into heel position. CR and feed your dog at the point farthest behind you. This encourages him to get back as far as necessary to come straight into the finish. For now, release your dog at this point. Spend many training sessions reinforcing him behind you to teach him he must go back far enough.

The same motivating techniques used in the *Teaching the Around Finish* section can also be used with the *side finish*. Use them as the dog starts his turn to heel position.

Figure 12.16 Lure your dog back past your left side as you turn to face him. Feed him at the farthest point behind you. This helps get him back as far as possible.

Teaching the Side Finish

You are still luring at this point (with food in your left hand) and may be using your CR in several ways. Use it as soon as your dog gets up in response to your command. We both use PLACE as our command for this exercise. Continue to use the CR as your dog passes you on the left and makes his turn and then again as he comes up into heel position. When first teaching this finish, do not demand a sit, since sits tend to decrease the dog's speed.

The Flip/Swing Finish

There is a variation of the *side finish*, sometimes called the *flip finish*, in which the dog leaps directly into a straight finish without doing any adjusting. With a very athletic dog, this looks flashy in the ring, but is hard to perfect because the dog may touch the handler, which results in lost points. We do not recommend the flip finish itself, but we do teach a combination of the *flip* and *swing finishes* in which the dog propels himself partway to heel position with a leap in the air and then completes the movement by swinging his rear into a straight sit. The leap in the air is not required, but we like the flash it lends to the exercise.

First, you must teach the dog to jump up to touch your hand. Most dogs will jump up for a treat held in your hand. You can also shape a

nose-touch to your hand just like you did to a clothespin or a dumbbell (Fig. 12.17). The goal is for him to leap upward, driving with his hind legs. Initially encourage a slight lift of the front feet by starting with your left hand just above your dog's nose. Then, on each

Figure 12.17 Teach your dog to leap up and touch your hand before adding a leap to either finish.

repetition, ask for a higher jump. Be sure to use your CR at the top of the dog's leap; otherwise you are reinforcing the takeoff or the landing. It is important to teach the dog to leap without touching you with his paws. You will lose points on your finish if your dog pushes himself off you in the process of leaping.

As your dog learns the leap, incorporate it into the *finish*. Give your hand-touching command followed by your finish command as you step back on your left foot and swing your hand out to your left side. Use your CR at the top of the dog's leap, then add the swing into heel position. CR and feed. Using the same technique, you can also teach a similar leap on the *around finish*.

Problems with Finishes

It may be hard to persuade your dog to move without a food lure or a moving hand. Make sure you do not use your command and luring hand at exactly the same time. Give the command a second or two before the lure. Expect to use the lure for a while and then gradually eliminate it. Occasionally, your dog will move without the hand signal, but the next time he may need the signal. This is not uncommon. Be prepared to use the signal, but be ready to celebrate if he works without it.

If your dog is motivated by toys, the following technique should help on the *around finish*. Hold a squeaky toy in your left hand behind your back. Give your verbal finish command and then squeak the toy. Release your dog to the toy as soon as he gets behind your back. Another option is to toss a toy out in front or slightly to your right to get your dog to finish by zooming around you.

Another aid is to hold a piece of food out to your right in your right hand. Hold your hand still, give your dog the command, and CR and give the food as soon as he gets to your hand. Gradually move your right hand farther behind you.

Slow finishes can be caused by a number of things, but most often they are the result of adding the sit to the exercise before working long enough on speed. Slow finishes also seem to plague the high-stress dog. Work to keep the training fun and make sure your dog always understands each step as you go along. Confusion can be a major cause of stress. Once the dog understands, continue to make the work interesting using food and toys for motivation. Always use your CR before the food and occasionally a leash pop or a gentle "boot in the rear" correction, as needed, to keep your dog responding promptly. Corrections are discussed in the next section.

Insist on faster finishes before adding a sit. The dog does not get his reward unless he continues to make a greater effort. If he is making an effort, use your CR but no food. The dog should try harder next time to get the food. If he does a particularly spectacular finish, be prepared to give him a jackpot.

Judy had trouble with slow finishes in the ring which she attributed to Alec's ring stress. A combination of backing up in training and working for more motivation, plus adding an occasional well-timed correction, helped Alec speed up.

If your dog slows down, do not revert to bribery with the food. Do the exercises described earlier to motivate him to speed up, and then use the food as a *reward*. This is extremely important.

Motivation can be in the form of moving more quickly yourself or backing up in your training until the dog is moving faster. Never be afraid to back up. You will usually move ahead more quickly if you do so. If your dog doesn't quite return to heel position, work on speed and motivation.

It is imperative that the dog truly understand heel position. *Many dogs don't finish properly because they don't know where to go.* It is up to you to teach heel position through maneuvers and other repetitive exercises where you do many *quarter turns, about turns* and *side steps* in heel position. Review the *Power Steering* and *Combination Words* chapters for ideas.

After working on finishes for a number of weeks, you may find that your dog tends to make a certain type of error. Perhaps he sits too far behind you or comes too far forward before he sits. We assume you have taught your dog the heel position steering words, so use them to help him learn how to straighten his finishes. It is important to use the steering word before your dog makes the mistake. This way, he has time to avoid the error rather than fix it after the fact. It is vital to do many *correct* repetitions, gradually fading out the extra cues.

Remember, practice doesn't make perfect. Perfect practice makes perfect!

You may want to use a chute for *finishes* as well as *fronts*. A U-shaped chute will help you correct most errors. Chutes help the dog develop muscle memory since each repetition is a duplicate of the past repetition. If your dog tends to come too far around, use a barrier in front of his paws. If he tends to swing his rear too far to the left, use a chute or a board on his left (Fig. 12.18). If his rear ends up tucked behind you, use a small barrier or your left foot to push his rear out (Fig. 12.19).

Figure 12.18 Use a barrier with the dog who over-rotates on the *around finish*.

Figure 12.19 Use your foot as a barrier with the dog who under-rotates on the *around finish*.

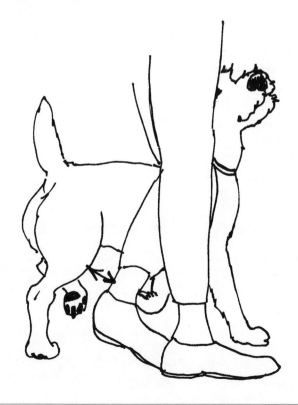

Another suggestion is to make a small turn as your dog is finishing. This helps him pay better attention. If your dog tends to forge on his finishes, turn left just as he comes up into heel position. If he lags, turn to the right.

Many dogs go through a stage where they anticipate the *finish*. Some stop briefly in front and then start to do a *finish* without a command. Others totally skip the *front* and try to go directly to *heel*. When this happens, react quickly to stop your dog from completing the *finish*. If you can, try to block him with your body. Put your foot in his path so he runs into your leg. Then sit him in front again and do some proofing. Stop the anticipation as soon as it happens and reinforce when he understands.

To proof against anticipation of finishes:

- Do some small body movements, such as a shoulder shrug. Use your CR and feed when your dog maintains his *front*.
- Use nonsense words instead of your *finish* command.
- Vary the amount of time before you give the command to *finish*.
- Take a deep breath, but don't give a command.
- Look at the dog as he *fronts*, then glance up as though you were looking at the Judge for a *finish* signal.
- Have someone else say *Finish* for you (which is what the judge says) and stop the dog if he does not remain sitting.
- Say *Finish* yourself in a variety of voices.

Adding Corrections to Your Finishes

When your dog understands the exercise but still needs a bit of correction to hurry him around, try tapping him on the hip with your foot just as he gets up to begin a finish. Make this a game. Tell your dog "hurry" or "gotcha" as you tap his rear. Your tone of voice will get him to move faster as he tries to avoid your tap. Use your right foot on his left hip for the *side finish* and your left foot on his right hip for the *around finish* (Fig. 12.20). We sometimes use a leash pop correction after the command for a dog who is slow to respond.

Figure 12.20 Tapping your dog on the hip helps to hurry him through a finish.

Proofing The Finishes

To proof your finishes, begin with a person acting as a distraction somewhere near your back. If your dog stops to look at this person, either motivate or correct. If the distraction confuses him or he doesn't understand that he is to ignore the distraction, help him by throwing a toy or by any of the other methods used when teaching the exercise. If your dog truly understands this exercise, it is time for a pop on the collar or a tap on the rear to speed him up. We sometimes use a "goose" on the rear for the gawking or distracted dog. If you do correct, do not have him sit in heel position. Instead, release him with enthusiastic praise and try again. It may help to work facing a mirror so you can see your dog's mistakes and react to them in a timely way.

Some other proofing ideas:

- Have your distracting person move closer.
- Add another dog or another person.
- Have the person hold food as a distraction.
- Work on finishes near a wall or ring gate.
- Work on finishes against another ring where another dog is working.

Don't use too many different distractions in the same training session if they are very stressful to your dog. Let him work through one type of distraction until he is confident, then move on to another. This should keep him motivated and willing to do the necessary repetitions.

Fronts and finishes seem to always be in need of maintenance or repair. By teaching a sound foundation and keeping your dog's interest high, you should have little trouble teaching and maintaining these two very important elements of advanced work.

Signals

In the Utility *Signal Exercise*, the dog must *heel, stand, stay, down, sit, come,* and *finish*. All actions must be done using only hand signals. *A hand signal must be a single, continuous gesture with one hand and arm, and your hand must be returned to its original position immediately.*

It is important to make your signals unique. Keep your signaling arm well away from your body so that your dog can see it clearly.

Your dog must respond correctly and promptly to each signal. Using a verbal command for any part of the *Signal Exercise* except the heeling and the finish will result in failing the exercise. In the ring, the signals are always done in the same order, as listed above. You and your dog are 35 to 40 feet apart when you signal the *down*, the *sit*, and the *come*.

Foundation Work

Before beginning the *Signal Exercise*, your dog should know the commands to:

- *Stand* from motion.
- *Stand–stay* with attention while you walk about 40 feet away.
- *Down* from a *stand*.
- *Sit* from a *down*.
- *Come*.
- *Finish*.

If your verbal commands are not firmly established in your dog's long-term memory, it is not possible to teach the signals that correspond to the commands. See the *Fundamental Words* chapter if your dog's foundation is not what you want it to be.

When working a dog with the proper foundation, you should be able to tell him to STAND, DOWN, SIT, or COME at any time, in any place, and know that he will respond correctly.

Adding New Cues

When you add a new cue to an action for which a cue has been established, present the new cue first and follow with the known one. For example, when adding a hand signal for *down*, give the *down signal* and then the verbal DOWN command. Do not do them at exactly the same time. Pair the signal with the command as soon as you think the dog has a firm understanding of the verbal command. Our dogs have seen the signal, along with the command, from the time they were puppies. The actual work of teaching and proofing signals for Utility is considerably shorter with a dog who has the proper foundation.

No Forward Movement

It is extremely important that you do not allow your dog to move forward on any of the stationary signals — not even one inch! By using our program, your dog has learned the *kick-back stand*, which taught him not to move forward on the *stand*. He has learned a *sphinx down*, which taught him to go backwards into the *down*. If you allow your dog to creep forward, even slightly, he might move too far forward to qualify in the ring. The "no creeping" rule must be enforced from the first command, and you should stay close to your dog until he clearly understands this.

Your dog should think "back up" during every signal. An enjoyable way to do this is to use your CR following a successful signal and then throw a toy or treat *behind* him for his release. Be sure your CR comes before the release and for the correct behavior. He will learn very quickly that good things can come from behind as well as from in front of him. Also, when you begin to add distance to the exercise, he will not be as likely to come to you for his reward. Stressed dogs often return to their handler for comfort. Help make your dog more confident by rewarding him for staying away from you during the signals.

The Stand Signal

When you are in the Utility ring at a trial, you will use a *stand signal* when the judge tells you to "Stand your dog." The judge's command typically comes immediately after a turn of some sort and at the end of the heeling pattern. You and your dog are usually at one end of the ring, in the center.

Use your right hand for the *stand signal* (Fig. 13.1) and your left hand for the *wait signal* (Fig. 13.2). Introduce the *stand signal* early in your dog's training when you teach the *kick-back stand*. By using your right hand to feed your dog, you condition him to the signal. If you have previously used different hands for these signals, it is not necessary to change. It doesn't matter which hand you use as long as you are consistent and your signals to *stand* and *wait* are distinct from each other.

When your dog responds correctly to your *stand signal*, he should freeze in place and not take *any* steps forward. The instructions in the AKC regulations say: "the handler shall signal his dog to Stand in the Heel position." Any deviation from heel position at the time you give the signal will be scored accordingly. Since losing points in Utility is fairly easy, getting this part correct is a way to save valuable points!

To introduce the hand signal, use your signal for the *stand*, followed immediately by your verbal STAND command. Use your CR the moment your dog's hindquarters move into the *stand* and give him a treat. As soon as your dog is responding well to the hand signal and command, stop using the verbal command and use the signal only. Should your dog fail to respond immediately to your signal, add a verbal command to help him. The use of your CR is extremely important at this point, since it signals your dog that he is correct and should continue what he is doing. *If you continue to use your verbal command paired with the hand signal, your dog will continue to rely more on your voice than on the signal.* It is important that he learn to respond to the signal alone. If you are having trouble getting your dog to transfer to the signal without the verbal command, do two or three rapid repetitions of the signal and verbal command, followed by your CR and food. Then do a quick signal without the verbal command, and give your dog a CR and a jackpot as soon as he responds correctly.

Initially, work the *stand* with no preceding heeling. Then heel one or two steps followed by the *stand signal*. Next do right and left turns followed by the signal to *stand*. In the Utility ring, the *stand signal* is almost always given following a *right* or *left turn*. Occasionally, it will be given after an *about turn*. Progress to training for the *stand* following a turn as soon as your dog is comfortable with the signal.

We train our dogs to stand at a distance, using either a verbal command or a signal. It is not required for the ring, but is convenient, fun, and adds flexibility to training signals. The *stand signal* at a distance should be one that is not easily confused with any other signals. Judy uses a signal like a touchdown — two hands in the air. Adele signals a

Figure 13.1 Use your right hand for the *stand signal*.

Figure 13.2 Use your left hand for the *wait signal*.

The Stand Signal

stand at a distance with her right hand near her right hip, using a small pushing motion towards her dog. We use this to practice signals from a distance in a random order.

The Down Signal

We first introduced a *down signal* in the *Fundamental Words* chapter when we explained how we teach *down*. If your dog does not have a reliable *down* command, go back and train it now. Remember, in the Utility ring, your dog will be about 40 feet away from you and a judge will stand behind him. Your foundation must be built slowly and carefully if you expect him to respond when he is in this stressful situation.

When you begin to teach the *down signal*, start with your dog standing and facing you. We use the right arm for the *down signal*. When you first taught the *sphinx down*, you commanded your dog to DOWN and fed him either from your left hand or by placing food on the ground between his paws. The right hand was the "praising" hand, but the praise was given by patting fairly hard on your dog's shoulders. At some point, you probably used this "patting" to correct your dog when he failed to go down. This means that your dog is used to your right hand moving when he is going down or just after he has done so. The signal can now be refined to the one you choose to use in the ring.

You may give the *down signal* in a variety of ways. Judy uses a pushing motion (Figure 13.3), like a traffic cop telling you to stop. Her right arm comes up from her side, bending at the elbow and at the wrist. Her hand is pointed up, and she pushes her hand towards the dog to signal him to stop and lie down. Adele raises her arm higher, but keeps her palm visible (Figure 13.4). In both the *down* and *sit signals*, it helps to have the flat part of your palm facing your dog. This makes the signal more clear to him, as your palm is the broadest part of your hand.

As you did when you taught the *stand signal*, use your *down signal* followed immediately by a verbal command. Repeat this series several times before trying the signal without the verbal command. Make sure you are using your CR correctly as you reinforce your dog's first efforts and then only his best efforts. Ask for doubles and triples, and give a jackpot when he does an exceptionally fast *down*. Remember, food is relaxing! If your dog is stressed, a bit of food on the floor will help him relax while in this submissive posture.

Figure 13.3 Judy uses a pushing motion for her down signal, like a traffic cop telling you to stop. Her right arm comes up from her side, bending at the elbow and at the wrist. Her hand is pointed up, and she pushes her hand towards the dog to signal him to stop and lie down.

Figure 13.4 Adele raises her arm higher when she signals a down but keeps her palm visible.

The Sit Signal

Perhaps you have never asked your dog to *sit* from a *down* position. We prefer that the dog do a *pop sit*, which means his rear end stays in place and his front feet move back towards his rear feet. This encourages him to move backwards rather than forwards.

If you have inadvertently taught your dog to move into a sit by moving his rear towards his front, you have two choices. The first is to accept this method and work hard to make sure your dog understands that he can move his rear forward but that he must never scoot his front feet forward. If you decide to accept the "moving the rear to the front" method, we suggest you keep a barrier in front of your dog until he has a complete grasp of this exercise. The barrier prevents him from moving forward.

To teach the *pop sit*, put your dog in a *sphinx down*. This is the position he will be in when you signal the *sit* in the ring. If he is rolled on one hip, as in the *long down*, it will be harder for him to smoothly come up into the sit. If you have followed our recommendations, you have taught your dog that the only time he should roll onto a hip is when he is in heel position. Whenever you are in front of him, he should be in the *sphinx down* position.

Hold the food in your signaling hand but between your fingers so you can keep your palm flat (Fig. 13.5). We use the left hand for the *sit signal*. Hold the food near his nose, as a lure, and slowly raise your hand over his head. CR the moment he starts into the *sit*. You are reinforcing his first effort! Again, add the verbal command after your signal if needed; then use your CR and feed him.

The actual signal is a scooping motion with your left hand. Start with your hand at your side, move it out to your left and slightly behind you as if you wanted to bring some water or sand to the front of you. Scoop your hand forward and stop the motion when it is in front of you and slightly off to your left (Fig. 13.6). Your wrist should be fully extended with your palm facing your dog. Stop the signal at or just above your waist level. Begin to use a *sit signal* while the food is still in your hand and you are still pairing the verbal command with the signal.

Keep your *sit signal* distinctly different from your signal to jump (see *Jumping* chapter). Some green dogs confuse the two signals and take the jump on your left instead of doing a *sit*.

Gradually condition your dog to doubles and triples and then to the signal without the verbal command. Eventually, you may hold the food in your right (non-signaling) hand for the reward after the CR.

Figure 13.5 Hold the food in your signaling hand but between your fingers so you can perform the sit signal correctly.

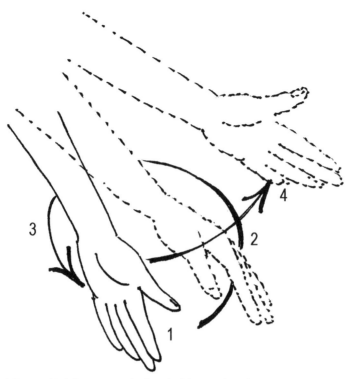

Figure 13.6 Start your sit signal with your hand at your side, move it out to your left and slightly behind you as if you wanted to bring some water or sand to the front of you. Scoop your hand forward and stop the motion when it is in front of you and slightly off to your left.

The Come Signal

The signal to COME should be one of the easiest to teach. You are finally allowing your dog to come to you after asking him to obey all the other signals from 40 feet away. Of course, in the beginning, he doesn't know that, since we teach all the signals separately. We put them together once the dog understands each signal.

We use the right arm to signal the dog to COME. Start with your arm at your side, move it out to your right to shoulder level or just below, and then bring your hand back across the front of your body. Your right hand ends up near your left shoulder (Fig. 13.7). It is the age-old signal used to get either animals or people to come to you. You want to emphasize the "arm away from the body" part the most, as that is the easiest part of the signal for your dog to see. Remember to keep your palm facing your dog as long as possible so he can see your signal clearly. Once your arm gets in front of your body, your dog will no longer see it as well.

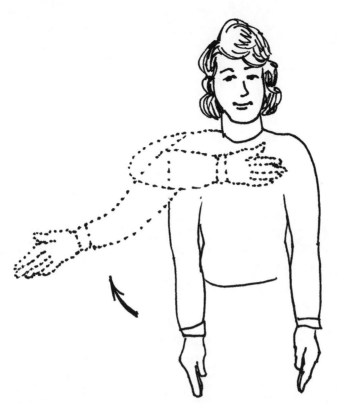

Figure 13.7 We use the right arm to signal the dog to COME. Start with your arm at your side, move it out to your right to shoulder level or just below, and then bring your hand back across the front of your body. Your right hand ends up near your left shoulder.

Start teaching the *come signal* with your dog sitting close to you and on a six-foot leash. Give the *come signal* followed by the verbal command. If there is no response, give a light pop on the leash. You may correct this exercise from the start because your dog should already understand the COME command but has failed to respond. If you are teaching the signals to a puppy and feel he does not have a clear understanding of the command, do not correct him but help him instead. If you are using a correction, use a buckle collar so the pressure for the recall is on the back of your dog's neck. Eliminate both the leash and the verbal command as soon as possible.

Train for doubles and triples, and use your CR at the moment of compliance, which is the instant your dog gets up to take his first step. This is when he should hear his CR. This will help speed him up and give him confidence. Don't get caught in the trap of having your dog depend on verbal feedback. As he gains understanding, delay the CR until he is closer to you and use your treats randomly.

The Heel Signal

You should not try to teach your dog the signal to *heel* until he has a good foundation in heeling. By the time you start training Utility seriously, most dogs start heeling as soon as your left leg moves forward. Try it, you'll see! If this works for you, you don't have to teach a hand signal. If you wish to teach the hand signal, move your left hand forward, command HEEL, and pair it with a *heel start* (see *Power Steering* chapter). CR as soon as your dog moves forward and feed after one or two steps.

If you are training a short dog, your signal can be over his head or next to your leg. If your dog's head is at or above the level of your hand, you may either signal on the inside or the outside of his head. For dogs who tend to heel wide or move away from you as you start, you may want to give your signal to the left of his head. If there is room, however, the best place is to the right of your dog's head and next to your leg (Fig. 13.8). This does not have to be a great sweeping motion if your dog works with focused attention! Try to use a flip of the wrist and immediately return your hand to your off-lead hand position, whether at your side or at your waist. Some trainers merely flip their hand from the "hand held at the waist position." If your dog does not catch on to this, attach a short leash and hold it tightly in your right hand. As you step off, bring your left hand forward so it catches the leash and gives your dog a little pop. We assume, at this point, that your dog responds well to your HEEL command.

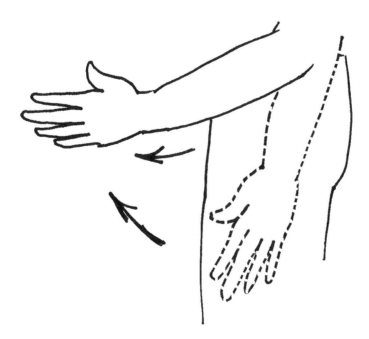

Figure 13.8 If there is room, the best place for your heel signal is to the right of your dog's head and next to your leg.

The Finish Signal

The *finish signal* was paired with your command to *finish* from the time you started to teach the exercise. Of all the signals it should be the easiest for your dog to remember and respond to.

While teaching the finish(es), you used your hands extensively, first to lure your dog and then to show him the direction he needed to go. These hand motions become your *finish signals* (Figs. 13.9 and 13.10). Some trainers use a higher signal to get a leaping finish, but this is not necessary (see *Fronts and Finishes* chapter).

Figure 13.9 We signal the *around finish* with the right hand...

Figure 13.10 ...and the *swing finish* with the left hand.

Corrections

Occasionally, as you teach the signals, you will notice a loss of understanding, attention, focus, or response. Something as simple as increasing the distance between you and your dog by one step can cause him to fail to respond to your signals. This means he hasn't generalized the signal to all distances yet. Go back and work the signals closer to your dog. You may want to add a verbal cue to the signal for a few days to help him over this hump. **It is better to err on the side of offering extra help rather than expecting too much too soon.** Your goal is to build your dog's confidence and have him *like* doing the work. Utility is a stressful class for both dogs and handlers. Your dog needs to be able to work farther away from you than he has in the past, and it requires him to think more independently. The more comfortable the training, the more confident your dog will be in the ring.

There will come a time, however, when you have done all the foundation work. You have backed up and moved forward, and you are positive your dog knows the signals. This is when we recommend adding corrections. Go back and work closer to your dog. When your dog errs, we suggest the following corrections:

- *Failure to heel:* Pop forward on his collar or a leash.
- *Failure to stay:* Return your dog to the place where you left him. Perhaps add a tap on his chest as a reminder.
- *Failure to stay standing:* Help your dog back into a stand with a hand under his belly.
- *Failure to drop:* Tap him on the top of his shoulders or pop him downward with your hand in his collar.
- *Failure to sit:* Pop up on the leash or his collar or brush his front toes with your foot.
- *Failure to come:* Pop towards you on a leash.
- *Failure to finish:* Pop your dog in the correct direction with your hand in his collar or on a leash.

When we add a correction, we release the dog immediately. We then repeat the same signal and reinforce with the CR and food when he responds correctly.

Putting It All Together

Dogs are creatures of habit, and they learn by repetition. Keep these two points in mind when you start teaching several signals in sequence. If you always repeat your signals in exactly the same order, your dog will anticipate them. Anticipation means only that your dog is thinking about what is coming next. This is not a bad problem unless it continues past the learning stage or interferes with his response to the next signal. It is best to train the signals separately and combine them in random order. *Be sure your dog is showing no hesitation when you work with one signal before starting to pair it with another.*

Your initial goal is for your dog to understand each signal alone and not necessarily in conjunction with another signal. Later, you may want to use the ring series (*stand, stay, down, sit, come, finish*) for pattern training. Pattern training sometimes builds confidence, especially in insecure or highly stressed dogs.

When you begin to pair signals, remember to CR and release a lot when your dog least expects it. Some pairs of exercises to work on include:

- The *down* followed by the *sit*.
- The *stand* followed by the *down*.
- The *sit* followed by the *come*.

The Utility Signal Exercise has more different parts than any other obedience exercise. You must be sure to reinforce each part randomly or you will end up with either anticipation or failure to respond to your first signal. To reinforce your dog, use your CR from a distance and throw food or a toy behind him. To help build confidence, use your CR and return randomly to your dog to feed him.

Backward Chaining the Signal Exercise

In the *Methods* chapter, we discussed *backward chaining*. As you recall, each successive step in a behavior chain reinforces the previous step. Backward chaining the signals often works well since most dogs like to do the recall better than the stationary signals. To backward chain the signals, use the following sequence:

- Do a *signal recall* from a *sit*.
- Do a *signal sit* from a *down*, followed by a *signal recall*.
- Do a *signal down* from a *stand*, followed by a *sit* and a *recall*.
- *Heel* a few steps forward into the *stand, stay signal, down, sit, recall*.
- *Heel* through an entire pattern, and do all the signals in order.

You should reinforce the *recall* with a treat or toy for many training sessions to keep your dog motivated. He is then usually more enthusiastic about doing stationary signals when he looks forward to doing a *recall*. Do not worry about *fronts* and *finishes* for now. Asking your dog to work on *fronts* will only slow him down, and your goal is for him to do speedy, reliable *recalls*.

Random jackpots used for each balance point of the exercise can help many dogs work confidently through the *Signal Exercise* (see *Methods* chapter and *Appendix A*).

Proofing

Proofing the Utility signals is probably the most important proofing you will ever do to prepare for obedience competition. This is because your dog will be alone in the ring, with a stranger behind him, and you will be 40 feet away. He is expected to ignore the stranger, pay attention to you, and execute the *Signal Exercise* perfectly. This is very difficult, and extremely stressful indeed!

We introduce distractions to the dog relatively early in our signal training while we are still close to him. Because we are close, we can help him respond properly, and add a correction if necessary. If he cannot respond when you are close to him, in spite of a distraction, he certainly will not be able to do so with you 40 feet away.

If your dog is easily startled or frightened, you should proof more slowly and carefully than if you are training a bold and confident dog. Do not fool yourself into thinking your dog knows more than he does. He will show you in the ring what he really knows!

Here are some examples of proofing exercises we have done with our dogs or have taught to our students. Make the proofing very easy at first and stay close to your dog. This increases the likelihood of success. You are trying to build confidence and have him succeed — NOT make him fail!

- Walk in an arc back and forth in front of your dog, giving signals at varying places in the arc and varying the distance between the two of you.

- Have a friend act as a judge and stand behind your dog. She should stand several feet away at first and then move closer as your dog focuses on you and ignores her.

- Have a friend walk around behind your dog. Again, she should start at a distance and gradually move closer.

- Have a friend train her dog nearby, throwing a dumbbell, doing *recalls, heeling,* and *jumping.*

- Have a friend deliberately distract your dog. She can squat down, pat the floor, or hold out her hand as though luring your dog.

- Have her stand close to and eventually bend over your dog.

- Have her pet your dog during the signals (Fig. 13.11).

- Glance away from your dog and then back to him, as you will when a judge is giving you the signals.

- Wait a long time between signals. Sometimes reinforce your dog for not anticipating. Sometimes reinforce for waiting and then responding to your next signal properly.

- Have a friend gently restrain your dog by the collar so he has to pull or push against the collar to perform the signals.

- Have your friend place her arms loosely around your dog's neck or body so he must again push against the pressure.

- Sit in a chair or on the floor when you give your signals.

Figure 13.11 Have a friend pet your dog during the signals.

Problem Solving

There are a variety of problems that you may encounter during your signal proofing.

Freezing

The dog who freezes often looks worried. His posture and the position of his ears and tail show his lack of confidence. Dogs usually freeze when they are not sure of what they are supposed to do. Perhaps you are combining your signals too soon, before each one is solid. When your dog started to make mistakes, you may have added corrections, making him hesitant to respond to the next signal. This can become a vicious cycle. If your dog is making a consistent mistake on a particular signal, take that signal out of the whole exercise and concentrate on it alone. Put it back into the complete exercise only when you regularly see a correct response.

A related problem is the dog who looks right at you but doesn't respond. This often happens with a green dog who is worried about the judge standing behind him. It's as though his eyes are engaged, but his mind is elsewhere. We have had this problem most often on the *down signal*; the dog freezes in a *stand* or responds with a *sit* instead.

Most dogs have a strong chase instinct. They enjoy chasing a moving object, whether it is a piece of food or a toy that the handler throws. When you can find a way to keep your dog's chase instinct strong, it makes the signals easier. Some exercises to increase your dog's chase instinct include:

- A *food-toss recall.*
- A *chase recall.*
- A release backwards, to food or toy, after completing the *stand, down,* or *sit signal.* The food or toy may be stationary on the ground behind your dog or may be thrown by you. Do several *signal recalls* in a row to build your dog's drive and motivation.

Think of games to play to motivate your dog and make him attentive, and incorporate signals into these games. Pretend to throw a toy in order to get your dog running away from you. When he turns to face you, give a *down* (or *sit* or *come) signal.* CR and toss him a toy or treat as soon as he responds correctly. As his abilities improve, have him do two or more signals in sequence before you toss the toy. Give the signals randomly, releasing your dog frequently to make it fun.

Attention

Obviously, your dog has to see your signal to respond to it properly. If he looks away frequently during your signal work, you need to work harder on maintaining his attention. Use the exercises discussed in the previous section to build his attention. This will keep him more focused on you. You should also add proofing to these exercises to help your dog understand what you expect of him.

A Perfect Signal Exercise

A perfectly executed *Signal Exercise* looks like this:

- The dog and handler move briskly to the starting line and set up for heeling.

- The dog sits attentively in heel position.

- On the judge's command, the handler gives her *heel signal,* and the team steps out briskly. They flow through the *heeling,* the dog attentive and responsive, the handler smooth in her turns, halts, and pace changes.

- On the judge's command to "Stand your dog," the handler gives a smooth *stand signal* as she stops with her dog standing in perfect heel position.

- The command to "Leave your dog" prompts the handler to give a smooth *wait signal.* She then walks briskly to the other end of the ring.

- While the handler is walking away, the dog *stands* with focused *attention* on the handler.

- The handler turns and faces her dog and looks to the judge for the *down signal.*

- The dog responds to his handler's *down signal* promptly, dropping in place, with no steps to the side, forward, or backward. His attention remains riveted on the handler.

- The handler immediately looks at the judge for the next signal.

- The dog pops up into a *sit* as signaled, again with no excessive motion in any direction.

- The handler again looks at the judge.

- The *recall signal* causes the dog to gallop to his straight sit in front.

- Finally, the judge cues the handler for the finish, and the dog responds smartly to the handler's signal.
- All of the handler's signals are done smoothly, crisply, and continuously, but not too fast.

Understand that this is our ideal. We have included many extras in our perfect picture! Rarely do we see such an ideal exercise, and seldom have we experienced one. Remember, the essential feature of the exercise is that you work together as a team for the heeling and the signals.

A crisply executed *Signal Exercise* is a joy to watch. It's also a joy to perform. Train with this image in mind.

Retrieving

etrieving is one of the first games we play with a new puppy or dog. In retrieving, you throw an object, your dog runs out, picks it up, and returns promptly to you. He should hold the object until you take it from him. It is a good way to exercise him, and it teaches him to work with people.

Many trainers never get beyond the Novice obedience level because they are unable to teach their dog to do a complete, ring-ready retrieve. Teaching a dog to retrieve can be a great mystery to new trainers, and it can be a source of frustration for both trainer and dog.

Retrieving is a crucial element of advanced obedience. The exercises that include a retrieve are:

- The Open *Retrieve on the Flat.* On your command, your dog retrieves a dumbbell, and delivers it to you.

- The Open *Retrieve Over the High Jump.* Your dog jumps over a jump, retrieves his dumbbell, jumps back over the jump, and delivers the dumbbell to you.

- The Utility *Scent Discrimination.* Your dog selects one item from eight other similar items. The correct item is the one you have handled, and your dog must recognize it by scent. Your dog returns the item to you as in the *Retrieve on the Flat.*

- The Utility *Directed Retrieve.* Your dog retrieves one of three gloves when directed with your hand-signal. The judge tells you which one your dog should retrieve. Your dog then returns the glove to you as in the *Retrieve on the Flat.*

Throughout most of this chapter, we will use the word *dumbbell* to simplify the text, instead of saying something awkward like *retrieve object.* In most cases, you may substitute *scent article* or *glove,* except when we are discussing specific exercises. We encourage you to teach your dog to retrieve a glove and each type of scent article, as well as the dumbbell. This early introduction to gloves and articles will be important later on when you teach *Scent Discrimination* and *Directed Retrieve*, because the retrieve foundation will already be in place.

When he retrieves perfectly, your dog gallops or trots briskly and directly to the dumbbell on your command. He picks up the dumbbell without fumbling and returns immediately to you without mouthing (shifting it around excessively in his mouth) or playing with it. He sits straight in front of you, continuing to hold his dumbbell until you take it from him. He sits close enough so that you can touch him without moving forward, but he doesn't touch you or sit between your feet.

Forced Retrieve

Many obedience trainers believe the only way to have a reliable retrieve is by using a *forced retrieve*, most commonly the *ear pinch*. The theory behind the *ear pinch* is that of negative reinforcement. You apply pressure to your dog's ear until he feels enough discomfort or pain to open his mouth, immediately place the dumbbell in his mouth, and stop the pressure the instant the dumbbell is in his mouth. This has proven to be successful for many dogs, but a handler with poor timing can ruin her dog's enthusiasm with misapplied force. This is especially true when it is introduced before the dog understands what he is supposed to do when presented with the dumbbell. The dog becomes stressed, learns to hate the dumbbell, and both dog and handler develop terrible attitudes about retrieving. Rather than putting their dog through such stress, many people simply give up.

Play Retrieve

People who don't wish to use a *forced retrieve* often rely on a *play retrieve*. For dogs with a strong desire to retrieve, the *play retrieve* can work well, but sometimes, dogs trained this way develop bad habits. They may mouth the dumbbell or pounce on it. This can result in many lost points in the ring. Bad habits develop when a handler does not teach her dog each of the skills he needs for a complete formal retrieve. She relies on her dog's excitement for the chase instead of thoroughly training the exercise.

Shaped Retrieve

Many people think that training the retrieve with food causes mouthing problems. *When done correctly, the use of food can eliminate mouthing and improve attitude.*

We have found that when dogs are taught in a positive manner, with food as reinforcement, most of them become eager retrievers. Our video tape, *Positively Fetching: Teaching the Obedience Retrieves Using Food,* covers this subject in depth.

We begin to teach the retrieve by reinforcing each time the dog touches any part of the dumbbell with his nose. Next, we limit reinforcement to when his nose is near or touching the bar of the dumbbell, not the bells. We simply ignore wrong behaviors while we wait for his current "best effort."

As discussed in the Methods chapter, an important part of shaping is to move quickly from constant to variable reinforcement. A good example is your dog touching the dumbbell with his nose. As soon as he frequently touches the dumbbell with his nose, wait for him to touch it two or three times before giving him his reward. This is variable reinforcement. Make sure you are truly variable. Reinforcing every second time or every third time is still a fixed schedule. A random schedule makes your dog work harder and accustoms him to not getting food for every performance. Sometimes use your CR but no food. Sometimes withhold both your CR and the food until he has touched the dumbbell two or three times. Do this carefully. If he gives up and walks away, reinforce for less effort the next time.

You know you are reinforcing often enough if your dog quickly offers the behavior again.

As you begin to move away from constant reinforcement, your dog will offer a wider range of behaviors. As long as he keeps doing something, reinforce the actions that are closest to your current goal. Ignore less accurate responses and unrelated actions. Pay close attention to your dog and strive to keep the reinforcement coming steadily.

Your dog will not make continuous improvements. Some days, you will need to back up rather than move forward. This is common in learning.

The timing of your CR is critical to the success of this method for teaching retrieving. Your dog must hear the sound while he is still doing what you want him to do.

When attempting to shape a dumbbell hold, new trainers frequently use the sound too late, just after the dog has let go of the dumbbell. This teaches him to barely put his mouth on it and then to quickly let go.

Remember that initially the CR "ends the behavior." Don't worry at first about what happens after the CR. Most likely your dog will let go of the dumbbell so he can get his treat. This is a problem only if you don't move on to the next step quickly enough.

Equipment

Before you begin to teach your dog to retrieve, you should gather various equipment (see *Equipment* chapter for more guidance):

- A dumbbell.
- A cotton glove.
- A leather and metal scent article.
- A chair for you to sit in.
- Many tasty treats.
- A hungry dog.

You may wish to wait to invest in gloves and scent articles, but find a cloth, a metal, and a leather object for your dog to learn to hold. A sock tied in a knot, a bent spoon, or a piece of an old belt may be used. Later, you may need a four- to six-foot leash and a retractable leash.

The Dumbbell

You may start teaching your dog to retrieve using a dowel or any dumbbell that is approximately the right size, but buy one to fit your dog as soon as possible. See the list of suppliers in the *Equipment* chapter for more information. You will not be able to fit your dog precisely for a dumbbell until he is full grown and can hold one for a short time.

The size of the dumbbell should be proportionate to the size of your dog. There are three elements to consider when fitting a dumbbell to your dog (Fig. 14.1):

- The height of the bells (the ends of the dumbbell).
- The width between the bells.
- The thickness of the dowel.

Many dumbbells are made with tapered bells to allow for a more comfortable fit. An "off-the-shelf" size is fine for many dogs, but some breeds require a custom fit due to the unusual length or width of their muzzle.

The ideal placement of the dumbbell is directly behind your dog's canine teeth (Fig. 14.2). He should hold it firmly. If the dowel is too long and there is too much space between the bells, it is easier for him to roll it back onto his molars. This usually leads to mouthing, which is excessive shifting of the dumbbell in his mouth. If there is too little space between the bells, his lips may get pinched. If the bells are too large, they

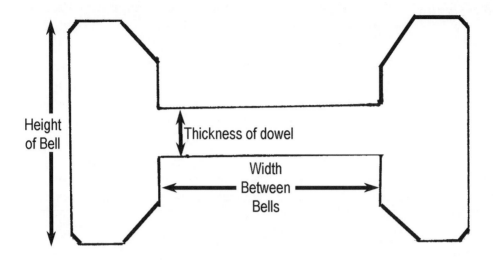

Figure 14.1 The size of the dumbbell should be proportionate to the size of your dog. There are three elements to consider when fitting a dumbbell to your dog: the height of the bells, the width between the bells, and the thickness of the dowel.

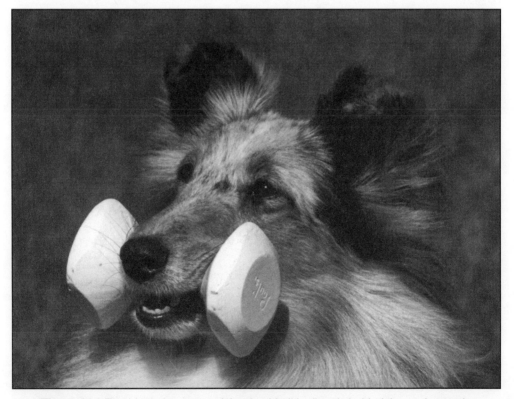

Figure 14.2 The ideal placement of the dumbbell is directly behind the canine teeth.

may interfere with his vision. If they are too small, he may have difficulty picking up the dumbbell smoothly without hitting his nose on the ground.

We recommend a thicker dowel to help prevent your dog from rolling the dumbbell to the back of his mouth. It is possible for him to roll a thin-doweled dumbbell with his tongue even when his teeth are tightly closed. Also, a thin dowel on a wooden dumbbell tends to break more easily.

A properly fitted dumbbell is easier for your dog to pick up from the floor. He needs to be able to close his teeth easily on the bar without hitting his nose on the floor. If he frequently picks up the dumbbell by an end, try one with larger bells.

A Chair

Begin to teach retrieving while sitting in a chair. This keeps you close to your dog's head and makes it easier for him to give you the dumbbell. If you are working with a small dog, you may want to sit on the floor.

Food

You will need a large supply of food that your dog finds especially interesting. Vary the type of food to keep his interest strong.

If you have a dog with extremely low food drive, work on the retrieve just before meal time. This type of dog may need to skip a meal or two when you first start teaching the retrieve. Put a dumbbell next to your dog's food bowl or your favorite chair. This will remind you to spend a small amount of time every day training the retrieve.

Some dogs cannot concentrate when they are hungry. If this describes your dog, work on the retrieve after he has eaten. Feeding half his meal shortly before training might help him concentrate better.

For a dog who loves toys, substitute a toy for food as reinforcement. Unfortunately, you may not progress as quickly because of the time lost while he plays with the toy. If your dog learns that he must retrieve the dumbbell to get you to throw the toy, you will build drive for the dumbbell and persuade him to retrieve. Using a toy as a motivator generally works better at a later stage of training (i.e., once he is taking the dumbbell).

Leash

You may prefer to keep your dog on a leash while training the retrieve. If you are working alone in a quiet place, off-leash is fine. If he frequently wanders off, or you are somewhere unsafe for off-leash work, keep a leash attached.

Muzzle Handling

Before you introduce your dog to holding the dumbbell, you should be able to:

- Hold your dog's muzzle with your hands around it for a count of five.
- Hold his chin up gently with one hand underneath.
- Hold his muzzle with a finger or two in the groove under his chin.
- Open his mouth and handle his muzzle without him struggling or avoiding your hands (Fig. 14.3).

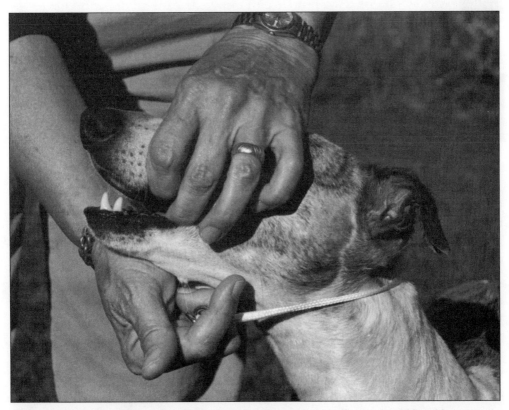

Figure 14.3 Before you introduce your dog to holding a dumbbell, you should be able to open his mouth and handle his muzzle without him struggling or avoiding your hands.

If your dog struggles when you handle his muzzle, start slowly and, when he is calm, use lots of praise and treats. Gradually increase the length of time you handle his muzzle each session until your dog accepts it calmly. With quiet, consistent work, you should see progress in a short time. If you have regularly handled your dog's mouth, you will probably be able to skim over this phase. If you have neglected it, spend some time teaching him to accept your hands around his muzzle.

Teaching Interest in the Dumbbell

Sit in your chair with your food readily accessible. A bowl of food on a counter or table works well. Your first goal is for the dog to touch the dumbbell with his nose. Hold the dumbbell near your dog's nose. He may sniff it immediately. Any movement towards the dumbbell earns a CR and food. Once he realizes you have food, you may have to be patient and wait for him to stop staring at you. It works best to keep the food in your closed hand resting on your knee. He knows it's there but must ignore it and work to earn the reward.

This is an important lesson for him to learn early in training. The food will always be nearby, but he can't have it until he does the next part of the exercise. If necessary, move the dumbbell in front of his nose or gently touch his nose with it. CR and treat. Repeat many times. As your dog catches on, he should return more rapidly to touch the dumbbell after each reward. As this happens, move the dumbbell a few inches in a new direction and to different locations, especially towards the floor. As your dog begins to understand, wait until he touches it two or three times before he gets the food. Initially, you may have to use your CR for each touch, but begin to fade that quickly.

Many dogs lie down when the dumbbell reaches the floor. Ignore this unless your dog believes it is part of the desired behavior. If he lies down each time or stays in the down position, teach him to lower his head to the floor without lying down. Slow down your shaping steps and, if he does lie down, get him back into a sit or stand before showing him the dumbbell again.

It is crucial for you to keep quiet, other than to use your CR for the right response. Resist the urge to say *anything* for now. **Don't add a verbal cue until your dog is taking the dumbbell from many locations.**

As your dog catches on to the nose touch, wait to reinforce him until he keeps his nose close to the dumbbell for longer periods of time. Wait for him to touch the bar of the dumbbell, not the ends. As he works to figure out what you want, he will experiment with different movements, seeing which ones earn reinforcement. Keep quiet until you see the behavior you want. One exception we make to this "quiet" rule is for a dog who paws excessively or one who barks. We sometimes respond with a quiet verbal reprimand such as AH-AH, WRONG, or TOO BAD.

The Take

The next goal is to teach your dog to *take* the dumbbell, though he is not required to hold it at this point. If you are very lucky, your dog may voluntarily take the dumbbell on his own. This response should earn a "jackpot," which means giving him a handful of food all at once. If not, the following steps should help.

Hold one end of the dumbbell in one hand and hold a piece of food in the fingertips of your other hand. Put the food behind the bar of the dumbbell and put the dumbbell near your dog's mouth (Fig. 14.4) so that the dumbbell is between his mouth and the food. He should open his mouth to try to get the food. When he does, slide the dumbbell past his canine teeth, use your CR, and push the food past the dumbbell towards the roof of his mouth as you withdraw the dumbbell (Fig. 14.5).

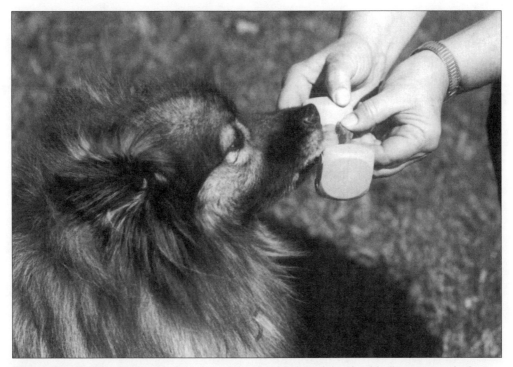

Figure 14.4 Put the food behind the bar of the dumbbell and the dumbbell near your dog's mouth.

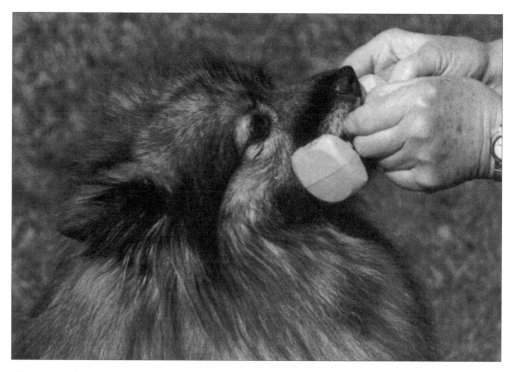

Figure 14.5 The handler has just started to pull the dumbbell out and to push the food past the bar of the dumbbell towards the roof of her dog's mouth.

Be patient while your dog works to figure out what to do. He will try to go under, over, and around the dumbbell to get to the food, but seldom through it. Wait! You may first need to reinforce his pushing the dumbbell with his nose as he tries to get the food. If you get stuck, you can speed up this step by opening his mouth with a finger, and then slipping the dumbbell into his mouth. Use your CR, and then give him a treat after you remove the dumbbell. *The CR tells him he is correct while the dumbbell is still in his mouth.*

When your dog consistently opens his mouth when the food is next to the bar, begin to hold the dumbbell and food an inch or so away from his mouth and wait for him to reach for it. *You are still not giving a retrieve command.* Gradually move the food away from the bar of the dumbbell and move the dumbbell farther from his nose, teaching him that he must reach for it. *Remember to keep quiet and let your dog work out what earns the CR and food.* Don't go too fast with this step. Some dogs will quit if you do.

Once your dog takes the dumbbell without the food next to it, begin to move the dumbbell to different locations, as you did when shaping the nose touch. Work until he will take the dumbbell from:

- Between your knees.

- Between your calves.
- Between your feet.
- Your hand while you hold the dumbbell in various positions.
- The floor, in front of you and as far as six feet away (you are placing the dumbbell, not throwing it).

Some dogs may only be able to succeed when the dumbbell is moved a short distance, perhaps one inch at a time. Others adapt to the different locations more quickly. Move the dumbbell slowly when teaching. Quick, jerky movements make it difficult for your dog to comprehend what you are trying to achieve.

The Lift

The *lift* introduces your dog to lifting and briefly holding the dumbbell. When he catches on, he should begin to help you lift the dumbbell, taking your hand, which is holding on to one end of the dumbbell, along for the ride.

Sit in a chair facing your dog or on the floor if he's small. Grasp the dumbbell by an end and hold it about six inches below his nose. When he puts his mouth on the bar of the dumbbell, slowly and gently lift the dumbbell straight up by the end, with your other hand or fingers under his chin. This helps keep the dumbbell in his mouth. Use your CR at the top of the lift (if the dumbbell is still in your dog's mouth), remove the dumbbell, and reinforce him with a treat.

The first few times you do this, your dog may pull his head back as though gagging. If so, try lifting a shorter distance the next time. Use your CR anytime you feel your dog grip the bar of the dumbbell.

The next step is to teach your dog to bring the dumbbell to the center of your body. Do this by using your CR when his head is centered in front of you. As your dog gets the idea of the *lift*, start with the dumbbell closer to the floor. Also, begin to move it off center. Your dog earns the CR and a treat when his head is at the center and front of your body.

Lifting from the Floor

After your dog gets better at lifting the dumbbell while it is still in your hand, gradually move the dumbbell to the floor (Fig. 14.6). Start with one end of the dumbbell on the floor and the other end in your hand. Next, keep your hand on one end but put both ends on the floor. Then keep just one finger on the end of the dumbbell, and finally, let go completely.

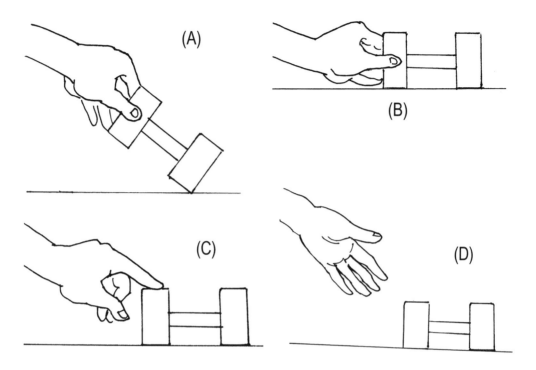

Figure 14.6 After your dog gets reliable at lifting the dumbbell while it is still in your hand, gradually move the dumbbell to the floor. (A) Start with one end of the dumbbell on the floor and the other end in your hand. (B) Next, keep your hand on one end but put both ends on the floor. (C) Then keep just one finger on the end of the dumbbell, and finally, (D) let go completely.

As mentioned earlier, be sure to use your CR when the dumbbell is still in your dog's mouth, not after he releases it. Randomize the position of the dumbbell so your dog practices pickups from a variety of locations around you. Don't work too long at this stage or he might continue to drop it soon after picking it up.

Pickup Style

Different dogs pick up a dumbbell in different ways; on the way out, on the way back, and turning either left or right.

Most dogs turn consistently in one direction. Use this to your advantage by throwing slightly off center to the opposite side (Fig. 14.7). This will help your dog return and sit straighter. As long as his pickup is brisk and clean, any method is acceptable.

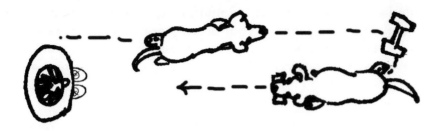

Figure 14.7 Throw your dumbbell off center to the opposite side from which your dog usually turns when he picks it up.

Adding the Release Command

Once your dog takes the dumbbell from a variety of places, add a release command, such as GIVE, OUT, or THANK YOU. Add the command just before he opens his mouth, but after your CR.

The sequence now looks like this:

- Your dog takes the dumbbell.
- You use your CR, immediately followed by your release command.
- He releases the dumbbell.
- You give him a treat.

Most dogs will readily give up the dumbbell for a piece of food. If you have a dog for whom the dumbbell is more reinforcing than the food, you may need to help him open his mouth. Use your fingers over the top of his muzzle to gently push his lips into his teeth.

Once you start to add your release command, don't give your dog food if he releases the dumbbell before the command. Wait for him to take it again, use your CR, and then use your release command. You may also use your CR two or more times while the dumbbell is still in his mouth before giving your release command. This is the way you start shaping the *hold* (discussed later in this chapter).

Most handlers take the dumbbell from their dog by reaching for both ends, gripping the ends as they give the release command, and pulling the dumbbell up and out. Your dog should not release it until he hears your command.

Adding the Retrieve Command

You should now add a retrieve command, such as GET IT, TAKE IT, or FETCH. You can do this as soon as your dog understands what he is supposed to do when he sees the dumbbell. However, if you find yourself repeating the retrieve command without your dog retrieving, stop using it until he takes the dumbbell on his own in a variety of places and in the presence of mild distractions.

Begin with easy goals. Present the dumbbell near his nose and give your retrieve command. Wait until he takes it in his mouth and immediately reinforce with your CR and food. Repeat this with the dumbbell in increasingly difficult positions, but don't expect to exceed what you have achieved with earlier shaping.

The Finger Hold

If your dog spits the dumbbell out the instant he takes it, we suggest you teach him to *hold* one of your fingers. This gives you a much better sense of what he is doing when an object is in his mouth. It allows you to give him immediate feedback (with your CR) when he relaxes his tongue and stops fighting your finger. This should help him understand what HOLD means.

Start by positioning yourself facing your dog. Show him a piece of food held in one hand. With one or two fingers and possibly your thumb of the other hand, open his mouth by putting gentle pressure on his lips just behind his canine teeth (Fig. 14.8). The food should be directly in front of his nose and, as soon as he opens his mouth, use your CR and give him the treat. Do this until he is relaxed with your hand opening his mouth.

Next, place the first finger of one hand behind his canine teeth. There is a space there for your finger! Use your thumb under his chin and other three fingers on the top of his muzzle. You can also hold your thumb on top and your fingers underneath (Fig. 14.9). Gently shut his mouth on your finger while commanding HOLD. Use both hands if it is easier for you. The instant he tightens his grip on your finger and relaxes his tongue, use your CR, remove your finger from his mouth, and give him a treat. You can time your reward correctly when you feel him begin to hold your finger. It is imperative that you use your CR *while* your dog is gently closing his teeth on your finger. This gives him the necessary information that he is doing what you want him to do. Remember, when you use your CR properly, you can give the treat later. This exercise readily transfers when you begin to work on *hold* with the dumbbell.

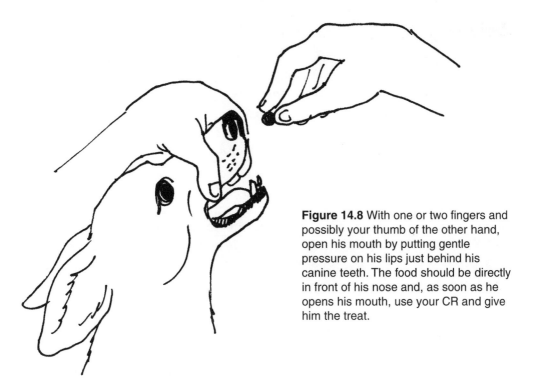

Figure 14.8 With one or two fingers and possibly your thumb of the other hand, open his mouth by putting gentle pressure on his lips just behind his canine teeth. The food should be directly in front of his nose and, as soon as he opens his mouth, use your CR and give him the treat.

Figure 14.9 Teach your dog to hold your finger.

The Hold

A proper *hold* requires the dog to hold the dumbbell just behind his canine teeth without chewing, rolling, or spitting it out. **When teaching the hold, you are not teaching the take.** Work on each separately. Get the *take* portion well established, but make sure you don't teach your dog that grabbing and spitting it out is what you want. Start the *hold* as soon as your dog takes the dumbbell reliably.

Many trainers and training books gloss over how hard it can be to teach a dog to hold the dumbbell. Most rely on physically holding the dumbbell in the dog's mouth and tapping him under the chin when he tries to spit it out. The *hold* is probably the hardest part of the retrieve to teach without force and for some dogs, a little physical help may be necessary. The essential steps your dog needs to learn for a reliable *hold* are:

- Hold after a clean pickup from the ground.
- Hold without mouthing while galloping or trotting briskly.
- Hold while coming into a sit in front.

Begin by holding the dumbbell with one or both hands. This allows you to feel when your dog clenches his teeth on the bar. You may be able to teach *hold* this way, simply reinforcing the longer *holds* and ignoring the shorter efforts. Do not reinforce every effort. Instead, do doubles and triples. The varying reinforcement should produce *holds* of varying durations. Reinforce the longer ones.

If shaping doesn't give your dog the idea of the *hold,* give him some gentle, physical help by opening his mouth and inserting the dumbbell. You must do all of the preliminary steps first, because some dogs become anxious when you restrain them in any way. If this physical help is done too soon, your dog may get stressed and avoid the dumbbell, and his excitement for it will disappear. If you see this start to happen, you are probably asking for too much too soon. It would be best to go back and review the muzzle handling exercises to make sure you can hold your dog's muzzle and chin *without* the dumbbell in his mouth.

When you are sure that your dog is comfortable with you handling his muzzle, the next step is to gently hold the dumbbell in his mouth. There are various ways to position your dog during this step. Either place him seated next to you, straddle him with one foot on either side of him (Fig. 14.10), or sit him in front of you with one hand in his collar and your fingertips under his chin (Fig. 14.11).

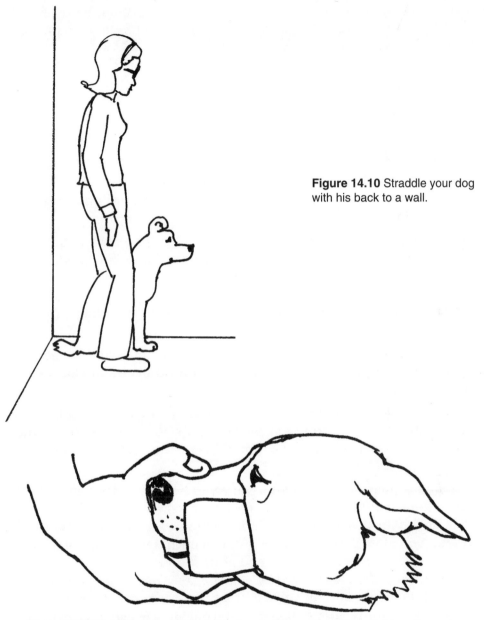

Figure 14.10 Straddle your dog with his back to a wall.

Figure 14.11 Position your dog in front of you with one hand through his collar and your fingers under his chin.

Try each position to see which is least stressful for your dog and most comfortable for you. Insert the dumbbell just behind his canine teeth and shut his mouth gently while commanding HOLD. Keep one hand firmly under his chin and the other hand on one end of the dumbbell.

After holding his mouth shut for about one second, use your CR, followed by your release command, take the dumbbell from his mouth, and give him a treat. Note the order here:

- HOLD command.
- Conditioned reinforcer (CR).
- Release command.
- Food.

Your dog should hear the CR while the dumbbell is still in his mouth. The CR reinforces the HOLD command, not the release. It is important that you do this correctly to help prevent mouthing in anticipation of the food.

Do not take your hands away from your dog's muzzle while the dumbbell is in his mouth. Doing so invites him to spit it out. Hold his mouth closed until you feel him gripping the dumbbell. This may take a few days or a few weeks, depending on your dog and your persistence. Remember, start slowly and work only as fast as your dog grasps the concept to *hold* the dumbbell.

If your dog struggles, slow down! Ask for a shorter *hold*. If he accepts the dumbbell quietly, don't hold his mouth shut firmly, but do keep your hands on or close to his muzzle.

Make sure you are not forcing his head up too high. His head should stay level with the floor during this stage. If your dog manages to roll the dumbbell onto his molars, remove it from his mouth and start over. He gets no reinforcement.

Gradually increase the length of time you help your dog hold the dumbbell. If he can hold it with help for about ten seconds, he should be ready to hold it for two or three seconds by himself. Give your retrieve command, and after the dumbbell is in his mouth, tell him to HOLD. You may want to keep one hand on the end of the dumbbell. If he holds it for one second, use your CR followed by your release command, take the dumbbell from his mouth, and give him a couple of treats. If he drops it before you give your release command, start again. He gets no treats for this, nor do you get upset. He is merely wrong! Gradually increase the length of time he holds before you reinforce him.

Some dogs stand up the instant they take the dumbbell. Since you want him to be able to sit calmly in front of you while holding the dumbbell, teach your dog to remain sitting after he takes it. With him sitting in front of you and you either standing or sitting in a chair or on the floor, present the dumbbell in front of his nose. If you get any sort of mouth contact and he remains sitting, use your CR and a treat. If your dog stands up, command SIT and start over. Gradually build a longer *hold* with him sitting. You may try wrapping your legs around him to keep him in a sit (Fig. 14.12). This is easy to do when you work from a chair, and it prevents him from standing. A STAY command given before he takes the dumbbell may also do the trick.

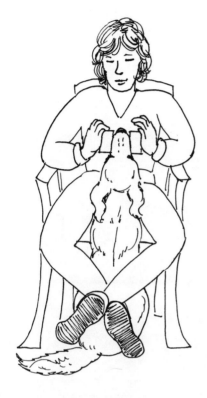

Figure 14.12 Wrap your legs around your dog to keep him in a sit.

Proofing the Hold

Once your dog is able to hold the dumbbell independently for five seconds, begin proofing his *hold*. This will show how completely he understands this exercise.

First, check to see if he continues to hold the dumbbell when you move your hands closer to the ends, but do not touch it. For some dogs, just seeing your hands approach the dumbbell is enough to cause them to drop it. If he is successful and holds, even for a split second, he gets a CR. Remove the dumbbell and give a treat. When he is successful with this step, touch the ends. Next, put gentle downward pressure on one or both ends. He may turn his head away or open his mouth when you reach for the dumbbell. If he opens his mouth to get rid of it or rolls it back on his molars, use a gentle verbal reprimand such as AH-AH, remove the dumbbell, and start over. You may need to keep one hand under his chin to help him hold the dumbbell when you apply the pressure. Work until he resists when you push or pull the dumbbell in all directions. He should not open his mouth until you give your release command.

You can tie a short piece of dental floss to the bar of the dumbbell and pull on it to test his *hold* (Fig. 14.13). He will probably let go as soon as you apply the slightest pressure, so be prepared to correct him verbally. You may also need to help him with a hand under his chin. The floss doesn't interfere with the pickup and is another way to proof the hold. Some dogs are more sensitive than others to hands on the dumbbell but do not object as much if you pull on it with a piece of floss.

Figure 14.13 Tie a short piece of dental floss to the dumbbell.

The Carry

Up to this point, your dog may never have taken a step while holding the dumbbell. To start him moving, have him walk with you, present the dumbbell just in front of his nose, and give your TAKE and HOLD commands. Once it is in his mouth, continue walking two or three more steps, use your CR, remove the dumbbell from his mouth, and give him a treat. If he tends to let go of the dumbbell before your release command, keep one hand on the dumbbell. You might also have to hold his mouth shut while he takes a couple of steps. Gradually increase the number of steps he walks while carrying the dumbbell. Then walk faster and encourage him to trot with you.

Next, step in front and turn to face your dog before you remove the dumbbell and feed him a treat. Do not ask him to sit.

As your dog learns to do the *hold* and *carry*, begin to assume a more formal posture. Begin with a *carry*, step in front, turn to face him, and ask him to SIT. As soon as his rear is on the floor, immediately use your CR, assuming the dumbbell is still in his mouth, remove the dumbbell, and give him a treat. Don't try to get a long *hold* at this point.

Fronts with the Dumbbell

When you first ask your dog to *sit in front* of you while holding the dumbbell, it is not likely that he will be able to do a straight *front.*

A useful exercise for training fronts with the dumbbell is the *scoot front* (see *Combination Words* chapter). Teach this first without the dumbbell and then add the dumbbell to the exercise. At first, ask for one *scoot front*, then add more repetitions as your dog gains skill.

As his *hold* becomes more reliable, begin leaving your dog in a *Sit-stay*, with the dumbbell in his mouth. Walk away a short distance and call him to *front.* Gradually build this exercise to a full distance recall as long as his *hold* remains steady. The longer distance usually helps him learn to come more quickly while holding. Some dogs have trouble moving briskly while maintaining the *hold.* Work on fast recalls without the dumbbell, and when you add the dumbbell, continue to insist on a steady *hold.*

Once your dog has some sense of what your HOLD command means, start putting it together with the full retrieve. He should also have learned a COME command before doing the complete exercise.

Review *chair fronts* in the *Front and Finish* chapter. Begin to add the dumbbell to that exercise, substituting a dumbbell retrieve for the food chase. Toss the dumbbell about four to six feet in front of you. As your dog picks it up, remind him to HOLD and tell him to COME. Encourage him to come close to you, between your extended legs. If he drops the dumbbell before you can take it from him, you have two choices. Use your *retrieve* command if it is well-established or keep quiet and see if he figures out that he should pick up the dumbbell and bring it closer. Once your dog is successful when the dumbbell is thrown straight out in front of you, work on tosses first to one side and then the other.

Restrained Retrieves

Restraining your dog by the collar while you throw the dumbbell often helps speed up his retrieve. Restrain him, throw the dumbbell, do some verbal and physical teasing, and then release him to retrieve. When he picks it up, use your CR and tell him to COME. Build the speed of his retrieve before combining it with either a *stay* or a *sit in front*. Once you have conditioned him to come back to you for food, reinforce only his faster returns. Many dogs get excited and motivated by this exercise.

The Wait or Stay

We assume your dog knows the commands STAY or WAIT at this point. If not, see the *Stays* chapter before proceeding. To add the *wait* to the retrieve, restrain your dog by the collar, command WAIT, and throw your dumbbell. Use your CR and a piece of food when he *waits* successfully. Release him to get the dumbbell with your *retrieve* command. As he waits more reliably, feed him less frequently. Some dogs focus on getting the food reward without doing the retrieve. These dogs may require a little push towards the dumbbell. If this happens too often, you may need to build a more focused retrieve by restraining him as described earlier. A correction of some sort may be appropriate at this time. Corrections are discussed in a later section.

Once your dog has learned the individual parts (the wait, the retrieve, the carry, the sit in front and hold, and the release), continue to combine them until you have an entire ring-ready retrieve. **If any of the balance points are weak, the entire retrieve will be weak.** Continue to concentrate on the weak parts until the exercise is balanced.

Handler Responsibilities

You have various responsibilities when showing in an Open class. You must throw your dumbbell at least twenty feet for the *Retrieve on the Flat* and at least eight feet beyond the jump for the *Retrieve Over the High Jump*. You should practice your throws so that your dumbbell lands in approximately the same location each time. A good way to practice this is to use a target such as a hula hoop.

Most people throw their dumbbell underhand, though the rules allow you to throw overhand. There are many different ways to grip and throw a dumbbell. You may try placing (A) your thumb on the top of the bell, (B) your fingers on the top of the bell, (C) your thumb closest to you or (D) gripping the dumbbell by the bar (Fig. 14.14).

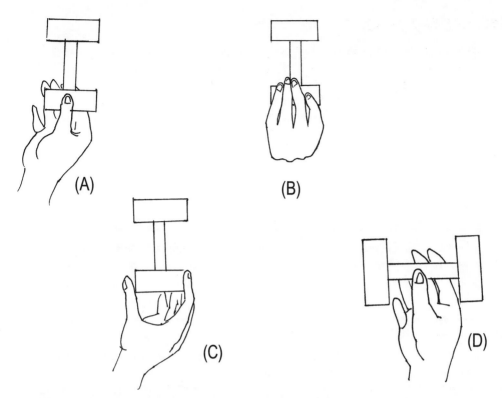

Figure 14.14 There are many different ways to grip and throw a dumbbell. You may try (A) placing your thumb on the top of the bell, (B) your fingers on the top of the bell, (C) your thumb closest to you, or (D) gripping the dumbbell by the bar. Note: these are all top views.

Sometimes throwing the dumbbell using a particular grip causes less bounce. Throws into grass are likely to bounce less than ones on matted floors and plastic dumbbells usually bounce more than wooden ones.

If you use a *STAY* signal before the throw, you must signal with the hand that is not holding the dumbbell.

A dumbbell with flat ends is more likely to land on its end than one with more rounded ends. If your dumbbell has flat ends, be sure your dog will pick it up when you place it on its end.

Decide where you will hold your dumbbell once you have taken it from your dog and during his finish. You may hold it either with both hands or with one hand. Adele holds her dumbbell in front with her right hand and drops her left hand back to her side so it is in the same place as during the non-retrieve exercises. Judy holds hers with two hands and leaves it in front of her while her dog finishes. Experiment to see how you are most comfortable and which position produces the best finishes.

Corrections

Here are some reasons your dog might not complete a retrieve:

- Forgets to retrieve due to a distraction.
- Lacks confidence to overcome a distraction.
- Cannot locate the dumbbell.
- Chooses not to retrieve.
- Chooses not to return.

What should you do when your dog does not retrieve? If your dog truly understands the retrieve and chooses not to do so, it is appropriate to add a correction. However, a correction at the wrong time can cause or add to your dog's confusion. **Be certain your dog understands the total retrieve before adding any form of correction.** You may not care to correct your dog and, of course, this is your choice. A correction used successfully for one dog may be completely useless for another. Some dogs respond well to a gentle push on the head while others require an ear pinch to make it clear that they must retrieve. **Begin with the mildest correction before progressing to a stronger one. Corrections should motivate your dog, not discourage him from trying.**

The following corrections are listed in the order that we consider the mildest to the strongest. Remember that your dog may not view them in the same way!

- Take your dog by the collar and put the dumbbell in his mouth.
- Push the back of his head towards the dumbbell.
- "Goose" him on the rear after your retrieve command (Fig. 14.15).
- Give a leash correction towards the dumbbell.
- Twist his collar towards the dumbbell.
- Pinch his ear towards the dumbbell.

When you introduce any of these corrections, hold the dumbbell in your hand. Gradually move the dumbbell to the floor and work toward short distance throws. Your correction will usually be more successful if your dog is on lead. Initially, you may need to put the dumbbell into his mouth after a correction so you can praise him for the correct behavior. Experiment with various corrections to see which is the most successful for you and your dog.

Figure 14.15 Give your dog a "goose" in the rear to speed up his retrieve.

The Ear Pinch

If you have shaped all the steps of the retrieve and your dog still acts as if retrieving is optional, you may choose to teach an ear pinch retrieve correction. Using the ear pinch to reinforce the retrieve is no different than using a leash pop to reinforce a *recall*. A correction is used after the dog has learned the basics of an exercise, but chooses not to do it on command. Many trainers who use the ear pinch like it because of the clarity of the correction.

Make sure you have not skipped any steps and that your dog understands what the retrieve command means. If your dog does not already know how to take the dumbbell, he will see the ear pinch as pain that he doesn't understand how to escape.

A properly used ear pinch is simply negative reinforcement. When your dog takes the dumbbell, the discomfort ceases. Many trainers swear it is the only way to have a reliable retrieve in the ring. We disagree with this statement, because we know many successful retrievers who have never been ear-pinched. We also realize there are times when this type of correction is appropriate. We try to use as little force as possible in all of our training and encourage you to do the same.

Judy had to ear pinch Alec, her Whippet. He was proofed through the flat retrieve and one day decided not to pick up the dumbbell and left the training area. She quit training for the day and went back to the same exercise the next day. Same behavior from her dog. Exit, stage left! Judy did try the lesser corrections before resorting to the ear pinch. She sat down in a chair with her food nearby and took Alec's collar and ear in her left hand. (Either hand will do, but the dumbbell is in the other hand.) She put her thumb inside his ear, down fairly deep, and pinched it between her thumb and first finger (Fig. 14.16). The other fingers held his collar, making Alec stay in a sit. She held the dumbbell in her right hand and pressed it against his lips. When he opened his mouth to yip, she pushed the dumbbell in, stopped pinching, and used her CR. He did it the next time without a pinch and received the food as well as the CR. He has gladly retrieved the dumbbell ever since. He understood all the steps, but thought he had a choice. Silly dog!

The most important elements to keep in mind when adding a correction are:

- Is it quick?
- Is the correction effective (i.e., is your dog more likely to retrieve the next time)?
- Do you have to use it frequently? If so, it is not an effective correction.

Figure 14.16 Giving the ear pinch with the thumb inside the ear.

Proofing

When you first introduce proofing, do so gradually. It is best to start with mild distractions so your dog will succeed.

Ideas for proofing include the following:

- Throw the dumbbell near a friend. She can stand near the dumbbell, put her foot on it or sit on the floor nearby. Also, have your friend stand between you and the dumbbell, hiding it from your dog's view.

- Throw it near or under a baby gate.

- Throw it against a wall.

- Throw or place the dumbbell on end.

- Throw it near distractions on the floor, such as toys, leaves, hairballs, or small scraps of paper.

- Throw it alongside a high jump. This teaches your dog not to jump during the *Retrieve on the Flat*.

- Use nonsense words instead of your retrieve command. This helps prevent anticipation. If your dog starts to retrieve when you use the wrong command, keep him on a leash so you can stop him. Reinforce him with your CR and food when he *waits* correctly.

The Retrieve Over the High Jump

The *Retrieve Over the High Jump* is just like the *Retrieve on the Flat*, except that your dog must jump the high jump on the way out to the dumbbell and again on the way back to you. The jump is sized according to your dog's height and breed.

When your dog is reliably doing the *Retrieve on the Flat* and he comfortably jumps a high jump that is two-thirds his full height (see *Jumping* chapter), begin to teach the *Retrieve Over the High Jump*.

First, teach him to carry the dumbbell over the jump. This should be done before he actually does the full retrieve over the jump. The weight of the dumbbell in the dog's mouth changes his center of gravity and makes jumping more difficult for some dogs. If you teach your dog to carry the dumbbell over the jump *before* adding the full retrieve over the high jump, he will be more confident with the entire exercise.

Start with a low jump, between four and sixteen inches high, depending on the height of your dog. Have your dog take the dumbbell and encourage him to hop over the jump with you. Next, if he knows how to *stay*, leave him in a *Sit-stay* with the dumbbell in his mouth. Step over the jump yourself and then call him to you with your *jump* command. Gradually increase the height until he carries the dumbbell over a full-height jump.

To begin the actual *Retrieve Over the High Jump*, return to using a low jump. Your dog should be able to see the dumbbell land on the other side of the jump. You may wish to have him on a six-foot or a retractable leash when you teach this.

Stand about eight feet away from the jump and restrain your dog by the collar or leash. Toss the dumbbell over the jump, move slowly towards the jump as soon as you throw it, and continue to move with him after the throw. This keeps him moving towards the jump. Release your dog as the dumbbell lands. Use your JUMP command, followed by your *retrieve* command as soon as your dog lands on the other side of the jump. After he has gone over the jump, walk up to it. When he picks up the dumbbell, command COME, tap the center of the jump to focus him, command JUMP again and, as he commits to jumping, move backwards out of his way.

To sum up, we use these commands:

- JUMP
- GET IT
- COME
- JUMP

Eventually, your dog must do each of these *balance points* with a single command. We use the command JUMP to distinguish between the *Retrieve on the Flat* (for which we use TAKE IT or GET IT) and the *Retrieve Over the High Jump*.

Angled Jumps

Once your dog retrieves reliably when you throw the dumbbell straight over the jump, prepare him for a dumbbell that bounces off-center. Practice angled retrieves in which you throw it to the right or left of center. When the dumbbell lands far enough off to the side, most dogs will try the obvious and head straight to it without jumping. Be prepared for this error. As the angle increases, walk towards the jump with your dog and stay there to direct him back over on his return. Keep the jump low until he can reliably jump from these angles. Later add height to the jump, but begin again with straight throws before proceeding to angled throws.

Solving Retrieve Problems

A number of errors can lose points during a retrieve exercise. You can solve most of these by carefully teaching all the steps outlined earlier. It is also important to continue to reinforce each *balance point:*

- The *wait.*
- The retrieve with a non-fumbling, fast pickup.
- The *hold.*
- The return.
- The *front.*
- The release.
- The *finish* with the dumbbell in your hand(s).

When your dog has retrieve problems, you must first identify any weak spots. Concentrate on the weak spots separately from the rest of the exercise until he consistently performs properly. Then put them back into the complete exercise.

Some common retrieve problems are:

- Your dog does not leave your side to retrieve on your first command.
- Your dog forgets the dumbbell because of a distraction.
- Your dog does not go directly to the dumbbell.

Some dogs fail to go on the first command simply because they don't understand what to do. This should improve with time and repetition as your dog gains confidence. Some don't go because they get distracted and are not listening to you. If he is distracted because of fear, work to build his confidence. You might try doing your retrieve work in a quieter location for a while. If your dog is simply paying too much attention to the environment, a correction is appropriate.

Other dogs don't go because they fear a correction for not waiting long enough or, conversely, expect a piece of food for waiting. In either case, a gentle push on the back of the head toward the dumbbell will usually solve the problem. If you have a dog who is waiting for assistance, try some of the restraint techniques outlined earlier, and then gradually fade the help you give him.

If your dog forgets to come back with the dumbbell, a correction is probably appropriate. Again, make sure the forgetfulness is not due to fear. A frightened dog may act timid and appear stressed. He moves slowly, often with both head and tail lowered. He looks at the dumbbell, then at the distraction, and decides that fleeing the situation is a better choice than retrieving. If fear is causing the problem, try quietly and calmly taking your dog to the dumbbell. Put it in his mouth and run backwards. Praise cheerfully and give him a treat. A dog of this type benefits from slow and careful proofing. If fear is not the cause, use one of the corrections discussed earlier.

If your dog does not go directly to the dumbbell, proof some more. This will make sure he understands that he needs to concentrate on the dumbbell and ignore the distractions. Try shorter throws or add an appropriate correction when needed.

Poor Wait

If your dog goes to retrieve without waiting for your command or signal, reinforce the *wait* portion more frequently. Sometimes, continuous feeding on the *wait* will relax him enough to cure the problem.

Other suggestions for fixing a poor *wait* include:

- Put a light leash under your left foot to stop his premature retrieve. Your dog will correct himself if he starts too soon. When he *waits* correctly, lift your foot when you send him so he doesn't correct himself.

- Use some nonsense words instead of your retrieve command. Stop anticipation with a leash, as above, or with a verbal reprimand. Be sure to reinforce him with a CR and a treat when he stops himself without your help!

- Have a helper give the same instructions that a judge would give in the ring — "Throw it" (you give your WAIT command and/or signal after this instruction from the judge). "Send your dog" (you give your retrieve command).

- Say the judge's instructions out loud when training alone with your dog.

Marking the Dumbbell

It is important for your dog to watch where the dumbbell lands; otherwise he will have to do a blind retrieve. Dogs with a strong chase instinct usually watch where the dumbbell goes. Others need to be taught how to *mark* (see *Fundamental Words* chapter).

Once your dog understands how to *mark* food, temporarily add the MARK command as you throw the dumbbell. When he looks where it lands every time, stop using the extra command.

Poor Pickups

Poor pickups include:

- Fumbling the pickup.
- Picking up the dumbbell by an end.
- Pouncing on the dumbbell with his front feet.
- Pushing the dumbbell around with his nose before picking it up.
- Hesitating and looking around before the pick up.

A dog who makes any of these mistakes does not have a clear understanding of how to pick up the dumbbell correctly. Many dogs whose owners have trained a play retrieve have these problems. A dog with a strong prey drive is also likely to do some or all of these things, particularly pouncing. Go back and review the *take* from many locations, starting with him taking the dumbbell from your hand.

If excessive prey drive is a problem, place the dumbbell on the floor, return to your dog, and release him to retrieve. Work on placing the dumbbell for several weeks before you throw it again. The sight of the flying dumbbell incites these dogs to crazy retrieving. Some other solutions include:

- Place the dumbbell on flattened chicken wire, which negatively reinforces his pouncing paws. Start by placing the dumbbell on the wire, return to your dog, and send him. Then toss it out and have a friend place it on the wire.

- Keep your dog on a six-foot or retractable leash so you can stop him from completing the retrieve as soon as he starts to pounce. Go out yourself to pick up the dumbbell and start over.

- Give a COME command just as your dog is reaching for the dumbbell. Be careful here, as he might skip the pickup.

- Place the dumbbell close to a wall, a gate, or in a corner. Your dog will naturally slow down.

Patterning your dog this way for several weeks should fix the problem.

Start these corrections with the dumbbell about six feet away and gradually extend the distance. Go slowly in the *take* phase of teaching, as this is a critical step for these enthusiastic dogs. Proper use of your CR and food is also important.

Hold Problems

A poor hold includes mistakes such as:

- *Rolling*: Your dog rotates the dumbbell with his tongue.
- *Mild mouthing*: He moves it around in his mouth.
- *Chomping*: He flips it to his molars and chews enthusiastically.
- *Chattering*: He chatters his teeth on the bar of the dumbbell.
- *Dropping*.

Dogs who do any of these do not understand how to *hold* correctly. Concentrate on teaching your dog how to hold the dumbbell under any circumstance. Reintroduce the retrieve itself only when he can do the *hold* exercises explained earlier. For a persistent chattering problem, check for teeth problems, especially in an older dog.

Poor Returns

Poor returns include:

- Looking around after picking up the dumbbell.
- Trotting slowly or walking on the return.
- Arcing on the return — not returning in a straight line to you.
- Shaking the glove.

A dog who makes any of these mistakes needs to learn that a fast return to you earns a treat. It may help for him to carry his dumbbell while you train recalls. Try having him face different directions. Start with him facing you and gradually move around until you are calling him while he is facing away from you (Fig. 14.17).

Put your dog on a regular or a retractable leash to help speed up the return. This gives him less time to make some of these mistakes. As soon as he picks up the dumbbell, give a COME command, followed by a pop on the leash toward you. Practice from six feet first, gradually extending the distance.

Figure 14.17 Call your dog while he is facing away from you.

Poor Fronts

The dog who does not sit correctly in front of you while holding the dumbbell might make these errors:

- Sits too far away.
- Sits on your feet.
- Bumps or crashes into you.
- Sits at an extreme angle.

A dog with one of these problems often sits the same way without the dumbbell. If this is the case, work first on curing the problem without it. If your dog sits too far away on the *front*, it may help to take a step backward just before he sits. To have any effect, you must do this for several weeks, not just for a day or two.

Spitting food to your dog when he sits in front may inadvertently cause him to sit too far away. This is especially true if you have a small dog. A chute with a back bar should help fix this problem (see *Fronts and Finishes* chapter).

If your dog sits on your feet and nudges you with the dumbbell, or worse, crashes into you, try taking a small step towards him when he is four to six feet away. A SIT command as you step towards him may help, too. The point at which you give the command will depend on how fast your dog is returning. Try placing a piece of plastic gutter or a broad jump board on end in front of your feet. This blocks access to your feet. Bending your knees slightly so your dog hits your knees may also help.

A dog who retrieves with enthusiasm, joy, and precision is a thrill to watch. It is a vital part of advanced obedience; make it a fun part!

For information on our video, *Positively Fetching*, which teaches the retrieves using the methods in this chapter, please see the order form at the back of this book.

Scent Discrimination

he *Scent Discrimination* exercise requires your dog to select the correct article by scent alone and to retrieve it promptly (see *Equipment* chapter for article information). He should go out to the articles and return at a brisk trot or gallop and complete the exercise as in the *Retrieve on the Flat*. The AKC ring exercise requires five leather and five metal articles.

Before starting any Scent Discrimination work, your dog should know how to retrieve a stationary metal and a stationary leather article. You need to train the stationary retrieve since articles are not thrown so the thrill of the chase is gone. If you have not already done so, review how to teach your dog to retrieve each type of article (see *Retrieve* chapter). If your dog does not retrieve articles reliably, *Scent Discrimination* will be much more difficult to teach. This is one reason we encourage introducing the articles and gloves, along with the dumbbell, early in the retrieve training.

Note: A common way to describe the set of articles from which your dog selects your scented one is "the pile of articles" or simply "the pile." This is not literal — the articles are not piled on top of one another! They are placed randomly about six inches apart.

Proper timing of any correction is essential for article work and usually requires an instructor who has "been there, done that" to help you. We recommend that you avoid correcting your dog at the pile unless you know exactly what you are doing. You can ruin a good dog with an ill-timed correction at the scent article pile. Again, it may be best to find an instructor to help if you have never taught scent work before and are having problems.

The balance points for *Scent Discrimination* include:

- Set dog up to watch articles placed by steward.

- Turn dog away from the articles and set up in heel position near a chair which holds the articles you will scent (Fig. 15.1).

- Sit dog in heel position during article scenting.

- Sit dog in heel position during article placement by judge.

- Send dog to pile:

    You and your dog turn 180° in place, and your dog sits in heel position. Another command sends the dog.

    -or-

    Do a *flying send*, in which you and your dog turn 180° in place. Dog does not stop.

- Dog gallops or trots briskly to pile.

Figure 15.1 Set your dog up in heel position near a chair that is used to hold the articles you will be scenting.

- Dog hunts for your scented article.

- Dog retrieves correct article.

- Dog returns to you.

- Dog fronts and holds article.

- Dog releases article to you.

- Dog finishes.

Your dog can learn many of these *balance points* long before you teach the scent work. This will allow you to concentrate on the scent work when you are ready to introduce it.

Using a Clock Face

Many trainers refer to the article pile as a clock face, with 12 o'clock farthest away from you, 6 o'clock closest to you, and so on (Fig. 15.2). Judges usually have favorite areas they place each article; commonly 12 o'clock, 6 o'clock, or in the center.

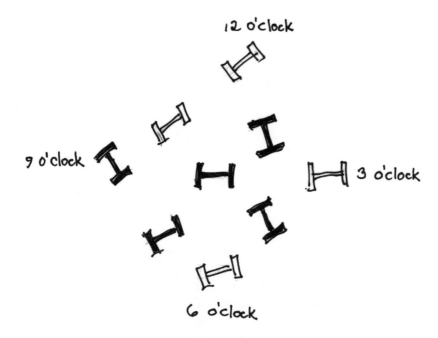

Figure 15.2 Many trainers refer to the article pile as though it were a clock face, with 12 o'clock farthest away from you, 6 o'clock closest, and so on.

Around The Clock

Our favorite method of teaching scent work is the *Around The Clock Method of Scent Discrimination* by well-known trainer, Janice DeMello. We recommend that you buy her video and teach your dog *Scent Discrimination* this way. Using this method, you train with a whole set of articles from the beginning. One of the goals of her carefully laid out program is to teach the dog to follow a search pattern as he looks for the correct article. "Squeeze cheese," or other sticky food like peanut butter, is spread on the bar of the article. This gives your dog strong motivation to go out to the pile and use his nose. As your dog catches on, you gradually decrease the amount of cheese. The video tape discusses a variety of common errors, as well as solutions for these problems. Information on ordering the tape is in Appendix B.

We have found this method to be the best one we have ever used, and it should be followed carefully for success. DO NOT skip steps! We have encountered problems when trying to modify the program for our dogs. We do not recommend changes for this reason.

Hot or Cold Scent?

There are two schools of thought about the use of *hot* or *cold scent*. Hot scent is giving the article a lot of scent by rubbing it until you can feel the heat. Cold scent is touching the article lightly, perhaps for just two or three seconds. Judy has used both; Adele has used only hot scent. You will use hot scent if you train articles using the *Around the Clock* method. Hot scent works well for many dogs, but yours may do better with less scent. Once you have trained your dog to do the exercise, experiment to see which method works best for him.

Be sure that you scent the bar only and not the ends. Your scent is more likely to be transmitted to another article when you put it on the ends.

Tie-Down Method

Before learning of the *Around the Clock* method, we used either a peg board or a tie-down mat to teach *Scent Discrimination*. We'll describe this method here for those who choose to use it instead of the *Around the Clock* method. You will need a piece of peg board or rubber matting, like that used in the ring. Your dog learns to take the correct article because the wrong ones are tied down. This prevents him from retrieving an incorrect one, as only your scented article is untied. We prefer to use the matting because it is easier to carry around and it duplicates the surface your dog will be working on if you show indoors. The peg board is heavy and awkward to carry, and many dogs won't walk on the surface. However, it is easier to tie your articles to a peg board and, unlike matting, the pegboard should withstand any attempts by a strong dog to yank an article free.

For simplicity, we will talk of training with a mat, although a peg board might be the best choice for your dog.

Dogs have a very acute sense of smell, and the problem is not so much teaching them *to* smell, but rather *what* to smell. Most people start teaching this exercise with a metal article, because metal has no strong scent of its own. This makes it easier to apply a strange scent. In addition, many dogs dislike picking up a metal article, so by starting with a metal one, you accustom your dog to it early in training. Metal articles can also be cleaned better than leather ones once your dog learns the routine.

You must first tie one, two, or three clean metal articles to your mat. Be sure to tie them down tightly at first! Tie these down the night before you start your training so there is less of your scent on them. You could also wear rubber gloves when tying the articles to the mat. Some dogs recognize the correct article by the absence of the string. If your dog does this, tie a string to the correct article as well. Tying the articles to the mat with clear fishing line sometimes prevents this problem.

We use the same two articles throughout the early teaching. Once the dog understands the concept of scenting, begin to scent fresh articles each training session.

To begin, place the mat with its articles about six feet from you and your dog. Add some food scent to your hands by holding some strong-smelling food such as hot dog or cheese. Rub this scent on the bar of the untied article. If you want to use hot scent, rub heavily to heat up the bar of the article. You may also put some food on the article itself. Food like Easy Cheese™ or peanut butter works well. Tell your dog to WAIT and place the scented article on the mat among the unscented ones. Step back to your dog and send him to retrieve the scented article. We use the command FIND IT to send the dog to the pile. Once he *indicates* the correct article, which he might do by stopping to lick the food or sniffing the food scent, we use his familiar retrieve command, like GET IT or TAKE IT. You can then eliminate the GET IT command when he understands the exercise.

Some dogs catch on to this game quickly. Others seem to need months before the light bulb goes on. Be patient! This is the only exercise in competition obedience where the trainer is not really sure what the dog is doing.

Do not always tell your dog he is correct each time he makes the right choice. He will learn to wait for your cue and not gain the confidence he needs to do the work himself. Vary the time in the exercise when you praise your dog as follows:

- As soon as he indicates the correct article.
- After he picks it up.
- One-quarter of the way back to you.
- One-half of the back to way to you.
- Three-quarters of the way back to you.
- When he gets to you.

Do not demand fronts and finishes early in the training, as this complicates the task and adds unneeded stress to the exercise.

Whether you tie down any leather articles among the metal ones or separate the two types depends on how quickly your dog learns the task and whether he is a "leather happy" or a "metal happy" dog. Some dogs will only bring back one type, so you may need to train the type he doesn't like separately and for a longer time. If your dog favors one type, use two different mats, one for leather and one for metal.

As your dog learns to sniff and reject the unscented articles on the mat or board, tie down more articles. When you add more articles, add them at the end of a session so that they will be free of your scent for the next training time. Also begin to use less food. The goal is for your dog to understand that he is smelling *your* scent and not the food. As your dog progresses, slowly withdraw all of the food scent.

We occasionally exchange the tied down articles for ones which have not been used as often. Again, change them at the end of a session so they will have aired out adequately by the next day.

Vary the places you put your articles among the tied down ones. Rotate the mat now and then before adding the scented one. Most dogs have favorite areas in the pile from which they retrieve. Place your scented article in his least favorite place more often. Some dogs dislike an article in the center of the pile, because it means they have to step between the other articles. Try spreading the "wrong" articles farther apart to make this easier.

Turn, Sit, and Send, or Flying Send?

When a judge takes your scented article from you and places it in the pile, you and your dog must face away from the pile so that neither of you sees where the judge places the article. You then have two ways in which to send your dog to the pile:

- The *turn, sit, and send*: You and your dog turn 180° in place using your HEEL or TURN command, and your dog sits in heel position. You may turn either to your right or left, though you must turn the same way for each article. You then use another command for him to FIND IT.

- The *flying send*, in which you turn clockwise 180° in place and your dog wraps around you as he does during a *dizzy spin*, and immediately trots or gallops to the pile.

We consider the *turn, sit, and send* the safer method for inexperienced dogs and handlers. This method helps your dog focus on where he is to go because he sees the articles before you send him to retrieve.

The *flying send* avoids the possibility of a crooked sit on the turn and gives your dog more momentum for the retrieve. We see two problems with the *flying send:* arcing and rushing. Your dog is supposed to turn and run straight to the articles and should be penalized for *arcing* or making a wide turn. If your dog is highly motivated, he may rush out and grab the first article he comes to. This method may be too exciting for some dogs.

The *flying send* is essentially a *dizzy spin* that your dog runs out of while you stand in place. Set up your dog in heel position. Use your HURRY command, spin halfway around, and throw food or a toy directly in front of you. You must turn in place, and your dog should wrap tightly around you. Use a gutter or a broad jump board just to your right before you turn so your dog does not arc (Fig. 15.3). If you teach this tight *flying send* correctly from the beginning, it should motivate your dog to retrieve a stationary article with more speed. We do not use this method but might consider it with a dog who wraps well but moves slowly to the pile.

Do not add either turn until your dog can scent and retrieve the correct article reliably.

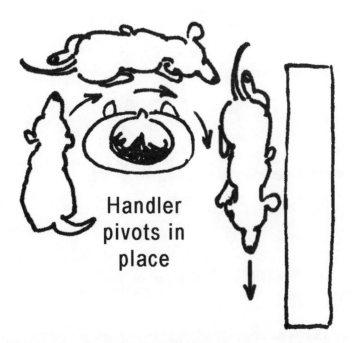

Figure 15.3 Use a gutter or a broad jump board just to your right before you turn so your dog does not arc during a *flying send.*

Proofing Articles

If your dog becomes stressed when you put your scented articles in different places, place the first one in the area of the pile where he sniffs first. He should find it immediately, which builds his confidence. Move the scented article to different areas, building on your dog's earlier successes. For instance: if your dog always starts at 1 o'clock and goes to the right (clockwise) around the pile, place your first article at 1 o'clock, the second one at 2 o'clock, and so on (Fig. 15.4).

When you teach articles using a tie-down method, it is a good idea to take the mat to different locations to proof the exercise while the articles are still tied down. You don't want your dog to slow down or stop when he gets confused, and using the mat makes the exercise more familiar.

Add someone else's scent to the articles that are still tied down, so your dog will still be successful while working under stress in this new situation. **Being "right" builds confidence!** When adding a new scent, have the person touch the articles lightly between her thumb and forefinger. Gradually have your helper add more scent as your dog shows you he understands this new part of the exercise.

Some dogs learn to do this exercise by trying to move the articles with their noses and rejecting the ones that don't move. Once your dog seems to understand the scenting, lengthen the strings on the articles,

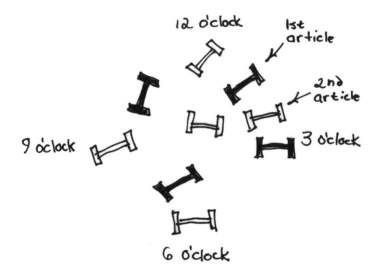

Figure 15.4 If your dog always starts at 1 o'clock and goes to the right (clockwise) around the pile, place your first article at 1 o'clock, the second one at 2 o'clock, and so on.

but keep them tied down. He may pick up the wrong article, but the string will either stop his retrieve or jerk the article out of his mouth. This can be a strong correction for some dogs!

When your dog consistently retrieves the correct article without trying to retrieve any tied ones, untie the strings, one or two at a time. Leave them in place since many dogs look to see which articles don't have strings attached. Continue until all are untied. Gradually fade the strings and the mat from the exercise.

If your dog has a solid, proofed retrieve, he should be able to do articles in the same brisk manner in which he retrieves the dumbbell. If his dumbbell retrieve is poor, his article retrieves will be also. *Any retrieve problem should be addressed separately from the scenting requirements.*

Be careful when proofing articles, because it may add too much stress for some dogs. Although we want the dog to work under duress, some difficult proofing may only make him hate the exercise or quit working. We recommend the following proofs:

- Place articles near a jump.
- Place articles near a baby gate.
- Use extra articles to make your dog search longer.
- Place one article, either the one you have scented or a different one, away from the pile.
- Place all of the articles in a straight line. There are many variations you can use, including the direction of the line and the direction of the articles within the line.
- Place the articles very close together or very far apart.
- Arrange the articles in different orderly configurations, such as different letters, squares, triangles, etc.
- Have someone stand close to the pile. When your dog works well with a person near the articles, add a dog near the pile.
- Have someone sit close to the pile.
- Have someone stand in the pile.
- Have someone sit in the pile.
- Put distractions near the articles, such as small scraps of paper, a toy, or a colander with food under it.
- Put an article or two on end. This is especially important for a dog who works fast and scatters articles in the process.

- Have someone toss a dumbbell nearby just as your dog gets to the articles.

- Have someone give extraneous commands while your dog is scenting the pile.

Above all, build your dog's confidence! Don't be afraid to reduce the number of articles or to shorten your distance from the pile. Sometimes you may have to extract the hard part, whatever it happens to be, from the whole exercise, and focus only on that part. Don't be afraid to work on leash. Some dogs need the confidence of a leash or, conversely, a correction to come quickly out of the pile on the return. This should be done carefully and probably with the help of a knowledgeable instructor.

Scent Discrimination Problems

The following mistakes are common during *Scent Discrimination* training:

- Retrieving the wrong article.

- Going to or returning from the pile slowly.

- Tasting the articles instead of scenting. This is especially tempting for dogs who are just learning scent work.

- Picking up and dropping either the correct or an incorrect article.

- Not starting to work immediately (i.e., circling the pile one or more times before starting to sniff).

- Sniffing the floor for a prolonged time.

- Air scenting.

- Refusing to pick up the correctly indicated article.

- Not leaving the handler.

- Doing a go-out instead of going to the pile.

- Jumping a jump instead of going to the pile.

- Taking the correct article to the judge.

Before you can solve a problem, you must pinpoint its reason. Your reaction to your dog's retrieval of an incorrect article will depend in part on how you originally taught the exercise. If you used the *Around The Clock* method, you will probably use the corrections described on the video tape. If your articles are still tied to a mat, the mat will make the correction for you. Once the articles are off the mat, you must have a plan for how to react when your dog makes a mistake. It is extremely important that you do not overreact when your dog brings back the wrong article. You have no idea what your dog may be scenting on any given day. Adele usually uses a verbal AH-AH correction when her dog has actually picked up and started back with an incorrect article. For some dogs, especially those without the proper correction foundation, this may be too much of an aversive. You may want to let him bring the wrong one all the way to you, take it calmly, and send him back to the pile. Judy prefers this latter method.

If your dog chooses the wrong article more than once, we recommend that you make the exercise easier for him

- Place fewer articles out so your dog has less chance of making a mistake.
- Work the exercise without anyone else's scent on the articles.
- Work in a quiet location.

Moving too slowly to or from the pile is a retrieve problem, but the stress of scenting can make it worse. Take the scented article out of the pile and work on faster retrieves with this single article. If your dog returns slowly with his article, it may help to use some special food each time he returns. Canned cat food and squeeze cheese are favorites. You may also try throwing an object between your legs as you did when working on a fast recall (see *Recalls* chapter). Your dog may drop the article, but again, you are working on a fast return and not a *hold*. You may also need to add a correction on a regular or retractable leash. Use your COME command, followed by a pop on the leash to speed him up. You may add your CR anytime, but save your treats until he delivers the article to your hand. And *do not* make him do *fronts* and *finishes*; instead CR and release when he gets to you.

Dogs who taste the articles usually outgrow this habit. Initially, ignore this behavior and see if your dog stops on his own. If you have been using food scent, try to get rid of it and teach him to work for your scent alone. When he is successful, he gets the food reward from you.

Picking up and dropping an article is usually a retrieve problem. Your dog has not mastered the *hold,* and you need to go back and review this (see *Retrieve* chapter). Dropping an article may also happen when a dog has been praised the moment he indicates or picks up the correct article and then the praise is withdrawn. When he is not sure he has selected correctly, he drops the article. Be sure to vary the timing of your praise early in the scent training.

Dogs dawdle at the pile for various reasons. If your dog doesn't start using his nose right away, motivate him to get to work faster with some food on the correct article. If you hot-scent your article, but your dog prefers a "colder" scent on the article, he may circle the pile waiting for the right one to cool off. Try using less scent. Dogs who do not start to sniff immediately are often stressed and are delaying or avoiding doing the work. Scent work should be fun, but many dogs have been forced too soon to do work they do not understand. Go back and review your teaching steps to help your dog gain confidence.

Sniffing the floor is often an evasive technique. If your dog doesn't work, he can't make a mistake and risk a correction. Correcting an insecure dog at the pile can cause this sniffing problem. Proofing for scent work in strange places, where the surrounding scent is unfamiliar, will help some dogs who make this mistake.

If your dog understands the scenting part of the exercise, even indicates the correct article, but makes errors on the pickup, temporarily suspend the scenting portion of this exercise and concentrate on the retrieve — especially the pickup. The metal article retrieve is typically more problematic. Always check for teeth problems in a dog that has a problem with the metal article. Nine times out of ten, however, the problem is the retrieve.

Judy had a severe metal article problem with Alec. He would scent it but not retrieve it because he didn't want the metal in his mouth. With Adele's guidance, she went back to the initial shaping of the pickup using a tennis ball. Judy placed the metal article on the floor and held the tennis ball. If Alec wanted the tennis ball, he had to pick up the article. Because he had been shaped to do all his retrieve work, he knew the drill. It was only a couple of weeks before Judy was able to introduce the scented metal article back into the exercise. The ball is still part of his reward for a correct scent exercise.

Doing a go-out, jumping a jump instead of going to the pile, not leaving your side, or taking the right article to the judge are all retrieve problems. Your dog is not going directly to the articles and not returning directly to you. Take the article out of the pile and work on retrieve proofing with the jumps in place and/or another person in the ring. Also make it worth your dog's while to return to *you!*

Scent work should be fun for you and your dog, but remember that we do not fully understand how the dog discriminates between scents. That is why you need to be especially cautious when using any corrections. Be careful to proceed slowly when teaching the *Scent Discrimination* exercise and do not be afraid to back up and work on your basic retrieving skills.

Directed Retrieve

T he Utility *Directed Retrieve,* sometimes called the *glove exercise,* requires your dog to retrieve one of three gloves according to the direction and signal you give him. You stand in the middle of the ring, between the two jumps, with your dog in heel position. A ring steward places the gloves behind you, about three feet from the ring barrier, one in each corner and one directly behind you. When your back is to them, the gloves are numbered as follows (Fig. 16.1):

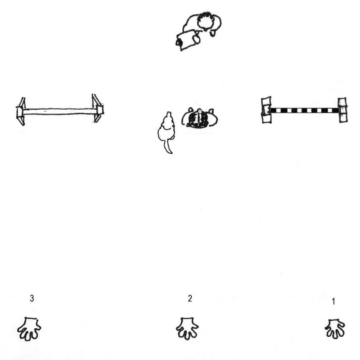

| 3 | 2 | 1 |

Figure 16.1 You stand in the middle of the ring, between the two jumps, with your dog in heel position. When your back is to them, the gloves are numbered in the order shown here. Note that this drawing is not to scale.

- Glove #1 is over your right shoulder.
- Glove #2 is behind you.
- Glove #3 is over your left shoulder.

The judge will tell you which of the three gloves your dog should retrieve. You and your dog pivot to face the correct glove and, with no further instruction from the judge, you signal and command your dog to retrieve it. He should return the glove to you as in the *Retrieve on the Flat*.

The balance points for the *Directed Retrieve* include:

- You and your dog set up in the middle of the ring between the jumps, facing away from where a steward will place the gloves.
- You both pivot to face a glove.
- You signal the correct direction and glove.
- Your dog marks the correct glove.
- He leaves you and goes to the correct glove.
- He retrieves the glove.
- He returns to you.
- He sits in front and holds the glove.
- He releases the glove to you.
- He finishes.

Your dog must have a solid mark in order to learn the glove exercise. He also must have a solid retrieve of a glove that is placed rather than thrown. Many young dogs get in the habit of mouthing or shaking the glove. This is easier to train correctly from the beginning than to fix later. If you already have this problem, go back and shape a solid *hold* as described in the *Retrieve* chapter.

When your dog is first learning this exercise, it will be easier for him to retrieve a glove that is bulkier than one that lies flat on the ground. One way to make a glove bulkier is to turn it halfway inside out. Another way is to stuff something inside it such as a tennis ball, another glove, or a piece of material. These methods make the glove more visible to your dog.

The Pivots

We introduced *pivots* and footwork in the *Combination Words* chapter. There are some details to add as you teach the *Directed Retrieve*. A correct pivot requires your dog to start in a sit, move with you as you turn, and sit in heel position when you stop. Work separately on the turning and sitting actions at first and then combine them. We use different commands for each turn; HEEL for glove one, TURN for glove two, and IN for glove three.

The pivots for gloves one and three are 135° from your starting position (Fig. 16.2). The pivot for glove two is 180°. You may choose to turn in either direction during the pivot. We normally turn to the right for gloves one and two and to the left for glove three. Your dog should keep his attention on you until you signal the glove with your left hand and arm. The footwork we use for each glove is explained in Figure 16.3.

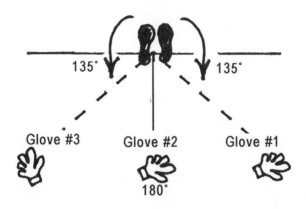

Figure 16.2 The *Directed Retrieve* pivots for gloves one and three are about halfway between ninety and one hundred and eighty degrees.

Allowable Mark Signals

When doing the *Directed Retrieve* in AKC trials, you are allowed to give your dog the direction with your left hand and/or arm along the right side of the dog's face. Your cue must be a single motion of your hand and a verbal command given either at the same time or immediately following the signal. We prefer to give the command just *after* we give the signal. This gives the dog a chance to see the glove before we send him. Using this option, the signal hand must remain motionless when you give your command. If you decide to use this method, make sure you don't move your hand as you give the verbal command. We see many beginning handlers use a double-pump signal — one signal to get the dog to mark and a second one to get the dog to retrieve the glove. The latter signal is not permissible and will cause you to fail the exercise.

Figure 16.3 The footwork for the glove pivots is shown here. **The black shoes show the foot that has just moved while the grey shoes show the foot that did not move.** Note that for each pivot, the second step points towards the glove (arrow). Just before you place your foot in step 2, glance up towards where the glove should be, and make any minor adjustments to make sure you are facing the glove. **Note: you must turn in place!**

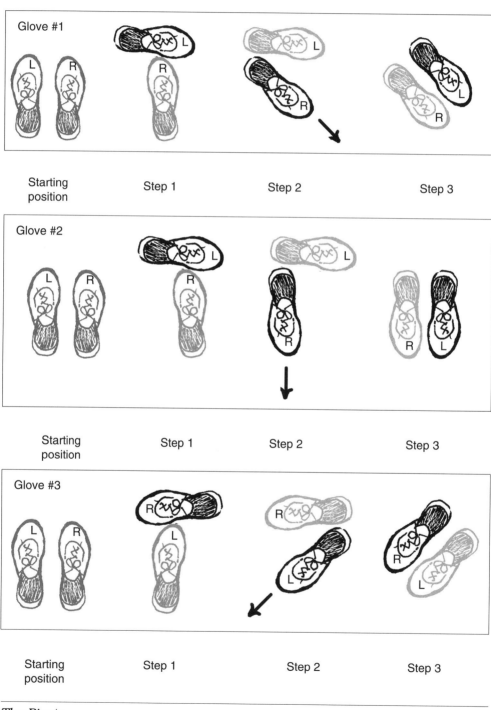

Glove #1

| Starting position | Step 1 | Step 2 | Step 3 |

Glove #2

| Starting position | Step 1 | Step 2 | Step 3 |

Glove #3

| Starting position | Step 1 | Step 2 | Step 3 |

The Pivots

You are allowed to bend your body and/or knees to give direction to a small dog. As soon as he leaves your side to retrieve, you must stand up and return both hands to your sides.

The Mark

We first explained how to teach MARK in the *Fundamental Words* chapter. Review that section if needed.

We teach and reward the glove mark separately from the retrieve. The *mark* will deteriorate if you only reward your dog after he has retrieved a glove. Be sure he understands the *mark* thoroughly before adding the retrieve to the exercise. When you add the retrieve, randomly use your CR and a treat for the *mark* to keep it strong.

A retractable leash is helpful when training gloves. It offers an easy way to stop a mistake. Use a mild AH-AH verbal reprimand before stopping your dog when he takes off in the wrong direction. If he responds quickly to your voice, he won't get a leash correction. If your dog won't work on a retractable leash or you are not familiar with it, use a six-foot leash. Do not yell at him or in any way discourage him. Just stop the dog and start again.

Use your left hand to throw a glove past the right side of your dog's face. This is the same motion you used when you threw the food to teach the *mark.* Leave your left hand beside your dog's face as you point to the glove (Fig. 16.4). Use your CR when he stares at the glove and let him

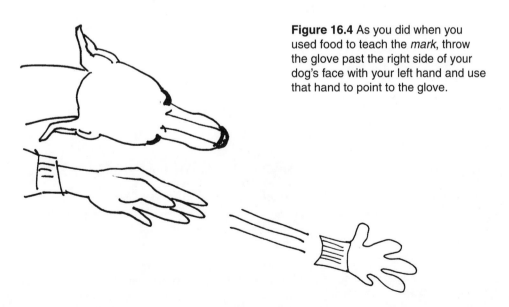

Figure 16.4 As you did when you used food to teach the *mark*, throw the glove past the right side of your dog's face with your left hand and use that hand to point to the glove.

retrieve it. The use of the CR is critical here! You want to reinforce your dog for looking at the glove, not just for retrieving it. Give him another CR and a treat when he returns with the glove.

Once your dog understands the *mark* when you throw a glove, place one about six feet away and tell him to MARK as you signal with your left hand along the right side of his head. If he can mark the glove when it is not thrown, repeat the exercise, but without your verbal cue. *Do not continue until your dog can mark a glove that is placed about six feet away, using only a hand signal.*

When your dog marks with only a hand signal, place two gloves about six feet away, one glove to your right and one to your left. You and the two gloves should form an equilateral triangle, so the gloves should be six feet apart (Fig. 16.5). Vary which glove you face, but keep both gloves visible to your dog. If he looks at the wrong glove or starts to move toward it, stop him at once and start over. Brief glances at the wrong glove are acceptable at this point, but do not use your CR until he *marks* correctly. This gives him the information he needs to go to the correct glove. If he keeps looking at the wrong one, make the next try easier. Step closer to the correct one or move the gloves farther apart. The sooner your dog learns that there will be more than one glove in view, the easier the rest of the exercise is to teach. Stop all wrong choices immediately.

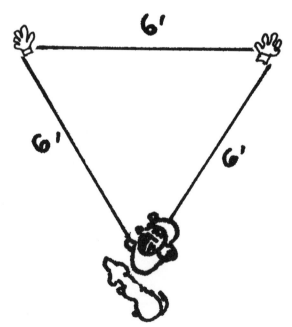

Figure 16.5 You and the two gloves form an equilateral triangle, so if you are six feet away, the gloves are six feet apart.

When your dog reliably retrieves the correct glove, teach him to follow your hand signal when you are not actually facing the glove he is to retrieve. This will teach him how to recover if he turns poorly in the ring and ends up not facing the correct glove. Face the midpoint between the two gloves, rather than directly toward one of them (Fig. 16.6). It is easier to teach your dog to mark the glove on your left as your hand will block his view of the glove to the right. You can help him by giving his muzzle a gentle push with your left hand in the direction you want him to look. Your dog should "sight" down your hand and lock his eyes on the glove at which you are pointing.

The glove on your right is typically harder for your dog because it requires that he ignore the one he can see on his left. When first training the glove on the right, reach under his muzzle with your right hand, pull his head toward the correct line, and gently help him *mark* the glove to your right (Fig. 16.7). If he continues to have trouble, move closer to the glove on your right or place the left one farther away. When he understands the *mark* better, without another glove in view, return to working in a triangle.

A final step is to face one glove and ask your dog to mark and retrieve the other glove.

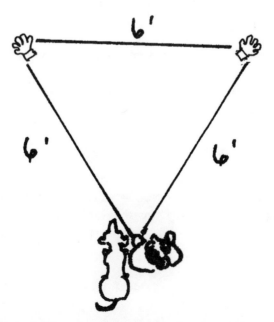

Figure 16.6 Face the midpoint between the two gloves, rather than directly toward one of them.

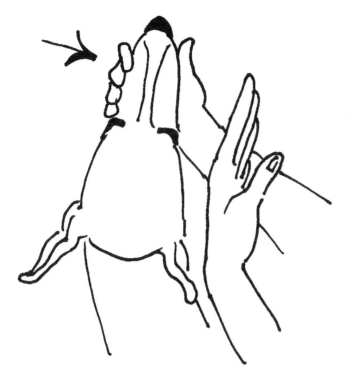

Figure 16.7 When first training your dog to mark a glove that is off to the right, if necessary, reach under his muzzle with your right hand, and gently help him *mark* the glove to your right.

Adding Distance and Gloves

When your dog understands the exercise up close, it is time to move the gloves farther away. As with all exercises, do this slowly and do not hesitate to back up if he has trouble. We generally work separately with gloves one and two, as well as gloves two and three before putting all three of them out at the same time. Work your pivots separately until your dog has a clear understanding of the *mark* and *retrieve* with all three gloves in place.

Problems with Gloves

Many dogs enjoy shaking the glove after they retrieve it. Unfortunately, this will lose points. Most dogs who shake vigorously also fail to return quickly to the handler. They are too busy "killing" the glove! If your dog is a shaker, go back and reteach the *hold* and *carry* (see *Retrieve* chapter).

Some dogs have the opposite problem. They try to pick up the glove by a single finger or by a tiny piece of the material. A dog with this problem will benefit from reworking a correct response to your TAKE IT command. Use a glove that is turned inside out or stuffed to make the pickup easier for a while.

Another problem is the dog who does incorrect pivots. This is a heeling problem and should be dealt with separately (see *Power Steering* and *Combination Words* chapters) from the *mark* and the *retrieve*. They should be taught early and reinforced frequently throughout your dog's obedience career. Good pivots are imperative for both the *Directed Retrieve* and the *Scent Discrimination* exercises.

Blind Retrieve

If you are planning to show your dog outdoors, teach him to do a *blind retrieve*. For a blind retrieve, you send your dog to retrieve a glove that he may not see until he is nearly upon it. Although the regulations say the gloves should be clearly visible, this is not always the case. Teaching a blind retrieve is fairly easy once your dog understands how to *mark*. If you train inside, place most of a glove under a corner of a mat about six feet away. If you train outside, place the glove in a small depression in the grass. Have your dog MARK the spot and, when you are reasonably sure that he sees the part sticking out, send him to retrieve it. Gradually hide more of the glove until he understands he must take the *mark* even though he can't see the glove. He must trust that it will be there when he gets to it. As your dog becomes familiar with the blind retrieve, go outside before training and drop several gloves into holes around your training area. Sometime during the training session, turn and send your dog on a blind retrieve to one of these hidden gloves. Many dogs like this blind retrieve work and it should improve the *mark*.

Proofing the Directed Retrieve

An interesting and fun test for your glove pivots is to work in the dark with a flashlight. Work this without your dog to see if *you* pivot accurately. Set the gloves out, stand at the appropriate distance from the gloves, and have a friend turn off the lights for you. Use the flashlight beam after you have made a turn, as you would to give the signal to your dog. See how close the beam comes to the glove. This may tell you a good deal about *your* turn and *your* mark. If the beam doesn't land immediately on the glove, you have some work to do on your pivots before you ask your dog to join you.

Other suggestions for proofing the *Directed Retrieve* include:

- Place gloves in a patch of sunlight.
- Place gloves against a white background.
- Have a decoy glove closer to you than the correct one.
- Have someone stand by the correct glove.
- Have someone stand by the incorrect glove(s).
- Have your dog retrieve a glove that was placed in a gated corner.
- Place several gloves in a circle or square, and stand with your dog at their center. After each correct retrieve, return that glove to its place and pivot counterclockwise to the next glove. It is easier when you pivot to your left because you can block your dog's view of the previously retrieved glove. After your dog has mastered pivoting to the left, pivot to the right (clockwise).
- Place the gloves out with the jumps in place. The purpose is to proof against your dog taking a jump on his return to you.
- Have your dog mark a glove that is about four feet away from you and then toss a decoy glove off to your right. The goal is for your dog to ignore this distraction and maintain his *mark*. You can toss this decoy yourself or have a friend drop decoys for you. Once he succeeds in ignoring one tossed to your right, toss a decoy to your left, either over his head or under his chin. Advance to tossing a decoy after your dog has left your side to retrieve. Start close to the correct one with the decoy farther away. Gradually reverse their respective positions.
- Attach a decoy glove to a retractable leash, which a friend slowly retracts, dragging the decoy glove across the floor while your dog marks the correct one. This sounds harder than it is! It is so obvious that most dogs quickly learn to ignore it. There are many variations of this exercise — your friend can drag the decoy toward a corner, away from you, toward you, and so on. Start with the decoy glove to your right, since you can block your dog's view of the decoy. When he does well ignoring it on your right, switch the decoy to your left.

The glove exercise is usually easy to teach and maintain, if you have taught the necessary foundation exercises. Remember, go back and review any weak balance points.

Jumping

Most dogs enjoy jumping over obstacles, whether a log in the woods, a puddle in your driveway, or a jump in the obedience ring. Some dogs and breeds, such as Dobermans and Whippets, are natural jumpers. Others, like some of the field breeds, were not bred to jump, so they need more careful training.

Exercises

Jumps are used in the following exercises:

- *Retrieve Over the High Jump* (Open)
- *Broad Jump* (Open)
- *Directed Jumping* (Utility)
- UKC Novice *Recall*

Commands

Adele uses the command JUMP for the *Retrieve Over the High Jump* in Open and both jumps in Utility. She uses OVER for the *Broad Jump*. Judy uses JUMP for all jumps. Other possibilities include:

- Jump it
- Hup
- Right/Left
- High/Bar

Jumping and Structure

Before beginning jumping training, you should assess your dog's conformation, especially shoulder layback and body type. These will help determine how well your dog will jump. Figure 17.1 shows two types of shoulders, those with good angulation and those that are too straight. A dog whose shoulders are too straight may injure himself jumping. This is especially true of the larger, heavier boned dogs. There is no "spring" in the shoulders to absorb the shock of landing, and the dog's spine takes the shock instead. We think it is a good idea to x-ray an obedience dog's elbows, shoulders, and hips before starting any jump training. These dogs are going to perform athletic maneuvers so you should be sure your partner is of sound body.

Figure 17.1 The shoulders on the left show correct angulation; the shoulders on the right are very straight.

Getting Started

We start to teach puppies the commands for jumping early; four to six months for most pups. Set the high and the bar jumps at four to eight inches for a medium to large puppy and two to four inches for a small puppy. We define a medium to large dog as one who will eventually jump 18 inches or higher and a small dog, 16 inches or lower. The height of the jump is not as important as the fact that there is a barrier to go over. We don't think puppies should be asked to jump very high. For some, the bar or broad jump board laid flat on the floor is enough.

Walk your dog up to the jump and let him investigate. Let him see and sniff the jump from both sides. This introduces the dog to the jump (Fig. 17.2). Use the bar and the high jumps, as well as one or two boards of the broad jump. We do not want the dog to develop a preference, so we introduce all three jumps right away.

Once you have introduced your dog to the jump, move about ten feet away from it. With your dog on your left side, though not necessarily in heel position, begin to walk slowly toward the jump. Just before you get to the jump, give your JUMP command and walk over the jump with your dog. You do not want your dog to watch you, but rather to focus on the

Figure 17.2 Introduce your dog to the jump.

jump and on what he is doing. Do not say anything except the command. You may wish to delay the command until your dog has some understanding of what he is to do.

It is important that you don't hurry your dog to the jump. If he is rushed, he may fling himself over trying to go too fast rather than lifting his body using his hind legs. Be careful not to interfere or lift the dog in any manner. Use your CR as soon as he commits to the jump and again when he has completed it. Continue to walk forward for at least ten feet beyond the jump and then reward him. By delaying the food reward, there is less interference with the smoothness of the jump, and your dog has a better chance to concentrate on the jump rather than on the food.

The jumps can be set up in a row or in a circle so you and your dog can move directly from one to another. *The dog should start at least ten feet back and do at least a ten-foot follow-through.* This should help develop smoothness, as well as get your dog into the habit of approaching from a distance and following through. Make sure he does not feel he has to fling his body over the jump. You want to see nice, easy strides to the jump and an easy arcing motion as he goes over it.

As quickly as possible, raise the jump height to about two thirds of what the full jumping height of your dog will be. At this point, you may want to walk past the jump rather than over it. A dog, especially a large one, will never learn to jump if he can simply walk over the jump. Do not raise the jumps for a dog under 18 months old to more than about 18 inches. This height would only be for a large dog who will eventually jump 26 inches or higher. Bones and joints are not fully developed until at least a year and a half, and you could cause serious or permanent injury.

Let your dog jump without a leash as soon as possible. He will more easily find his own stride over the jump. The best way to get your dog jumping off-lead is to leave him in a *Sit-stay* or have someone hold him while you do the following:

- Step over the jump.
- Turn and touch the top center of the jump.
- Tell your dog to FOCUS.
- CR when he looks at the jump.
- Back up and give your JUMP command.

You may want to stay close to the jump until you see your dog commit to jumping it, but remember that dogs do not have good depth perception. If your dog feels he is going to crash into you, and if you are not fast enough getting out of the way, he may refuse to jump.

The purpose of the FOCUS command is to call your dog's attention to the top of the high or bar jump and the back, center, top edge of the last board of the broad jump. He should be looking at these focal points before he jumps. Use your CR as soon as your dog commits to the jump, and give him a treat when he gets to you. Be careful not to use your CR too soon or he could change course and go around the jump. Keep the food out of sight so your dog looks at the jump instead of at you. He should be so motivated by jumping that he does not even think of going around.

Set-Up Distance

Once your dog is able to jump from a *Sit-stay*, moving easily with two or three strides before taking off, you should be able to determine what we call the *set-up distance* (Fig. 17.3). This is the distance from the

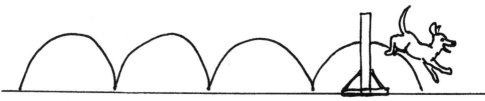

Figure 17.3 The *set-up distance* is two to three of your dog's strides away from the jump.

jump that allows your dog to take two to three cantering strides and then jump smoothly and correctly. The *set-up distance* is the place where you will always stand to throw your dumbbell or send your dog over a jump.

To determine the best *set-up distance* for your dog, make a series of marks on the floor or ground, starting at eight feet from the jump. Add marks at nine feet, ten feet, and so on to about fifteen feet. Have your dog sit at the eight foot mark and call him over the jump. If possible, have an observer stand at the side to see how your dog handles this distance. You want to see comfortable strides, each about the same length rather than either an extra long stride or a short, choppy stride just before he takes off. The dog's take-off and landing points should be at approximately the same distance from either side of the jump (Fig. 17.4).

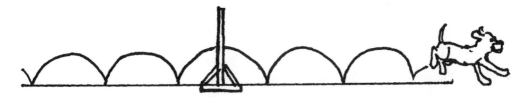

Figure 17.4 The dog who jumps correctly takes off and lands at approximately the same distance from the jump.

Restart your dog at the next mark back until you find one from which he jumps using two or three comfortable strides. For most small dogs, this point will be at eight feet, which is the minimum distance allowed in the regulations. For larger dogs, nine to eleven feet is generally a good distance. Two strides should be sufficient, but some dogs prefer three. A longer distance may help your dog sit in front of you more accurately when he returns over the high jump with the dumbbell. You must be able to find the right distance to have a successful jumper. If you do not understand or are unable to do this, either find an instructor who understands what your dog is doing or videotape him as he takes off and lands to help you analyze his style.

Jump Height

When we started showing in AKC trials, the jump height was set at one and one-half times the height of the dog at the withers (Fig. 17.5) for most breeds, with a maximum of 36 inches. While some dogs handled this relatively easily, it was impossible for others. It was also a simple matter to run under a bar jump. In 1989, the AKC lowered the jumps to one and one-quarter the dog's height. In 1998, the jumps were lowered

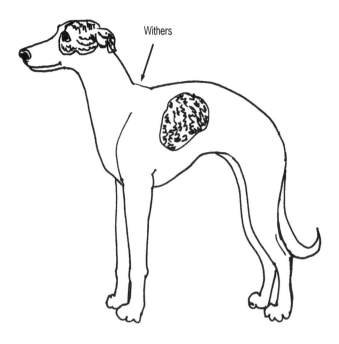

Figure 17.5 The height of the jump is dependent on your dog's height at the withers.

again so the minimum jump is set to the nearest two inch increment to the dog's height, with a minimum of eight inches and a maximum of 36 inches. Certain breeds now jump only three-quarters of their height at the withers. Note that these are minimum heights; the 1998 regulations give you the option to raise the jump to any height above the withers that suits your dog. Because some dogs jump better when the jump is higher than their shoulder height, this allows the dog's handler to make the decision of what jump height to use.

As soon as your dog is jumping properly, set the jumps at approximately two-thirds of the required ring height. With a puppy, use two-thirds of his current height at the withers, not what you think he will be when full-grown! The full jumping height for your dog can only be estimated when he is a puppy.

Angled and Directed Jumping

In preparation for the *Directed Jumping* exercise and for dumbbells that bounce off-center when you throw them, we teach the dog how to jump from off-center. We call this *angled jumping*. For many dogs, it is a good idea to lower the jump height when introducing angles. This helps keep them motivated and puts less stress on their joints.

Your ultimate goal when training *Directed Jumping* is for your dog to jump the correct jump when you signal and/or command him. Figure 17.6 shows the dog positioned perfectly. Train him to jump from any place within the grey area in Figure 17.7.

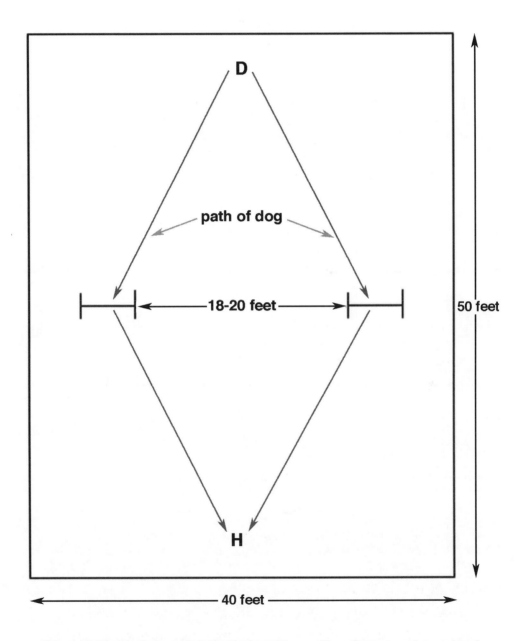

Figure 17.6 In this diagram, D is the dog's starting position after a correct *go-out,* and H is the handler's position. The grey lines show the two possible paths the dog travels when taking a jump on the way back to his handler.

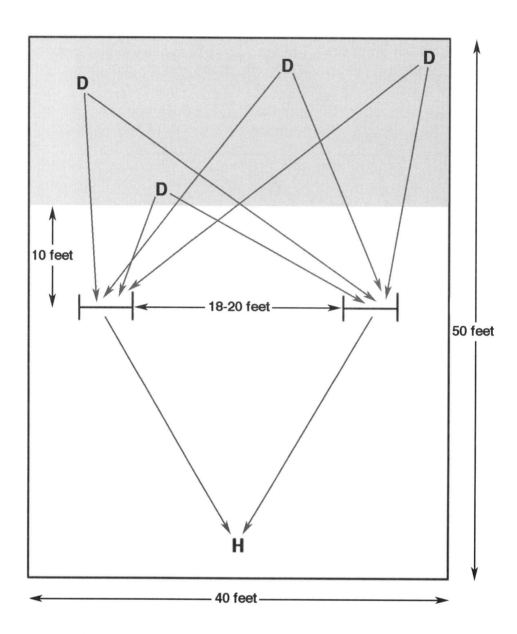

Figure 17.7 In this diagram, the Ds are the dog's starting position after poor *go-outs*, and H is the handler's position. The dog must go to somewhere within the grey area in order to pass the *go-out* portion of the exercise (i.e., at least 10 feet beyond the jumps). As you can see, the jumps can become very difficult for the dog to do successfully when his *go-out* is poor.

We introduce the signal for *Directed Jumping* at the same time that we introduce angled jumping. Begin by having your dog on a *Sit-stay* at his *set-up distance*. Walk around the jump, use your FOCUS command and move quickly to a point just opposite the inside upright (Fig. 17.8). Stay near the jump until your dog commits to jumping. Start with your arms against your sides and your palms facing inward. Begin the signal by turning your palm toward your dog, thumb on the top (Fig. 17.9) and then raise your arm straight out from your side to shoulder height. You might also try to move your arm slightly forward of your body.

Command your dog to JUMP *after* your arm has reached full height. He will get two complete signals before hearing a verbal command: (1) the hand turning outward, followed by (2) the raising of the arm and the command. You may decide to eliminate the verbal command altogether. Some trainers believe the dog is more likely to choose his own jump when the handler uses a verbal command. You need to see what works best for you and your dog.

You may also want to experiment with *when* to give your verbal command to JUMP. Some dogs do better when you give the verbal command when your hand signal is about half completed. Some do better when you give the command at the end of the signal.

Do not get in the habit of using the dog's name, the signal, and the command to JUMP. Using all three commands may cause the dog to anticipate, and if you plan to show in Canada, you are not allowed to use the dog's name in conjunction with a signal and a verbal command.

Figure 17.8 Position your dog at his *set-up distance* and yourself just opposite the inside upright.

Angled and Directed Jumping

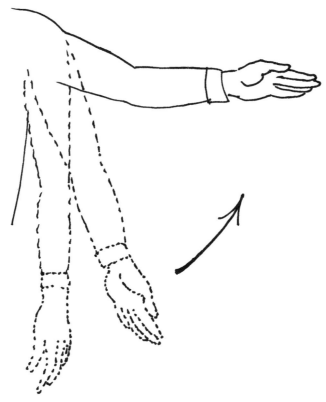

Figure 17.9 Begin the signal by turning your palm outward, thumb on the top and then raise your arm straight out from your side to shoulder height. You may also move your arm slightly forward of your body.

Signal the high and bar jumps randomly so your dog does not develop a preference or a fear of one jump or the other. Alternate sides so he sees the signal from both sides of both jumps. Don't get in the habit of starting with one side or one type of jump.

You may also set your jumps in a "V" (Fig. 17.10) to begin your signals. Stand at the bottom of the "V" and give the signal and command. You may tap the jump from this position so that your dog sees clearly which jump he is supposed to take. Teach this with the jumps set very low (eight to ten inches), since you will do many repetitions. Use proportionately lower jumps for a small dog. As soon as your dog commits to the jump, use your CR and reward him with food after he lands. He needs this positive feedback for making the right choice. This exercise can be done with a young dog or puppy and is best done off-lead. We are only teaching response to a directional signal, not jumping style.

Figure 17.10 You may also set your jumps in a "V" to begin your signals.

When your dog has grasped the concept of signal jumping, begin to move him farther away and more toward the center of the ring so he is taking the jumps at increasingly sharper angles (Fig. 17.11). When he consistently takes the jump rather than coming directly to you, begin to move yourself farther away and more toward the center of the ring. Do this gradually, no more than a foot at a time. If at any time your dog tries to come around the jump, you have moved too far too fast. You will eventually be about 20 feet away from the jumps and your dog about 20 feet away on the opposite side. You may want to begin with the jumps only a few feet apart, but progress to 18 to 20 feet apart as soon as possible. This exercise may take a long time to teach correctly, but it is so rewarding to see your dog take the signal and jump the correct jump confidently. Remember to vary the type of jump (high or bar) as well as the direction (left or right) when you give the signal.

Experiment with your arm position. Some dogs do better seeing the arm come up straight out from your side and some with the arm pointed slightly toward the jump. In any event, keep your wrist straight and your fingers together. Also experiment with eye cues. You should not turn

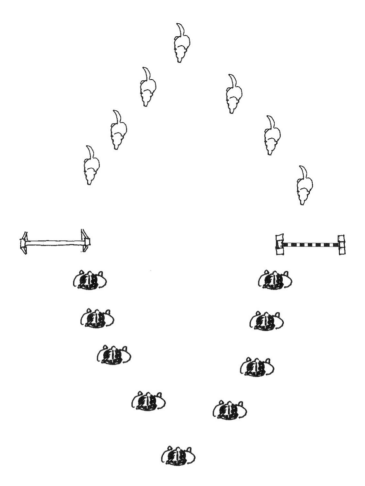

Figure 17.11 Begin to move farther away and more toward the center of the ring so the dog is taking the jumps at increasingly sharper angles.

your head to look at the correct jump, since this may be construed as an extra signal, but many dogs pick up an eye shift towards the correct one. See if this helps your dog.

Common handler errors seen during *Directed Jumping*:

- Holding the jump signal too long. This is a judgement call on the part of the judge. This can be a failure or just points off, depending on how the judge interprets it.
- Giving the jump signal too quickly. This does not lose points, but it will cause you to fail the exercise if your dog doesn't respond to it.

- Leaning your body towards the correct jump. This should not be a failure and may be worth the points off if you think your dog needs it to qualify.
- Stepping towards the correct jump. This is a double command and is a failure.

Dog Choosing The Jump

A common problem in the *Directed Jumping* exercise is a dog who decides on his own which jump to take. If you have taken the time to teach and proof the *Directed Jumping* exercise well, this can be easily corrected.

- Make sure your dog is paying strict attention to you when he turns and sits after his *go-out.*
- Make sure he understands the direction signal clearly.
- Vary your jump signal slightly to see what works best for your dog. Is it better when your arm is straight out from your shoulder or better when you point slightly toward the jump?

Many trainers believe that if you use only a signal and no verbal command, the dog will pay better attention to which jump you are signaling. Experiment to see what works best for your dog.

If your dog has done the *Directed Jumping* exercise well for a long time and suddenly either refuses to jump or takes the wrong jump consistently, you probably should get his eyes checked and have an orthopedic exam, including x-rays. Many dogs are getting up in years by the time they get into Utility so make sure your dog is in good health to do the work.

Retrieving and the High Jump

Once your dog is comfortably jumping two-thirds his full height, and can do a recall carrying a dumbbell, begin to teach him to carry the dumbbell over the jump. This should be done before he actually does the full retrieve over the jump. The weight of the dumbbell in the dog's mouth changes his center of gravity and makes jumping more difficult for some dogs. If you teach your dog to carry the dumbbell over the jump *before* adding the full retrieve over the high jump, he will be more confident with the entire exercise. To do this, your dog must understand the HOLD and STAY commands and be able to walk with the dumbbell (see *Retrieving* and *Stays* chapters).

Adding Height

While teaching the *Directed Jumping* exercise, your dog has been jumping no more than two-thirds his jump height. You should raise the jumps to full height before completing the *Directed Jumping* work and the *Retrieve Over the High Jump* work. We believe the dog should be at least 18 months old and well conditioned before raising the jumps to full height. When you begin to raise the height of the jump, add a maximum of two inches every week or two, and work outside whenever possible. Jumping on grass usually provides the softest, safest surface while your dog is learning to jump the higher jumps. This is especially true if he is large boned or is not a natural jumper. As he becomes confident at each height, continue to raise the jumps slowly at the same rate until they are at full height. The full height for your dog is specified in the regulations.

If your dog develops a jumping problem, reduce the jump height for a week or two until he gains enough strength and/or confidence to jump correctly. If you continue to have trouble and the dog is in good health, seek the help of a qualified instructor. If a dog becomes afraid of the jumps, it is difficult to fix the problem. When your dog can jump full height with ease (Fig. 17.12), you need only train at this height a couple of times a week to maintain his focus and confidence.

Figure 17.12 Bristol, the Pharaoh Hound, shows her excellent arc over the High Jump.

Problem Solving with the High and Bar Jumps

Going Under the Bar

Some dogs seem to have a "sight-picture" problem with the bar jump as it is raised and find it more convenient to go under rather than over the jump. This was more of a problem when the jump heights were higher. First, make sure there is no physical reason for the dog going under the jump, such as a vision problem. Remember to raise the height of the bar more slowly to help your dog gain confidence. Some dogs do better with a visual guide such as a broad jump or high jump board propped on its edge under the bar jump. If this helps your dog, by all means use it. When he is jumping confidently every time, begin to lower the height of the "sight" board from eight to six to four inches, until you can remove it altogether.

Vary the background your dog sees behind the bar jump, since he may perceive the background as actually being in his landing path. Have him jump fairly close to baby gates or to a wall. This helps him learn that even though the barrier is there, he can still jump correctly without injury. This proofing helps create trust.

Ticking the Jump

Some dogs have a persistent problem of *ticking*, or gently hitting, the jumps with either the front or the rear toes. This may occur only on the way over the jump. On the way back, he usually makes a better effort to clear the jump since he has corrected himself with the ticking. There are several methods of dealing with the problem of what we call a "lazy" jumper. Dogs will often put just enough effort into the jump to get over. Having the dog jump a slightly higher jump once a day may help him pick up his feet.

Sometimes you can best help your dog by making the top board an unpleasant surface for his toes to hit. Some suggested surfaces include:

- A piece of fishing line stretched across the top of the jump.
- A line of clothes pins on the jump that stick up from the top board (Fig. 17.13).
- A thin dowel resting on the top board that rolls off when the dog ticks (Fig. 17.14).
- Small brushes on the top of the jump.
- Heavy-duty rubber bands stretched between the uprights.

Figure 17.13 A line of clothes pins on the jump that stick up from the top board help to cure the dog of ticking.

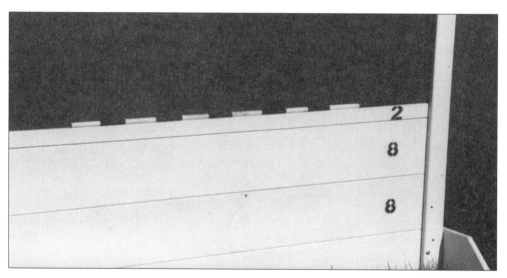

Figure 17.14 A thin dowel resting on the top board that rolls off when the dog ticks may also be helpful.

When using one of these, be careful not to frighten your dog. A dog who is afraid of the jump is not going to jump well. Ticking can also be dealt with by teaching the dog *spike jumping*, described later in this chapter. If he actually climbs the jump (lands on the top board and then pushes off) go back to the first steps of jump training and start over. This is a much less common problem than it was when the jumps were one and one-half times the dog's height. Make sure you do not skip any steps, no matter how much your dog likes the work. If you cannot correct the problem yourself, seek the help of an experienced instructor.

Charging the Jumps

If your dog runs at the jumps too fast, he will often either crash into the jumps or tick them because he is jumping flat. *Do not* encourage your dog to run too fast when teaching jumping. Allow him to gain his confidence and he will gauge his own speed correctly. If you already have one of these problems and you think it is due to too much speed, reteach jumping and make your dog slow down. The cavaletti exercise described later in this chapter should help the dog who takes off too soon.

Running Around the Jump

If your dog tries to run around the jump, you must stop the behavior immediately. We use an AH-AH verbal reprimand to stop him as soon as he starts to go around. If your dog believes he has a choice about whether or not he should jump, remove this choice and retrain the exercise. **Remember, retraining an exercise takes longer than training it correctly the first time because you are dealing with a learned habit!**

Some hints for fixing this problem include:

- Work in an inside hallway to block both sides of the jump.
- Use baby gates or objects like picnic table benches to block the sides of the jump.
- Lower the jump and start over.

If your dog has always jumped over the jump but suddenly begins to go around or not return over the jump, take him for a veterinary exam, as he may be in pain. Sometimes the only way he can tell you he is in pain is by not doing what it hurts him to do.

Proofing Directed Jumping

When your dog understands the *Directed Jumping* exercise, it is time to add proofing. This exercise requires that your dog be attentive to you following his *go-out* (see *Go-Outs* chapter) in order to see the direction you give him. Since your dog is about 40 feet away from you when he has finished his *go-out*, it is likely that he may be distracted before you give your *jump* command and/or signal.

One of the best ways to proof this exercise is with another person standing in the ring. Ultimately, when you show, a judge will be standing at the same end of the ring as you are when you direct your dog to a jump. To start, have the person a fair distance away from your dog and not looking at him. If your dog pays no attention to this person, have her move closer to him the next time. When beginning this proofing, skip the *go-out* to save time and to make it easier for your dog. Just place him at the go-out spot. It is also possible that you are proofing the jumping portion of the exercise before your dog is competently doing his *go-outs*. In any case, have your distracter gradually move toward your dog until she is finally standing between your dog and the jump you are signaling. The only place she shouldn't stand is directly between you and your dog as he then would be unable to see your signal. This will take a number of training sessions.

Another important proof is to place your dog in various areas where he might end up if he does a poor *go-out* (Fig. 17.7). For instance, he might run to a corner. He needs to be able to take the jump on that side as well as the jump on the far side. Put your dog in increasingly difficult locations. We like to use another area apart from where we usually train to proof this exercise so the dog does not get the idea that going out to a corner is okay. By proofing for jumping after a poor *go-out*, you may very well save a leg in a trial! Do not jump him from a corner if he runs poorly on a *go-out* in training; correct the go-out problem separately.

A proof for an advanced dog is for you to lean and later move toward one corner of the ring while signaling the jump on the opposite side.

As discussed earlier, vary the background your dog sees behind the bar jump, since he may perceive the background as actually being in his landing path. Have him jump fairly close to baby gates or to a wall.

Jumping as a Conditioning Exercise

For a thorough discussion on conditioning your dog, we highly recommend Chris Zink's book, *Peak Performance: Coaching the Canine Athlete.*

Many obedience exhibitors overlook the fact that we are asking our dogs to perform as athletes. We sometimes pay little attention to preparing them physically beyond what is needed for skill training.

Zink discusses the three important phases of conditioning:

- *Skill training* — the actual obedience exercises.
- *Endurance and distance training* — exercise, such as swimming or trotting, for an extended period of time.
- *Strength training* — needed for rapid acceleration and for the speed required while running and jumping; trained via hard running and jumping.

The book lays out a conditioning program for a variety of dog sports.

Jumping From A to Z: Teach Your Dog to Soar, by Chris Zink and Julie Daniels, also has a thorough discussion of conditioning, in addition to being an excellent guide to jumping. We have followed their conditioning program with our own dogs and found it highly beneficial.

Before using jumping as a conditioning exercise, make sure your dog has a clean bill of health from your veterinarian. We keep stressing this point because we want only the best of health and happiness for your dog! A physical examination might include x-rays of his shoulders, elbows and hips, patella checks on small dogs, and a general physical to determine the dog's fitness (i.e., weight control and muscle development to withstand the stress of jumping). For any dog over the age of two, a yearly eye exam is also a good idea.

Keep your dog's toenails short, and if he has a lot of hair on his feet, cut away the excess hair between the pads to prevent slipping. If you find that he slips frequently, you may want to get some "no-slip" spray to put on his pads before jumping.

It is sometimes difficult to keep dogs in good jumping condition, especially in the winter, but it is important to keep them physically fit. This includes weight control and regular cardiovascular exercise like running or swimming. Teaching a dog to jump requires the dog to use muscles not usually needed in daily living. It also requires a little knowledge of canine anatomy. This is why you may find an experienced instructor helpful with this phase of your training.

Horse cavaletti exercises, modified for dogs, are helpful for teaching timing. They are also good body conditioning exercises. Cavalettis are a series of jumps of various heights that are set at varying distances from each other. A course can be set up in a hallway, a living room, or a training room, as long as the footing is secure. Whatever space you have to work with can be utilized. Start with objects of varying heights, depending on the size of your dog, such as a cardboard box, a ladder, a chair on its side, a table or bench laid on the floor or ground and, of course, the traditional, high, bar, and broad jumps. You can make a jump using two bars crossed to give the dog yet another sight picture.

Depending on space, set these jumps a varying number of strides apart to encourage your dog to learn to time his takeoff correctly. When training a large dog, vary the height of the jumps from eight to twenty-four inches; for the medium and small dog, use jumps that are proportionately lower. This exercise encourages the dog to judge variable distances and takeoff points. Work him off-lead if possible. If your training area isn't safe for this, use a six-foot or a retractable leash. *Keep your dog in good jumping condition and maintain his confidence to produce a sound, confident, stress-free ring performance.*

Spike Jumping

Another winter training exercise is to teach your dog *spike jumping.* "Spiking" the jump is when the dog lifts himself from a position very close to the jump and does not use or maintain an arc when he jumps. It is physically hard on the dog and is not a good jumping style. However, *spike jumping* produces excellent rear strengthening and is especially good for a dog who continually ticks the jump or has a flat style of jumping. It does not promote "spiking" the jump in competition as your dog is approaching from a distance. It will help him learn to maintain an arc.

Set the high jump at your dog's chin level when he is sitting directly in front of it (Fig. 17.15). You are going to ask him to jump from this sitting position. If your dog cannot do this, lower the jump to a height where he is successful and then gradually raise it until he is doing his full height from a sit. This exercise encourages your dog to lift himself using his hind quarters and enables him to jump more smoothly and correctly. Remember to use your CR and food or a toy the instant your dog is successful.

Figure 17.15 In preparation for *spike jumping*, set the high jump at your dog's chin level when he is sitting directly in front of it.

The Broad Jump

The *Broad Jump* exercise in the Open class requires your dog to jump two, three, or four boards. It is a "wide" jump instead of a vertical or high jump. The number of boards (and therefore the width of the jump) depends on the height of your dog and is twice as wide as the height of your dog's high jump. The handler leaves the dog, goes to a position to the right of the jump (somewhere between the first and the last boards) and stands with her toes about two feet back from the jump. She commands or signals the dog to jump. The dog jumps all of the boards in one leap and turns to come and sit in front of the handler. The handler makes a quarter turn to the right while the dog is in the air. The dog then finishes as in other exercises.

Target Training the Broad Jump

We teach the *Broad Jump* with a combination of targeting and avoidance. Targeting is placing a target, like food or a toy, out beyond the jump. Avoidance is done by using a barrier in the "Bad Zone", which is the area just beyond the last board of the broad jump and to the right of the center (Fig. 17.16). The size of the *Bad Zone* will depend on your dog. The farther to the right the dog lands in the *Bad Zone*, the harder it is for him to turn and do a straight front. Carried to excess, the *Bad Zone* extends around the sides of the jump, and landing in it becomes a failure of the exercise.

We teach the dog to avoid the *Bad Zone* by placing a visible object such as a traffic cone or jump upright in the place where we do not want him to land. As he gets comfortable and appears to be thinking "jump straight", we make the barrier smaller. Eventually the barrier becomes nearly invisible. We use a rectangle of fencing wire or a baby gate lying flat on the floor in the *Bad Zone*. Place wire on a bar, just beyond the last board to make an even less pleasant place to land (Fig. 17.17). With a small dog, the barrier is invisible until he is airborne, so it typically has excellent carry-over to the ring. Be careful about what you use as a barrier. You don't want the dog to get scared or injured! Adele once used a ring gate upright. Treasure landed on it, slipped, and hurt herself. Fortunately, her injury was slight and an important lesson was learned.

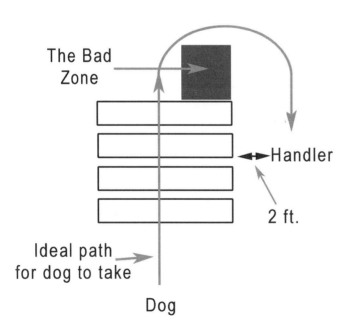

Figure 17.16 The Bad Zone is the area just beyond the last board of the broad jump and to the right of the center.

Figure 17.17 We use a rectangle of fencing wire or a baby gate lying flat on the floor in the Bad Zone. Placing the wire on a bar, just beyond the last board, makes an even less pleasant place to land.

We use a foot to direct the dog to the center in proofing this exercise (Figs. 17.18 and 17.19). The dog will stay in the center if he never knows when "big foot" is coming to get him. We do not kick the dog! Just the sight of a foot coming up helps him focus on going straight over the jump.

If your dog loves toys, use one to help move yourself to the side of the broad jump. Adele starts with recalls over the jump, but fairly soon turns her left shoulder towards the dog and tosses a toy to her right for the dog to retrieve. Sometimes she tosses it before the OVER command, sometimes while the dog is in midair, and sometimes just after landing. Toss the toy as straight as possible beyond the jump.

If your dog isn't much interested in toys, you can use food in a similar way. Some trainers put the food on a target, such as a plastic lid. The dog focuses on the target, jumps, and then gets the treat. We recommend some kind of targeting in combination with a *Bad Zone* barrier.

Figure 17.18 Judy uses her foot to direct Alec to the center in the proofing of this exercise.

Figure 17.19 Here Alec avoids Judy's foot and jumps properly.

Stick Jumping in Preparation for the Broad Jump

Judy teaches stick jumping in preparation for the *Broad Jump*. There are three reasons for this. First, by using the stick, you can move directly to the side of the *Broad Jump* instead of moving gradually from the end of the jump to the side, as you would do when using the "call over" method. Second, the stick gives your dog the idea of arcing from the beginning of learning the exercise. By jumping in an arc, he is better able to make a quick turn to come into a straight front. Finally, most dogs find that stick jumping is fun! If, later in your training, you want to get rid of the stick in your hand, you can easily use a bar jump over the *Broad Jump* or just lay the stick on the jump as a reminder to the dog.

As you begin to teach stick jumping, you should remember a few points:

- The dog only jumps the stick from left to right as if he were doing the *Broad Jump*. We are pattern training and teaching at the same time.
- The stick is held in the left hand.
- The dog should be off-lead and can be lured or rewarded with food that is held in the right hand. If circumstances require that you use a leash, hold it in your right hand along with the food.

Any wooden dowel or piece of one-half or one-inch PVC pipe will work as a jump stick. It should be about three feet long. We use white PVC pipe with a three-inch stripe of black electrical tape placed every three inches to simulate the bar jump and make it more visible to the dog. You can, of course, purchase a collapsible jump stick from one of the obedience supply companies. These are portable and fold to fit easily in any training bag.

The first step in stick jumping is to put the stick on the floor. If your dog is suspicious of anything new, let him see and sniff the stick before you use it. Keep your left hand on the stick while your right hand holds some food. Sit or stand your dog on your left, with the stick directly in front of you (Fig. 17.20). Remember, he moves from left to right only. Use your jump command and lure your dog over the stick. Give your CR and feed.

Begin to raise the stick an inch or two at a time. You may want to place the end of the stick against a solid surface like a wall to keep from moving it. It is very hard for a dog to jump a moving target! The maximum height you want to achieve with a tall dog is about eighteen inches and for a small dog, eight to ten inches (Fig. 17.21). Early in the teaching

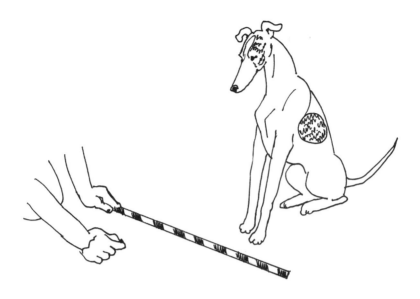

Figure 17.20 The first step in stick jumping is to put the stick on the floor. Keep your left hand on the stick, with some food in your right hand. Leave your dog sitting or standing to your left, with the stick directly in front of you.

Figure 17.21 The maximum height you want to achieve when teaching stick jumping to a tall dog is about eighteen inches and for a small dog, eight to ten inches.

The Broad Jump

of this exercise, begin to ask for doubles and triples. Since jumping itself is extremely motivating to most dogs, the action of jumping may be as reinforcing as the food.

Adding the Broad Jump Boards Under the Stick

When your dog jumps the stick comfortably and responds every time to your jump command, it is time to place the broad jump boards under the stick. It is best to hold the stick at the back of the jump, over the last board, or between the second-to-last and the last board (Fig. 17.22). Remember, the dog has been jumping the same two or three boards since his initial introduction to the broad jump. For a dog who will eventually jump two or three boards in competition, start with one or two boards under the stick. For the four-board jumper, use three boards. At first, the width is not as important as getting the dog to approach the jump smoothly and go over it with a nice arc (Fig. 17.23).

If your dog does not have a solid *Sit-stay*, you will need someone to hold him until you command him to jump. Remember to teach only one exercise at a time. If your dog's *Sit-stay* needs work, do it separately from the jumping. When you first place the boards under the stick, the set-up distance is not critical. As you lengthen the jump, pay more attention to

Figure 17.22 It is best to hold the stick at the back of the jump.

Figure 17.23 The final product.

your set-up distance as described earlier in this chapter. The minimum set-up distance is eight feet, and this is usually a good distance for a small dog. Larger dogs may need ten to twelve feet. Remember to use your FOCUS word and touch the top center of the last board for the first week or two before you send your dog (Fig. 17.24). As you give your *jump* command, he sees the same sight picture you used when starting with the jump stick. Your dog is on your left, the broad jump boards are directly in front of your feet, the stick is in your left hand, and the food or toy is in your right hand. The only difference will be the presence of the boards.

Adding the Turn

The new part of this exercise, the turn, begins when your dog has completed his jump and you have given him his CR. Command COME as your dog lands, and run back to his starting point. Let the stick drop to your side out of the way. CR again and give your dog the food or toy. You can throw the toy or food between your legs to maintain your dog's speed and enthusiasm after the turn. You may also want to use your CR as soon as he commits to the jump. The exercise is now "roughed in."

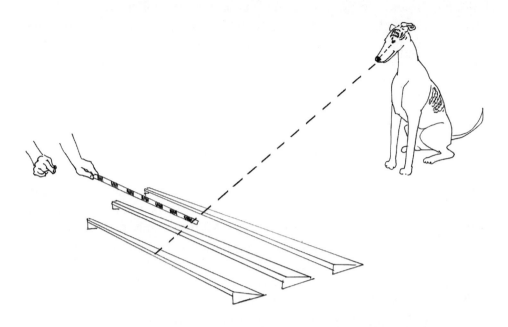

Figure 17.24 Your dog should focus on the top center of the last board.

What's Next?

The next step depends on your dog's age and stage of training. For a young dog, you may want to leave the exercise in its rough form for a period of several weeks or months. If you are actively preparing for your CDX, continue.

At this point, your dog should be able to do a reliable *Sit-stay* or *wait* until commanded to jump. Dogs who run haphazardly at the jump, rather than taking two or three full strides, will jump flatter and have a harder time making a correct and safe turn. With a dog who jumps flat, continue to use a bar or stick over the jump for a longer period of time. If possible, use a video camera to help you see how your dog jumps. Perhaps you will want to find an instructor who understands the mechanics of jumping to help you.

The Turn

Many dogs that are trained to do the broad jump with food or toys turn too quickly in their eagerness to get the reward. Turning too quickly may cause him to slip or put too much stress on his right shoulder. A barrier in the *Bad Zone*, as discussed in a previous section, will help your dog stride forward a couple of steps and slow his forward momentum before he makes the turn.

The opposite problem is the dog who goes too far forward and too far to the right after he completes the turn. This dog does not return directly to you due to his wide turn and will usually lose points for this in the ring (Fig. 17.25). Generally, you can overcome this problem by using the proper motivator to encourage your dog to come quickly to you. You might also put a broad jump board, bar, or gate just past and to the right of the place where the dog should turn. You do not want to introduce a *front* at this point, because they tend to slow a dog down. Your goal is to encourage the jump, turn, and quick return to you.

If you are using a stick, continue to hold it in your left hand, place it on top of the jump, or substitute a bar jump. If you use a bar, it is a good idea to place it over the last board so the dog knows where the end of the jump is and doesn't jump the bar and crash into the boards. The bar seldom needs to be more than eight or ten inches above the broad jump to get the dog to elevate properly. Place it lower for small dogs. As you refine the exercise, lengthen the jump, using your stick or bar as needed, and pay attention to your dog's jumping style.

Gradually begin to move away from the jump to attain the required two-foot distance (Fig. 17.26). As you move away, use a bar or stick laid on the jump. Begin to randomly use your CR and food or toy and begin to add a *front* after the turn.

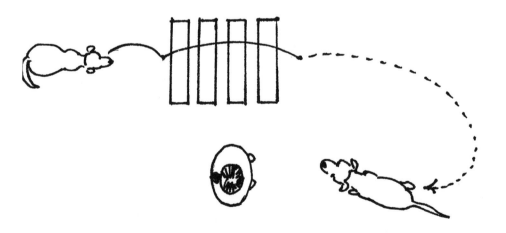

Figure 17.25 The dog who doesn't turn quickly enough may lose points not only for a poor front, but also for a wide turn.

The Broad Jump

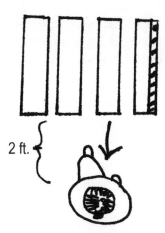

2 ft.

Figure 17.26 Begin to gradually move away from the jump to attain the necessary two-foot distance as required by the regulations.

Where Should You Stand?

The regulations tell us that the handler should stand with her toes *about two feet back* from the jump and somewhere between the first and last boards.

We stand somewhere between the first and the third board for a dog who jumps three or four boards. Generally the more space the dog has to turn and move straight toward the handler, the straighter his fronts will be. However, the closer you stand to the dog, the more likely it is that he will cut the corner and land in the *Bad Zone*. Experiment by standing in several different locations and figure out which one produces the most consistent fronts. This also proofs the dog's complete understanding of the exercise.

Making the Turn

There are two legal ways for you to turn in place to give your dog the best advantage for a straight front. You can pivot slightly away from the jump or slightly toward the jump, depending on which foot you start your pivot. Either is considered pivoting in place. Pivoting away from the jump may help a dog who has developed a wider turn. This would be called "good handling." It is not especially good training, as you want your dog to make a tight turn and return immediately to a straight front.

The Broad Jump Finish

For the *Broad Jump*, we prefer the *around* finish (see *Fronts and Finishes* chapter). If you use the *side* finish, some dogs, especially big ones, find it difficult to go between the edge of the jump and your side to get lined up for a snappy, straight finish. When you make a slight pivot in towards the jump on your turn and use an *around* finish, your dog has a chute to guide him into a straight finish.

Proofing the Broad Jump

- Jump on grass, different colored mats, dirt, and other surfaces. The different sight picture may confuse some dogs.
- Jump with cracks or bumps in the mat where the dog is expected to sit in front.
- Use ring barriers or walls to the left of the jump, with or without people and dogs sitting or standing there.
- Use curtains to the left of the jump, such as those sometimes used in Canada.
- Work with a solid white background beyond the jump. The broad jump looks like a solid white platform to most dogs. A white background can add to the confusion.
- Have a person standing about ten feet beyond the end of the jump. The judge usually stands at the end of the jump to watch the dog jump and complete his front and finish. Your dog may perceive this as a person standing in his way, so he should learn to jump with people standing near, but not in, the landing area. Some overly social dogs may also visit the judge, so this is an important proof for this type of dog.
- Have a table beyond the end of the jump. Often the steward's table may be at the end of the ring, and more than one dog has failed by "going to visit" after he jumped.
- Have the high jump positioned to the right of the broad jump. Some rings are smaller than others and, for the dog who makes a wide turn, the high jump may suddenly be in his visual path. His tendency is to jump the high jump. He becomes confused, as he is now behind the handler. Teaching a tight turn after the jump should eliminate this problem. Teach your dog that the high jump may be right beside you but that he is not to go over it after jumping the broad jump.
- Have a table with people and chairs right behind or next to the spot where you set up your dog for the exercise.
- Have a person standing beyond and to the right of the jump, luring the dog with food or a toy. This is especially useful proofing for the dog who makes wide turns.
- The handler should stand in a variety of places, such as four feet back from the jump rather than two feet.

- The handler may stand on the left side of the broad jump. You can either call the dog to a front or let him go to a target for this proof. This helps the dog truly understand the exercise.

Help your dog perform correctly, even when he is stressed. This is the purpose of proofing. Make it clear to your dog that he can and must jump properly under a variety of circumstances. This helps him focus on the task and become more confident.

Broad Jump Problems

Walking On or Between the Boards

One of the most common problems that dogs have with the *Broad Jump* is walking through the jump rather than jumping over it. A related problem is the dog who comes directly to the handler instead of jumping the jump. Both of these problems result from poor basic teaching of the exercise and a lack of confidence. There is also a possibility that the dog is in pain or having vision problems. If he has done the exercise correctly for a period of time and suddenly starts having these problems, it is time for a thorough orthopedic and eye checkup.

If your dog is in good health, back up in your training and figure out where you went wrong. Maybe you took away the guide (stick or bar) too soon. Unless the problem is physical, the problems are generally ours, as trainers, not the dog's. By shaping the exercise correctly and *slowly*, most serious problems can be avoided.

Two weeks before Rio's Open debut, Adele realized that he had to jump a 24 inch broad jump rather than the 20 inches on which they had trained. The additional four inches gave Rio the opportunity to step between the boards and he took full advantage of the increased space. He was cured quickly of that behavior by a fairly hearty scruff shake correction. The correction was followed by motivating a couple of jumps and a jackpot for success. He rarely stepped between the boards again.

Instead of making the correction yourself, you might fix the problem by adding some chicken wire or other unpleasant material, such as double-sided sticky tape, under the boards. Dogs usually choose to jump rather than walk on these unpleasant surfaces.

Loss of Enthusiasm

Loss of enthusiasm is another problem for some dogs. The *Broad Jump* is not a difficult exercise for most dogs, and the thrill of the retrieve is not there to stimulate them. After the jump and turn, the dog suddenly has to stop and do a straight *front* and *finish*, and this can be very demotivating to some dogs. Balance the precision work with the motivational work. As with all exercises, remember to make the work interesting and fun for the dog. You should continuously build and maintain enthusiasm.

Poor Turns and Fronts

If you feel you need to drill *fronts* after the turn, stand the dog facing away from the end of the jump as if he had just completed the jump, and call him to FRONT. He is then doing only the part of the exercise that is "broken," and it won't be nearly as boring or physically stressful for him as repeating the full exercise. This exercise can also help the dog who makes a wide turn after the jump. You may wish to do this without the jump in place. Have the dog face away from you and perhaps use an interesting distraction, such as a piece of food on the ground, on which he can focus. Call him to FRONT, and see how quickly he turns and responds. By doing this, you do not run the risk of "breaking" another part of the exercise.

You may want to use a long line or a retractable leash to give the dog a reminder pop as he lands. We do not recommend this method for teaching, but it may be needed to retrain some dogs whose habit of making a large turn has become ingrained.

Teach jumping slowly, one step at a time, and teach a correct style. Build enthusiasm and confidence. Teaching your dog to jump correctly and safely may require assistance from someone knowledgeable in the mechanics of jumping. Seek help if you are having trouble.

Go-Outs

T he *go-out* is the first part of the Utility *Directed Jumping* exercise. The dog and handler begin the exercise standing at one end of a 40 X 50-foot ring on the center line, about 20 feet back from the jumps, which are 18–20 feet apart (Fig. 18.1). When performing an ideal *go-out,* the dog runs straight away from his handler, between the jumps, to a point about 20 feet beyond the jumps, and, on his handler's command, stops, turns to face his handler, and sits.

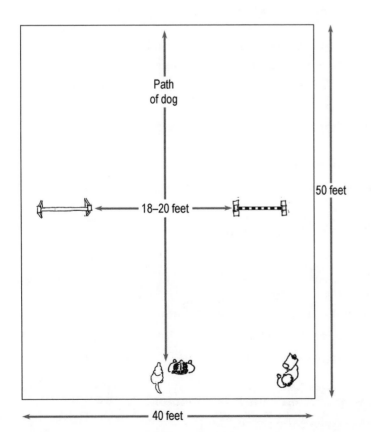

Path
of dog

18–20 feet

50 feet

40 feet

Figure 18.1 The dog and handler begin the exercise standing at one end of a 40 X 50-foot ring on the center line, about 20 feet back from the jumps, which are 18-20 feet apart.

Judy has always used food to train go-outs. She teaches the dog to *mark*, or stare intently, at a piece of food on a small plastic lid or paper plate (a target) and then to run to this target on command.

Adele trained her first three dogs this way and has since started teaching a touch-based *go-out*. In the *Fundamental Words* chapter, we explained how to teach your dog to put his foot on a target such as a plastic lid or a paper plate and how to touch his nose to a clothespin or a similar small clip. If you take the time to teach one or both of these to your dog, it can help make your *go-out* training less tedious than if you must frequently walk out to put food on a target. Using a touch method also transfers much of the responsibility to the dog earlier in the training. Adele still uses food on the target occasionally to keep her dogs' interest and motivation strong. While most of our discussion is on the food-based *go-out*, you can substitute a touch for the food in most instances.

If your dog is not strongly motivated by touch or loses motivation easily, use a combination of food and touch. If a toy is a powerful motivator for your dog, you may wish to train *go-outs* using a toy as his target. What is most important is to find a method that helps make *go-outs* understandable and motivating to your dog.

One of the tricks to teaching solid *go-outs* is to do several thousand of them before your dog is ready to show! *Go-outs* involve a great deal of pattern training. You should start training *go-outs* early in your dog's obedience career and continue to practice them often.

Remember that even though your dog seems to understand *go-outs*, you will need to reinforce them frequently. *Go-outs* seem to deteriorate faster than most other exercises.

There are several points to consider when beginning to teach a reliable *go-out*. We recommend that you:

- Teach your dog to *mark* a target that will eventually be at least 40 feet away from him.
- Teach your dog to run very fast to that spot.
- Teach him to *turn and sit* promptly in place on your command when he gets to the target.
- Teach him to focus his *attention* on you after he sits so he can see and correctly obey your signal to *jump*.

A team will receive a zero if the dog:

- Anticipates a command or signal to leave your side, to *sit*, or to *jump*.
- Does not leave your side on your first command.
- Does not go out between the jumps.

- Does not stop and remain at least ten feet past the jumps.

It is also a failure if *you* give a second command to *sit.*

Teaching Targeting

You may teach puppies as young as eight to ten weeks the following targeting exercise. They usually love it and, if you introduce it early, they seldom forget their early exposure because it is *fun.*

Use a small target for a puppy, such as a paper plate or a lid from a margarine container. Some people use a raised target, such as a bucket turned upside down. This is fine for a puppy, but keep in mind that whatever you use must eventually be faded from the *go-out.* All you are doing at this stage is teaching your dog to *mark* a specific location. When he is focused intently on this location, let him run to get the food from the target. We refer to this intense focus as the *vulture* look. *Until your dog stares in the direction he is to run, he does not get to run to the food.*

Begin with your target on the floor about three feet away from you and your dog. Throughout most of your *go-out* training, place the target next to a barrier of some sort, such as a wall or a baby gate. Hold your dog with your left hand, either by a leash or by his collar, while you place a treat on the target with your right hand (Fig. 18.2). The dog does not need to know a STAY command, so you may do this with a young puppy. As you place a treat on the target, pair a word with the food placement. The dog should assume the *vulture look* when he hears this command. This "look" eventually helps the dog see where he is supposed to run when he marks the end of the ring 40 feet away. We use the command SEE IT? Other commands are TARGET or LOOK.

Place the food on the target and use your focus word, SEE IT? When your dog is staring at the food, use your CR to tell him he is correct to look at the food. Then let him run to the target by using a GET IT command. You are using the food as a *delayed primary reinforcer,* since your dog does not get the food as soon as he is right, which is as soon as he looks at the target. Do not introduce a *go-out* command at this point, since you are merely teaching your dog to look at the target. He will quickly learn to look at the food as soon as you place it on the target. If you are doing this with a puppy who does not yet know a *Sit-stay,* either hold him while someone else puts the food out or have another person hold him while you put the food out. If your dog knows how to *stay,* have him do so while you walk forward and put the food on the target. You may reinforce the LOOK or SEE IT command with your CR just as you

Figure 18.2 Hold him with your left hand, either by a leash or by the collar, while you place a treat on the target with your right hand.

place the food on the target and your dog looks at it. Since your dog will not get the food immediately, it is extremely important to use your CR the instant he looks at the target.

Return to your dog and tell him to SEE IT? again. As soon as he drops his head to look at the target, give your CR and let him get the food by using your release command or GET IT.

Follow your dog to the target every time so he does not get in the habit of running back to you. He should stay at the end of the *go-out* in preparation for learning the *turn and sit*.

Adding A Command To The Go-Out

When your dog has learned these early steps — the *vulture look* and running to the target for the food — begin to use a command to send him. He should already understand that, after he focuses on the target and the food, he will be allowed to get it. At this point, it is a simple matter to introduce a command such as RUN, GO-OUT, AWAY, or GET LOST!

You may want to say both RUN and GET IT the first few times and then drop the GET IT command. You may also want to use your CR again just as he begins to run.

Do not forget to use your CR when your dog looks at the target or the spot where you intend to send him. Occasionally give him a food reward from your hand before you send him to reinforce the focus word.

How To Use A Signal For The Go-Out

While we do not use a signal for the *go-out*, it is legal to do so. There are dogs who do the exercise better when their handler uses a signal. The most common signal is to move your left arm directly along the right side of your dog's head as you command RUN (Fig. 18.3). This signal may help your dog leave your side and run straighter. If your dog does better *go-outs* with a signal, by all means use one.

Figure 18.3 The most common signal for the *go-out* is simply moving your left arm directly along the right side of the dog's head as you command RUN.

Teaching The Turn And Sit

The primary goal of the go-out is for your dog to sit far enough beyond the jumps (at least 10 feet) to be able to safely take either jump. Your dog is supposed to *sit* at the end of the *go-out* and, while it is not required by the rules, it is best if he turns in place to face you before he *sits*. This makes it easier for him to see your signal as well as take either jump.

Judy has found that many dogs do better when learning the turn if they are taught to turn in the opposite direction from their natural "pawedness." That's not a real word but is analogous to handedness in people. In other words, if your dog repeatedly turns to the right when running out to pick up a toy, food, or dumbbell, he needs to be taught to turn to the left on the *go-out*. Many dogs seem to understand the *turn and sit* in place better when they have to think about the direction they are turning. Our goal, when teaching this, is to prevent the dog from arcing or traveling to either side before he sits. We assume, for this discussion, that your dog is "right pawed" and you will teach him to turn to the left.

Stand your dog in front of you, facing away from you. Hold food in your left hand and use it like a magnet. Tell your dog to TURN and lure him around in a tight circle to the left (Fig. 18.4). Once he is facing you,

Figure 18.4 Hold food in your left hand and use it like a magnet. Tell the dog to TURN and lure him around in a tight circle to the left.

tell him to SIT. Use your CR twice before giving him the food; once for the *turn* and again after the *sit*. When your dog understands the *turn*, drop the TURN command, although you may want to reinforce it randomly if he needs help. This is especially important to remember when you combine the *turn and sit* with the *go-out*. *Your goal is for the dog to promptly turn and sit in place on command.* There should be very little delay between your command and the planting of your dog's bottom on the ground. You will need this immediate response later when proofing your dog to *turn and sit* on command while ignoring a treat or a toy.

We start training the *turn and sit* portion of the *go-out* early in a dog's training. He must know a SIT command first. Pretend to throw a toy. When your dog runs out in front of you, expecting you to throw the toy, command SIT and, when he obeys, give your CR and throw him the toy. When your dog understands that a quick sit brings the toy, it becomes an enjoyable game.

Adding A Barrier And A Chute

To perform a correct turn and sit at the end of a go-out, your dog must neither walk back towards you before he sits nor move off to either side. You may find that having a specific place to sit helps your dog understand his job better. He should go to this specific place on each *go-out* and turn and sit quickly.

If your dog has problems turning in place and sitting promptly, you may want to use barriers of some sort. Only the simplest barriers are needed for a dog who turns well but walks towards you before he sits. We use a bar jump bar, a broad jump board, or any of the other barriers we have recommended in earlier chapters. Introduce this barrier by having your dog stand facing a wall or a baby gate with the barrier between the two of you (Fig. 18.5). You should be about six feet from the wall. Use your target so the scene is a familiar one. Repeat the *turn and sit* exercise so it is clear to your dog that he can perform this exercise with a barrier in place. If he tries to step across the barrier to get closer to you, block him with your body or with a leash. You may also wish to use a verbal reprimand just as he starts over the barrier.

If your dog does not go straight to his target, or if he adds a little hook at the end, make a *go-out* chute using plastic rain gutters or two broad jump boards. Use the barriers as suggested above, another piece of rain gutter, or a dowel across the front to act as a barrier (Fig. 18.6).

Figure 18.5 Introduce the front barrier by having your dog stand facing a wall or a baby gate with the barrier between the two of you.

Figure 18.6 Make a *go-out* chute using plastic rain gutters or two broad jump boards. Use another piece of rain gutter or a dowel across the front to act as a barrier.

You may want to enlarge your target to include a piece of carpet or cloth on which your dog sits or a box made of PVC or wood for him to sit inside. If you make a box, it should be just large enough for your dog to turn and sit tightly inside it. Because you will use these aids for quite a while, choose something lightweight and portable.

Combining the Go-Out With the Turn and Sit

Next we combine the *go-out* with the *turn and sit* into a shortened version of the entire *go-out* exercise. Put food on the floor or the wall, or place your target on the floor. Placing the food at different heights and against different backgrounds helps your dog generalize the *go-out* spot. Some suggestions for "sticking" the food to the wall or gate include:

- A clothespin with food on it placed at the right height.
- Sticky food such as squeeze cheese or peanut butter that the dog can lick off the gate or wall.
- A food holder made from a piece of dowel, which is stuck on the wall or gate with poster tack (Fig 18.7).
- A finishing nail on a gate stanchion (Fig 18.8). Be sure the nail is pounded in far enough to prevent your dog from swallowing it!

You and your dog should start about six feet from the target. Depending on the size of your dog, the barrier should be about two to four feet from the target. Send your dog to the target with your RUN command. Follow him out and, just before he gets to his target, use your CR. This tells him he has just run correctly. After he has eaten the treat from the target, tell him to SIT and, when he obeys, give him another CR and a treat. At this stage, he needs a lot of reinforcement to build his confidence.

Do not ask for a *sit* at the end of the *go-out* until your dog has gone all the way to the wall or gate. ***If you ask him to SIT before he has gone all the way out, you are teaching him it is okay to stop short.*** Later, during the proofing stage, we suggest that you stop him short of the wall or gate. For now, wait until he goes all the way to his target.

Some dogs are confused by the need to go over the barrier to get to the target and try instead to go around. Stay close until your dog is readily hopping directly over the barrier to get to his target.

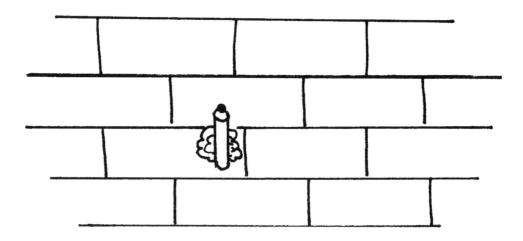

Figure 18.7 You can make a food holder from a piece of dowel, which is stuck on the wall or gate with poster tack.

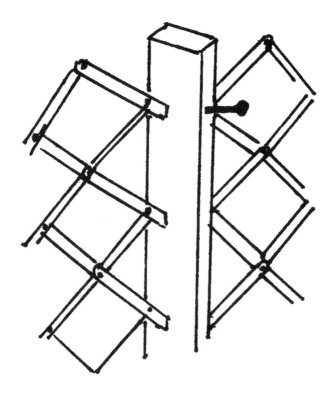

Figure 18.8 A finishing nail on the gate also works to hold a treat.

Combining the Go-Out With the Turn and Sit

We suggest that you use your CR:

- When your dog looks at the target.
- As he runs.
- As he turns.
- After he sits.

Your dog gets food:

- When he reaches the target. This treat comes from the target.
- After he *turns and sits*. This treat comes from you.

To make your job easier, put another treat on the target after you release your dog from the *sit* but before you take him back to the current starting point. This treat placement is less obvious to your dog than leaving him on a *stay* while you walk out to place a treat.

Lengthening The Go-Out

The eventual goal is for your dog to run a minimum of 40 feet on his *go-outs*, but we suggest you train so he confidently runs at least 60 feet. Once he shows he is able to run your current training distance, with a *turn and sit* at the end, have him run farther. Before you tell him to RUN, make sure he looks at the spot where he is going. Use your CR and send him to his target. Remember, he doesn't go out unless he is staring intently at the spot! CR and follow him. Tell him to SIT, CR, and feed him when he complies.

Gradually lengthen the distance until your dog drops his head to see the food on the target when it is 60 feet away. Follow him every time until he understands what he is doing. This may mean running up to 60 feet at a time, but it is very good exercise! Depending on how frequently you train, it may take several weeks to reach this distance.

When you match and show your dog in Utility, he will repeatedly run about 40 feet on his *go-outs*. Dogs learn distances quickly, so again, during your training sessions, do *go-outs* that are longer than 40 feet to help your dog understand that he must run until you tell him to SIT. Some trainers put their targets and food just outside the ring to encourage their dogs to go all the way. We do not do this, but it is another way to proof the long *go-out* and the SIT command.

Be careful as you lengthen the distance that you ask your dog to run. If you lengthen it too fast, he may start to wander or stop short. You do not want him to think a short distance is the final goal. This is a training area where an experienced instructor may offer useful help.

Phasing Out Following The Dog

When your dog runs out to his target eagerly and responds promptly to your SIT command, stop yourself three to six feet short of the end of the *go-out* while letting your dog go to the end. He should still get food on the target each time he runs, as well as after a quick *sit*. If he continues to respond promptly, stop sooner so there is more distance between you and your dog and a longer food delay. Many dogs begin to walk back toward the handler at this point, so it is important either to use a barrier or to stay close enough to your dog to stop him and enforce the SIT. Each time he *sits* promptly, CR and walk in calmly to feed him. When he is slower, praise him, but don't give him a treat. When he sits extremely slowly, he needs more training on the *sit* exercise, perhaps adding either a correction or positive motivation. Take this lesson out of the *go-out* and work on it separately. When adding it back into the *go-out*, vary how closely you follow your dog to the *go-out* spot, increasing the distance only when your dog reliably *turns and sits* promptly on command.

Adding A Correction To The Sit

When training the *go-out*, a time is likely to come when your dog obviously understands the *turn and sit* but decides not to respond promptly to your command. By following him closely, you will be in a position to give him a tap on the rear just after you command SIT. If this is too stressful and confuses him, back up your training and again work on the SIT command without a *go-out* for a few days. *Backing up is often the fastest way to move forward!*

Food Removal

As with all obedience exercises, your dog will have to do the *go-outs* in the ring without food. Many dogs stop running when you remove the food. If you have this problem, consider two possibilities:

Is your dog confused because you have removed the food and/or target too soon and therefore he doesn't understand the exercise without it?

If this is the case, begin to remove the food on a random schedule, but leave the target in place. When you teach any exercise, we recommend that you go to a variable schedule of reinforcement as soon as you can. This teaches your dog early in his training that food will not always be there, but you will still reward him when he performs correctly.

Does your dog understand what you want but decides not to run because there is no food?

If you have taught with food for such a long period of time that he has learned not to run unless there is food present, it is probably time for a correction. Calmly take your dog's collar and run him out to his spot. This is a mild correction and all that some dogs need. You should begin with a mild correction and go to a stronger one only if your dog needs it. A stronger correction would be using several pops on his collar, on lead, as you run him out. Praise lavishly, but do not give him food. Next time, move closer to the target and, when he runs out correctly, use your CR, go to him, and give him a treat. Repeat without food on the target, but follow him to quickly reward compliance.

The name of the game is repetition! Encourage speed, which will encourage him to run straight, which will encourage distance.

If your dog doesn't understand, or if you don't know why he isn't doing the exercise properly, help him. If you correct a dog who is confused, you add stress, your dog may refuse to work, and you will find yourself in a vicious cycle. Learn to pay close attention to your dog's body language. He will tell you when he needs help and when he needs a correction by his responses to your commands.

If you are teaching *go-outs* to a very young dog, you may have to wait many months or even years before you perform them in the ring. Randomly reinforce as you gradually remove the food from the target, reduce the size of the target, and don't worry about doing more than a dozen or so repetitions a week. This will be enough to maintain your dog's interest in the exercise.

Although the *Directed Jumping* exercise ultimately requires two jumps (Fig. 18.1), we teach the *go-out* without the jumps in place. Jumping should be taught separately (see *Jumping* chapter).

Proofing Go-Outs

Proofing *go-outs* can be a long process, but if you want your dog to truly understand that he must run in a straight line until told to sit, you will take the time to do it! *Go-outs* require more proofing than most other exercises, but with patience and creativity, the proofing can be fun.

Go-Outs Following Gloves

Even though the *Moving Stand* is performed between the *Directed Retrieve* and *Directed Jumping* exercises, dogs have an uncanny way of remembering where they retrieved the glove, and they sometimes run back to that spot on the *go-out*. This may especially be a problem if your dog retrieved a corner glove (i.e., glove one or glove three). To clarify this for your dog, teach him to do a glove retrieve followed immediately by a *go-out*. Expect him to be confused when you first try this, and be prepared to help him.

Start with one glove in the corner to your right, and use your *go-out* target in place in the center. Set up for the *go-out* fairly close to the target, perhaps ten to fifteen feet away to help your dog succeed.

Before you send him on the *go-out*, make sure your dog is focusing straight ahead and not toward the glove corner.

Use your CR when your dog looks at his *go-out* target. This tells him he is right, and you can reward him with food either in heel position before you send him or after he completes the *go-out*, or both.

Gradually start the *go-out* farther from the target and at the same time, slowly move the glove closer to the center, until it is as close as fifteen feet from the target.

When your dog can successfully do a full length *go-out* with a glove to the right of his *go-out* path, start close to the target again, but with a glove in the left corner. Repeat the steps you used with the glove on the right. Teaching your dog to do a *go-out* with the gloves in view is the first step toward avoiding the going-to-the-corner problem.

Once your dog understands this simple exercise, do repetitions of a glove retrieve followed by a *go-out*: glove number one, then a *go-out*; glove number three followed by a *go-out*, and so on. After the dog retrieves a corner glove, put it back in the corner, but send him to do a *go-out*. Gradually move the glove closer to the *go-out* spot until it is clearly in his line of vision from the start of the *go-out*. When he can do this without faltering, scatter more gloves throughout your training area and teach him to ignore them all. Put other items out as well: a dumbbell, a scent article, a toy, etc. He is supposed to ignore these distractions and think only about the *go-out*.

Toys

Adele has used Treasure's beloved ball to proof *go-outs*. She tosses a ball off to the side of the *go-out* path and, after a successful *go-out*, she releases Treasure to get her ball with the command GET YOUR BALL. It is hard and stressful, because the ball is a huge distraction, but the release to the ball helps dissipate the stress.

Adding More Targets

For the advanced dog who is trained to a target, it is fun to put at least one more target along the *go-out* path, in addition to the one at the end. Start with the extra target about ten feet closer to you than the end one. Place food on the target that is closest to you. You can do this exercise with a touch-based *go-out*, too. Send your dog to this close target with your normal SEE IT? and RUN commands. After he eats the food from the target, tell him to SIT. Yes, this is stopping him short. We do this to see if he will run past this point on his next *go-out* to the other target at the end of the ring. We want him to run until commanded to stop and sit. If your dog stops to look or sniff at the dummy target, he is wrong. He needs to continue running to the correct place at the end of the ring. You might simply tell him NO, RUN. If he keeps stalling at the closer target, take him to the second one and show him that there is food there. Keep sending him to the one that is farther away until he runs past the first one without pausing. Then put food on the closer one again and repeat the exercise until he understands.

You can also send him without food on either target. This tests whether or not he promptly obeys your *sit* command. Add more targets along his path once he has mastered one extra one. Your dog learns to go-out when told, to sit when told, and not to decide for himself when to do either.

Taking The Go-Out On The Road

Much of your early teaching was probably done in a familiar area. Most of your proofing must be done in new locations.

When you first go to a new place, lower your expectations to be sure your dog will succeed. Before you take him out to train, put out your target and food without your dog seeing you do so. Begin at the new location about six feet from the barrier and target. This barrier can be a wall of a building, a baby gate that you have taken with you, a baseball backstop, a tennis court fence, a tree, or even a stake in the ground. Whatever you use will show your dog that the *go-out* has an end. Cue your dog with your SEE IT? command and, when he drops his head to look forward, tell him RUN to this new spot. If he doesn't leave your side, move closer to the target one step at a time, until he sees it and "vultures."

You may use a chute if your dog has trouble going straight and turning and sitting promptly. Many trainers keep the chute in place for the dog's entire career. However, this proofing exercise is designed to be a blind *go-out* (i.e., the dog runs out without a target), so try to work without guides. If your dog requires a chute, you might consider postponing the proofing until he is more sure of the exercise in a familiar environment.

Lengthen the distance and repeat until he is able to run 50 to 60 feet to the barrier. Repeat the *go-out* exercise 15 to 20 times in the new location. Use random food rewards to keep your dog's interest high, but at the same time accustom him to going out without food.

The next day, return to the same location, set out your target without food, again without your dog seeing it, and try the *go-out* from six to eight feet. If your dog goes, run to him and have a celebration.

Ask for a sit at the end of the *go-out*, but not until he has gone all the way to the wall or gate.

Begin to randomize the food reward at the end of the *go-out* by going out and giving it to him for the correct behavior, rather than putting the food out as a lure. We recommend that you continue to visit this new location every day and continue to lengthen the position from which you first start the *go-out*. Proceed to lengthen the distance, randomize the food, and work toward perfection.

At some point, you must try the first *go-out* and then the first two *go-outs* without food or a target in place. If you do enough repetitions in each session, your dog will be more likely to go correctly even without food the next time you return. When you are seriously proofing *go-outs*, it is very important to train on consecutive days. It is much harder for your dog to generalize if several days or a week go by between training sessions.

Eventually, your dog will do the first two *go-outs* perfectly without food or a target, starting 50-60 feet from the now familiar barrier. You must then move to another new location and start the same procedure all over again. Expect that your dog will require the same slow, easy steps that you used at your first new location. Don't skip steps! As your dog gains experience with many new locations, you *may* be able to skip steps, depending on your dog's skills and confidence.

Keep changing the background to which your dog runs, and eventually add people and dogs to the end of the *go-out* on the other side of the gate, as if you were at a dog show. There are times when there may be another dog working in the adjacent ring, so proof for that as well. Have people and dogs sit along the side of the ring. Perfecting *go-outs* is a long process but very much worth it to get that wonderful Utility Dog title!

Teaching The Dog To Ignore Food

We recommend that you teach your dog to ignore food even though it is in plain sight on the target or the gate. It is best to teach this separately from the *go-out*. With your dog on a four-foot leash, standing nearby, toss a treat about five feet away and immediately command SIT. You can use the leash to stop him from diving at the food. If you do not have control when you are up close to your dog, you will certainly not have control when he is 40 feet away. If necessary, help him *sit*. You can reinforce prompt *sits* with either a treat from your hand or by releasing him to get the food from the floor following your CR. Gradually drop the treat closer to you until your dog *sits* quickly even with food at your feet.

Once your dog does this exercise well, do a short *go-out* with the food clearly visible, either on a target, on the floor, or on the gate or wall. Follow him out, command SIT before he gets to the food and, if he does not *sit* on your command, tap him on the rear. If you use more interesting food for the *sit* reward than for the *go-out*, it may help him respond to your SIT command more quickly.

Another way to help him go all the way out, but without eating the food, is to have a friend cover the food as your dog gets there and you command SIT. He may be allowed to get the food if you tell him to GET IT, or you can go to him and feed him yourself. This is the time to put an end to the "searching for food" behavior. If you take the food away too soon, you will lose speed and enthusiasm for the exercise. If you leave it in the exercise too long, without going to a variable schedule, your dog will never learn to go out without seeing the food or a target. We use food on a variable schedule for this exercise for the dog's entire career. Whether you make the target smaller, keep a chute in place, or use or don't use a target depends on the dog and how he is responding. You need to read your dog and make decisions based on what he is telling you he does or does not understand.

People Distractions

A challenging exercise for an advanced dog is to have a friend stand nearby while your dog does *go-outs*. Have your friend start about 20 feet away, but within the ring boundary, and gradually move closer to the *go-out* line. Have her start with her back to your dog. When he succeeds, she can become more and more distracting. Some dogs will go to your friend; some will avoid her. Help or correct as needed. When your dog succeeds with your friend standing or sitting still, have her wander around randomly. This exercise is likely to cause some confusion. Stay cool and help your dog do his *go-outs* correctly.

Problem Solving

Dogs err on *go-outs* in similar ways. They may not go straight, they often stop short, they don't sit promptly, they don't sit at all, they lie down instead of sitting, or they may jump a jump on a *go-out*. We have experienced every one of these problems with all of our dogs. The following sections discuss how we deal with them.

Crooked Go-Outs

Your dog will probably veer off the desired straight path or run to a corner at some point. *Do not take him from the wrong place and run him to the center.* This has no meaning to your dog and teaches him to do something you don't want him to do: run off center and then veer back to his *go-out* spot. Instead, go to him and take him by the collar to the correct *go-out* line, about ten feet from his *go-out* spot. Command SEE IT?, use your CR when he focuses, and run him to the spot at the end of the ring *with your hand in his collar*. This is a correction! Praise your dog, but do not feed him and do not ask him to SIT. You should work only on the problem, which is a crooked *go-out*. If this correction, mild as it is, causes him to quit trying, reduce your demands and move closer to the target. When he does a correct *go-out*, use your CR the instant he is right and go to him and celebrate!

Whenever your dog shows stress or a lack of confidence, help him rather than correcting him. Be sure he knows the instant he is right or wrong. **Understanding builds confidence and confidence is the key to successful Utility training.**

Dogs Who Will Not Leave The Handler

If your dog will not leave your side when you tell him to RUN, he may be unsure about what you are asking or he may be afraid of the consequences of making a mistake. If he is unsure, help him until you see his confidence return. If he is afraid of the consequences, figure out why. You may have either corrected a confused dog or lost your temper or both. See *Food Removal* section earlier in this chapter.

To help improve your dog's speed when he leaves your side, you may want to try *restrained go-outs*. This should sound familiar because it is based on the *restrained recall* and *restrained retrieve* discussed in earlier chapters. Begin fairly close to your target, holding your standing dog by his collar or with your arms around his neck and his chest. Do some verbal revving up, such as SEE IT? SEE IT? and, when your dog gets excited, release him with your RUN command towards the target. You may want to add a small collar pop or a goose on his rear as he leaves your side. These are both mild forms of corrections, so don't use them unless necessary. If you have used either or both of them in the context of your retrieving work, they should make sense to your dog. Sometimes we run beside the dog for a few steps with a hand in his collar and then release him to do the rest of his *go-out* alone.

If you have combined the *go-out* with the *Directed Jumping* and your dog is having difficulty understanding which jump to take, he may refuse to *go-out*. If he doesn't *go-out*, he won't have to jump and risk being wrong. **Dogs love to be right!** Help your dog with the jumping portion of the exercise separately from the *go-outs,* and do not put the two exercises together again until your dog can do both exercises separately and reliably.

In Utility, more than any other class, there may be negative carryover from one exercise to another. This is why we recommend keeping each part of the exercise separate until the dog thoroughly understands it. We frequently work parts in isolation even with an experienced dog.

Short Go-Outs

A dog who stops short on his *go-outs* needs to be reconditioned to run farther and not stop until he is told to do so. Many trainers fall into the habit of telling their dog to SIT because he stops and begins to turn around. Make it clear to your dog that he must keep going until you tell him to do something else. The target, with or without food on it, encourages this. Try the multiple target proof discussed earlier.

Set the jumps more than the required 25 feet from your barrier to test whether your dog is stopping on your command or at some spot he picks himself. If he stops before you tell him to, run him out the rest of the way with your hand in his collar, praise him when you get to the barrier, but don't give him any food. Repeat the *go-out* and celebrate with a jackpot when he does it correctly by himself.

Dogs Who Don't Sit On Command

A dog who refuses to *sit* on command, who hunts for food, walks back towards you, or makes other mistakes, such as lying down, needs to have the SIT command reinforced separately from the *go-out* until he responds promptly to the SIT command. Reteach the *turn and sit* separately and do not recombine it with the *go-out* too soon. We do add a correction (a leash pop or a tap on the top of the hindquarters) for a dog who consistently sits slowly.

Jumping On Go-Outs

It is very common for inexperienced dogs to attempt to *jump* on the way out, instead of doing a correct straight *go-out*. When this problem occurs, start your *go-outs* between the jumps and gradually back up to the regulation distance.

To proof for this problem, do four to six *go-outs* and *jumps* in one direction and then do them in the opposite direction. Many dogs will try to jump a jump on the *go-outs* in the new direction. We stop the dog verbally and bring him back to start again, perhaps either moving closer to the target or running him part way or all the way out with a hand in his collar.

If you have a dog who frequently makes this mistake, especially at trials, train him on a 15-foot light line. Put your foot on the end of the line. If he goes out straight, lift your foot. If he starts over a jump, the line will stop him. Bring him back and help him run correctly by either starting closer to the jumps or running part way with him.

Another way to address your dog's confusion is to do some retrieves over the high jump and then do *go-outs*. This may cause the problem again, but that's what proofing is all about!

Be patient when he errs, stay cool, and help him be right. Remember: **CONFIDENCE!**

When you regularly combine *go-outs* with jumps, remember that your dog does not always have to jump following a *go-out*. Our rule of thumb for a green dog is about four *go-outs* for every jump. The *go-out* concept is typically harder to teach and maintain than the jump concept.

If you want fast, straight go-outs and prompt turns and sits, you cannot skimp on the amount of time you train them. The proofing alone can take several months. It is better to proof and have a confident dog than to go to trial after trial and fail repeatedly. The dog quickly learns that you cannot correct him in the ring during a trial. In Utility, more than any other class, it is important to take your training back to the drawing board and help the dog through any confusion before you continue to show.

Moving Stand and Examination

T he *Moving Stand and Examination* exercise combines *heeling*, a *stand* from motion, a *Stand-stay*, and an examination by a judge. It has a new component at the end when your dog returns directly to heel position instead of sitting in front.

This exercise can be taught in a relatively short period of time, as long as the dog has a solid Novice foundation in the commands and/or signals to *stand*, *stay*, and *finish*.

For teaching, we break this exercise down into three phases: the *stand from motion*, the *examination*, and the *call to heel*.

The Stand from Motion

A well-performed *stand from motion* starts with your dog sitting in heel position. On the judge's "Forward" command, you and your dog should move forward briskly. After you have heeled about 10 feet, the judge commands, "Stand your dog." You may use a command and/or signal to stop your dog in a *Stand-stay*. He should stop immediately, though minor foot movement to adjust to a comfortable position is acceptable. You must not pause, but should continue to walk straight ahead about 10 to 12 feet and then turn in place to face your dog. You may turn in either direction.

Introduce the *stand from motion* by heeling slowly for a few steps. Signal a *stand* by swinging your right hand, in which you are holding a treat, towards your dog's nose, stopping your hand motion where you want him to stop. Say your STAND and WAIT commands simultaneously with your signal. Stop your hand in front of your dog's nose and let him eat the treat while you take one step and pivot to face him (Fig. 19.1).

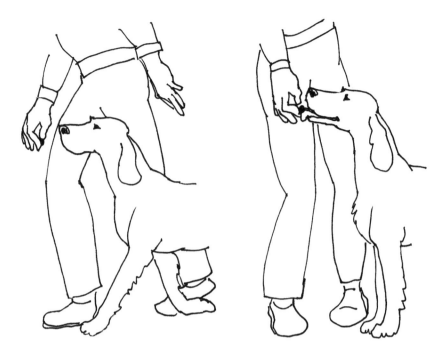

Figure 19.1 Stop your hand in front of your dog's nose and let him eat a treat while you take one step and pivot to face him.

Keep your treat-holding hand still while you continue to move forward. He should learn immediately that he must stop and that you will keep moving.

When your dog stops promptly as you heel slowly, gradually increase your speed. Continue to speed up until you are heeling at your normal pace. Once he responds promptly to your STAND and WAIT commands, use only the WAIT command.

When your dog understands that he must *stand* and *wait* when commanded, add steps to your straight line heeling before adding your WAIT command. When you fade one of your verbal commands, you may want to touch your dog's nose with your signaling hand to help stop his forward progress.

The Examination

When you have turned to face your dog, the judge will approach him from the front or side to examine him. This exam is more extensive than the Novice exam, and the judge may touch all parts of your dog except for his mouth and his testicles. She will probably touch the dog's head, ears, back, sides, all four legs and his tail (if he has one). Some judges are more thorough in their exam than others. Some are gentle, almost to the point of "tickling" the dog, and some use a firmer touch. It is important to prepare your dog for any type of exam by exposing him to the various types in your training and proofing. Earlier, we recommended that you teach your dog to accept a more thorough exam during his Novice training so he is used to it by the time you get to your Utility training.

Calling Your Dog to Heel

The final portion of the *Moving Stand and Examination* exercise may be entirely new to you. We teach our dogs two finishes (see *Front and Finish* chapter). We prefer to use the *around* finish for most regular exercises, and Judy saves the *side finish* for the *call to heel* portion of this exercise. It simplifies the exercise considerably for the dog, as he only uses this finish when he goes directly to heel without doing a *front*.

Start with your dog *standing* in front of you. Since you are allowed to use both a command and a signal for this exercise, we teach it this way. Use your finish command and signal together, and help him comply if he needs it.

When your dog reliably finishes from a *stand* directly in front of you, leave him farther away and motivate a brisk return to you, just as you would motivate a brisk *recall*. If you use a *side* finish, toss a treat or a toy off to your left. If you use an *around* finish, throw a motivator off to your right. This gets him moving correctly in the desired direction and should encourage speed. Sometimes the farther away you are from your dog, the easier it is for him to come quickly to you on his return, since distance often encourages speed. Gradually fade throwing the motivator.

Once he reliably zooms past you, run forward just as he passes you and encourage him to turn and catch you. Finally, add a *sit* in heel position to the exercise. Use your steering words as needed to produce a straight *finish*. You may also wish to use a chute of some kind. (See *Fronts and Finishes* chapter for proofing ideas).

Problem Solving

Some problems you may encounter with this exercise include:
- Not heeling.
- Anticipating your WAIT command or stopping on the judge's command.
- Not stopping on command.
- Moving during the examination.

- Moving feet repeatedly.
- Not coming to heel position when called.
- Anticipating *call to heel.*
- Walking in on the recall to heel position.
- Handler pausing when cueing her dog to stop.

If your dog doesn't heel when commanded or signaled to do so, you need to go back and work on *heel starts* (see *Fundamental Words* chapter).

If your dog responds to the judge's "Stand your dog" command, you need to have someone call this command repeatedly for you as you and your dog disregard the command and continue heeling. Don't forget to use your CR and a treat when he continues to heel without hesitation. Next, vary standing your dog with heeling straight forward after the command until he understands he should *stand* only when told to do so.

If your dog does not stop and *stand* on command, review your commands and signals to STAND and STAY (see *Fundamental Words* and *Signals* chapters). Remember, we started this chapter by reminding you that this exercise is nothing more than a combination of *solid* Novice foundation words.

Moving during the exam, such as repeatedly shifting feet, indicates that your dog does not understand the Novice *Stand for Exam.* You may need to stand closer to your dog during the exam. Go back and review the instructions in the *Stays* chapter.

Problems with the *call to heel* portion of this exercise may well be new ones, since it is likely that you have not taught this specific exercise at any other time in your training. If your dog anticipates the *call to heel,* or responds to a judge's command, proof his *Stand-stay,* since that is the broken part.

If your dog has slow *recalls,* he will probably return slowly on the *call to heel.* Go back and work on speeding him up on his regular *recall.* Review the sections on *restrained* and *motivational recalls* in the *Recalls* chapter. It is extremely important that you start with him standing directly in front of you and gradually work up to the 10-to-12-foot *recall.* Forget the perfect finish when first training this and reward your dog with his CR and a treat for coming quickly to approximate heel position. When he arrives, release him.

When your dog returns directly and briskly to *heel position*, add precision to the exercise. However, as with all precision exercises, do not dwell on the precision too much or your dog will develop a slow return. Instead of thinking about the fast *recall*, he will be thinking about a perfect *finish*.

When a handler pauses when commanded to "Stand your dog," she is generally worried that her dog will not stop as commanded. Review your teaching steps so your dog will be secure. Leave slowly at first, but do not build in a delay for long or you will have a hard time moving out of position quickly.

We have found this exercise easy to teach to a dog *with the right foundation*. We have seldom needed more than couple of weeks to teach the entire exercise. If you have trouble, go back in your training and rework the part that your dog does not understand.

Are You Ready?

How do you know when your dog is ready to enter a trial? For that matter, how do you know when *you* are ready? You are the only one who can answer these questions, but you should follow some guidelines.

When showing in an obedience trial, you and your dog must perform according to the regulations. You are not allowed to use food, toys, extra verbal help, or physical corrections in the ring. Extra verbal commands usually cost you a substantial number of lost points and, depending on when you give the extra command, can even result in a zero. Sometimes it is better to give an extra command during heeling and take the substantial point deduction than it is to let your dog get completely lost. This choice is possible only if you have taught your dog to find heel position on command.

Even though food, conditioned reinforcers, and shaping are central to our training philosophy, our goal is to train our dogs to work well in the ring without these aids. This is a form of proofing and you must go through a period of fading the training aids before entering an obedience trial.

Some dogs need more ring preparation than others. If your dog is very distractible or easily frightened or stressed, you will need to take more time to prepare him for the ring. If your dog is easy going and has the "What, me worry?" attitude, you can probably get by with less proofing — except perhaps in Utility!

Setting Goals

What is your goal when you walk into the obedience ring? Do you simply wish to qualify, even if the score isn't very high? If so, you can let many details slide. Just make sure you understand what causes you or your dog to pass or fail. Read your rule book carefully! *Remember, when you sign your entry form, you are stating that you are fully conversant with the rules of the class you have entered.*

If your goal is to earn class placements, a *High In Trial*, or a *Dog World Award* (which means earning three scores of 195 or higher in your first three trials at a given class level), you must prepare more completely than someone who is not concerned with high scores. You should:

- Know the rules.
- Proof each exercise adequately.
- Prepare yourself mentally.
- Be efficient and smooth in your handling rather than abrupt on turns, halts, or pace changes.
- Eliminate any errors for which you lose three or more points.
- Use consistent footwork so you are a good team leader. You should not be the one to lose points for your team.

If your dog consistently fails the same exercise or repeatedly loses a substantial number of points from an exercise, be honest with yourself, stop showing, and retrain the exercise. As the trainer and handler, you need to assess your own problems and proof accordingly. You might have to go back and retrain one or more exercises if your dog is unable to perform them in public.

If you have followed our teaching program, you have taught all the exercises with food and you have progressed to using food as a random and variable reinforcer rather than a lure. You have repeatedly asked your dog to perform an exercise, or part of an exercise, many times without giving him any food. *He understands that he will get a reward, but that he may have to wait until he has worked for more than just a few minutes. This is essential if your dog is to show reliably and with anima-tion.*

To proof for the ring, weaning your dog from frequent food is simply a matter of delaying the food a bit longer for each exercise until he can perform the entire routine without food. When you first begin "show weaning," keep the food with you so you can reward him quickly. As soon as you see him performing the exercise correctly and with animation, move your food to a container outside of or off to the side of your training area. When he performs an exercise satisfactorily, run to the container, get one or more treats, and feed him.

Teach your dog a command for this delayed food such as JACKPOT! A *jackpot* is a substantial quantity of food delivered all at once. The quantity will depend on the size of your dog, and can be as little as three or four pieces or as much as would fill a small plastic container. It is usually a special food rather than the usual training treats. It tells your dog that he was "super correct!" Start using the term JACKPOT when you are still carrying the food to get him used to the term. Most dogs learn this in one lesson!

Chaining

As discussed in the *Methods* chapter, a long string of behaviors, which follow one after the other, is called a *behavior chain*. Each successive step in a behavior chain reinforces the previous step.

Moving from the *Stand for Examination* to the *Heel Free* is a difficult chain for many novice dogs. Your dog does a static exercise — one where he is expected to *stay* — and must then move with you and set up for an attentive *Heel Free*. Static exercises tend to be "downers" for dogs. To help get him out of "static" mode and into "active" mode, run out of the *stand* to the *Heel Free* set-up spot and give your dog a jackpot — without asking him to *sit* in heel position. This prepares him to move away from the *stand* and be alert and ready to heel again. Build on this by adding the "set-up in heel position" to the "stand and run out of the stand." Immediately give him a jackpot. Then add "heel a couple of steps" before the jackpot, "heel a few steps and halt," JACKPOT, and so on until you have chained the exercises from the stand through the entire off-lead heeling pattern without the use of food.

Some extra talking may be needed during the heeling pattern as you extend the time your dog works without food, but this can be faded later. Do not shock your dog by removing the food and verbal help at the same time!

Backward Chaining

As discussed in the *Methods* chapter, if you build a behavior chain by training the final segment first and then working backwards, you are *backward chaining*. You can backward chain each of the individual exercises required in AKC obedience.

You must create a far more complicated chain before you actually show your dog. You should combine all of the individual exercises into a complete routine. To backward chain the entire Novice routine, start with a complete, formal *Recall*, after which you leave the ring to jackpot your dog. Then do a *Heel Free* pattern, the *Recall*, and leave the ring for a jackpot. Continue adding the previous exercises until the *Heel on Leash* is added. Jackpots may lose their effect if given too often in one training session, so this chain will probably require multiple sessions to complete. This requires a fair amount of time, but most dogs love it and look forward to the end result — the jackpot!

Back chaining the Open or Utility exercises is more challenging, but it will help keep your dog focused through the more difficult exercises. In Open, you would start with the *Broad Jump* and a jackpot. Then go to a *Retrieve Over the High Jump* followed by a *Broad Jump* and a jackpot. Continue until you have done the entire routine. After each *Broad Jump*, you would leave the ring and go to the jackpot.

When you regularly use backward chaining with a jackpot at the end of the chain, your dog usually becomes more animated as you near the end of the routine. Sometimes this animation leads to anticipation. Make sure your dog does each exercise in the chain properly, though perhaps not perfectly, to get his jackpot. Remember, you control the jackpot! Give one only for your dog's best work.

One of the benefits of jackpots is that they usually intensify your dog's enthusiasm for the work. Dogs often try much harder the next time you ask for an exercise that you have recently jackpotted. Random, unexpected jackpots are one of our favorite ways to keep our dogs keen about working with us.

Taking Your Show on the Road

Once your dog knows an exercise in a familiar training location, you need to take him to different training places for proofing. You must be sure that he really understands your commands and that he can perform the exercise correctly on your first command in a new environment.

Start by moving from your normal training area to a slightly more distracting location. This may be nothing more than moving from your backyard to your front yard. Take these steps slowly because you want your dog to succeed and you should see him exude confidence. Next, move to a neighbor's yard or to a school yard or park where the distractions are minimal.

Gradually increase the distractions near which your dog must work. Perhaps add a few children or adults or someone playing ball, and finally, work where there are other dogs. Sometimes you can do this by working on the perimeter of a training class. Also have a friend call commands for you. Make sure you have baby gates or other ring markers set up so a trial is not the first time your dog sees them.

Give your dog time to get used to any new place. You will probably find that he needs to spend some time sight-seeing, sniffing, and generally investigating. This is called *habituation*. It is entirely normal and should be expected. Instead of fighting it, let your dog have a look around. If you don't, you are likely to become frustrated over his lack of attention, both in training and in the ring. Within reason, give him as much time as he needs. He may need anywhere from a few minutes to half an hour or more.

Watch your dog carefully and reinforce him when he looks at you, but don't demand it. Stand still and wait for him to relax enough to focus on you. He should start looking at you more frequently and for longer periods. Once your dog attends to you more than his surroundings, he is ready to get to work.

You won't know how long it takes your dog to *habituate* until you try it. The day of your first trial is not the time to find out that your dog needs thirty minutes to gawk before he even thinks of looking at you. Once he starts focusing on you, ask for simple behaviors such as looking at you for a few seconds, a *sit*, a *stand*, or a *down*.

When he responds well to simple commands, start asking for more complicated ones, such as *heeling* or *recalls*. If a distraction captivates your dog and he totally ignores you, move farther away from the distraction and try again for a simple behavior.

If your dog continues to have trouble in new situations, you must take him to new places more often. Be sure to use especially delicious food on these trips. Take along a generous supply, and when you use it up, quit for the day. You will find that the same amount of food lasts longer on future trips, as your dog should be able to perform for longer periods of time with less reinforcement.

If your dog acts fearful in new places or is severely distracted by the surroundings, he may not be interested in eating. For dogs like this, road trips are *critical* to your future success in the ring. Offer an interesting treat from time to time to see if he has relaxed enough to focus on you. Try different tasty treats such as roast beef, chicken, or canned cat food.

Keep going to the same place to train until your dog is familiar with the area and no longer distracted. Then start over in a new location. *Dogs don't usually generalize commands immediately in each new place. You must teach him to respond everywhere by training him in many locations.*

Many dogs who won't eat when they are stressed will still play. Use toys instead of food if your dog responds better to them. Try teaching your dog a trick to help him relax. Tricks like jumping your leg or barking on command are good stress relievers.

A Show and Go or a fun match may be helpful, especially if you do not have an opportunity to practice a formal ring procedure any other way. These matches do not offer prizes and are generally less formal than a *sanctioned match*. Before you enter a match, attend at least one with your dog where you can both watch. Watch heeling patterns and ring procedure. At these first matches, do some simple training with your dog on the side lines. If you haven't trained and proofed your dog in many strange locations, you may be horrified to find how poorly he performs. Keep at it and his responses should improve!

We like to start attending matches with a new Novice dog long before the routine is polished. Our expectations are not high, but we want to see if he can maintain his attention and position. We usually give extra commands, as needed, in order to achieve the smoothest routine possible. We might do two heel patterns on-leash, rather than one on-leash and one off. We might ask the judge to not call any halts so we can get into the rhythm of our heeling. We take along some jackpots that we can pull out of a pocket after an especially well done bit of the routine. We want these early exposures to the ring to be *fun!* Since we enter before we expect the dog to be *really* ready, we use a "training mind-set" and are not very formal. We are always ready to help the dog through a difficult situation.

We also use matches to check our training progress. We may make notes of the weak areas of the routine so we can focus on those areas in training. It is important that both you and your dog get used to having a stranger call commands and follow closely while you work.

When you feel you and your dog are ready to enter a match, enter the first few times for exhibition only. This takes the pressure off to try to score well or win awards. The purpose of the match is to see if your dog is ready to show and if he still needs help in the ring. You want to make it easy for him to succeed, and if you are worried about winning a ribbon or trophy, this is not always possible. Sometimes, you may want the judge to score you, but if your dog needs help, forget about the score and help him.

Match Scores and Judges

How does the score you receive at a practice match, whether it is a Show and Go or a Sanctioned match, relate to the score you might get in a real trial? Generally, though not always, match scores are higher. The scores are only as good as the person judging you. If the judge is just learning the job, the scores may be a little lower than you would get at a trial. If the judge is a volunteer who doesn't want to hurt your feelings, the score may be higher.

It is not realistic to expect someone to score you correctly when you are talking to your dog or giving corrections or food in the ring.

You should be able to enter a trial and pass if you follow these guidelines:

- Take your dog to a new place. This can be a match or a run-through at a park.

- Use the equipment allowed in an actual trial (i.e., no pinch collars, food, or talking).

- Use only allowable commands; no extra commands and no praise except between exercises.

- Pass all the exercises in the class on three different occasions in a way that pleases *you*. Remember, you have your own goals!

Self Help

A video camera is invaluable for assessing your performance. Ask a friend to tape you and perhaps you can return the favor. Learn to critique your own performance rather than relying on someone else's opinion. Your instructor or other knowledgeable person can help you the first few times until you know what you are looking for.

Have your instructor, training buddy, or friend at ringside give you an honest opinion. It is important that the person giving you this information knows at least as much as you do about what you are trying to accomplish. Well-meaning people sometimes do not have the same goals as you do. High scores require attention to details. Inexperienced trainers may not even notice details that are obvious to an experienced trainer. Learn to evaluate your own performance while in the ring and pay attention to your dog!

Once you become familiar with some typical ring patterns and the order of the exercises, train regularly at places such as school yards, parks, and strip malls. It is generally best to stay home when teaching new exercises, but the more you train and proof away from home or training school, the easier the transition to the ring becomes.

Dressing for the Ring

When you are planning what to wear to show your dog, think *neat, clean, comfortable,* and *easy to move in.*

We recommend pants for anyone who shows in obedience. Skirts or dresses might flap in your dog's face, especially smaller dogs. We like to match the color of our pants to the color of the dog, if possible. Judy has a great collection of brindle pants! Your dog should blend with you rather than stand out. Avoid excessively baggy pants, especially when showing a small dog.

If you are wearing a long shirt or sweater that hangs over your pants, make sure it doesn't swing in your dog's face. *A shirt or sweater that contrasts with the background may help your dog see you better during the Utility Signal Exercise.*

Whatever shoes you pick, think *comfortable*. You are likely to stand a lot at a trial. We recommend athletic shoes that are easy to run in. Another consideration is how quietly you can walk and run in the shoes. Avoid shoes that clunk! Adele prefers to wear all-black running shoes to go with her black pants and black socks. Leave the sandals for the beach. In our opinion, they are not appropriate for the obedience ring.

In Figure 20.1, Judy and Alec are well dressed for the ring. Adele and Treasure are not. Study the photo and see if you can find what Adele should change before entering the ring at an obedience trial.

Grooming Your Dog For the Ring

When you walk confidently into the ring, neatly dressed and with a well-groomed dog, you give yourself an immediate edge in the judge's eyes. It shows you are prepared and care about what you are doing. The handler who shuffles into the ring, dressed sloppily with an ungroomed dog, does not present the sort of image *we* want to portray. Even if your dog is not conformation quality, he should still be a pleasure to touch and look at. Trim his toenails and any extra hair from his feet and ears. Give him a bath. You want him to look his best when you have your picture taken with him when you do well!

Your Trial Routine

If you have shown your dog in conformation before entering your first obedience trial, you have an advantage over an exhibitor whose dog has never been to a dog show before. Showing in the conformation ring is a great way to teach your dog to enjoy the ring. It allows you and your dog to get used to the environment and teaches you how to plan for a day at a dog show. Attending conformation shows or obedience matches also helps you determine how often your dog needs to go outside to eliminate before performing. You can see how he handles the stress and noise of other dogs, exhibitors, and spectators. He learns to hear applause, barking dogs, equipment being moved, and other dog show noises.

You can also determine whether he will work better if he is hungry or whether you should feed him his regular meal before showing. Per-

Figure 20.1 Judy and Alec are well dressed for the ring. Adele and Treasure are not. Can you find all the things Adele should change before she and Treasure enter the ring? The answers are on the bottom of the next page.

haps half a morning meal is better than a whole one. Your dog might work better if he is crated before showing. We prefer to crate our dogs. Some owners like to keep their dog nearby, either on the floor or in their laps. Some dogs do best waiting in the car.

Most dogs do better if allowed to walk around the show grounds for a while before either being crated or settling down to wait their turn. How much time do you need from when you arrive until entering the ring? Our goal is usually to allow *at least* one hour to park, unload the car, set up our crate and chair, walk the dog around both inside and outside, find the restroom for ourselves, and study the ring pattern. Matches are excellent places to learn how much time you and your dog require.

Visit at least one obedience trial before you enter your dog for the first time. Take your chair, your lunch, and a rule book. Sit at ringside and watch the appropriate class level for an hour or so. Watch more than one or two dogs. This gives you a chance to see a number of different handlers and dogs and how the judge handles any problems. You will usually see a higher percentage of passing performances in the B classes than the A classes, although not always. If you have questions about scoring, check your rule book for the appropriate passage.

Pay attention to the heeling pattern and ring procedure. Most judges are consistent about where they call halts, turns, and pace changes. Where does each exercise start? Does the judge use verbal cues, hand signals, or both?

The trial secretary or superintendent usually posts the pages from each judge's score book after the class is completed. Go look at the *breakdown* of the scores of the dogs you watched. These are the points earned on each separate exercise for each dog in each class. Did their scores come close to what you thought they should earn?

Nerves

How nervous do you get when you perform in front of your peers? If you prepare yourself and your dog thoroughly for your class, you should be able to relax more than if you aren't sure what your dog will do. Every-one handles nerves in a different way. Some appear calm on the outside while their insides are churning. If you get excessively nervous, learn some positive imaging techniques, as well as how to relax while perform-ing. There are many good books and tapes on this subject for athletes (see *Appendix B* for suggestions). You and your dog *are* athletes!

Some people fuss excessively over their dogs, adding to the jitters. If this is your tendency, put your dog in his crate or your car to rest com-fortably while *you* pace around the trial site by yourself. This is part of your "pre-ring routine" you need to figure out at practice matches.

Referring back to Figure 20.1, Alec is wearing a handsome choke chain and Judy is dressed neatly. Treasure has on a pinch collar and a big, fat leash. Adele has on clunky hiking boots, torn jeans, a bait bag, and a shirt with the name of her school. Her hand is in her pocket, and she is not paying attention to her dog. The pinch collar, bait bag, and shirt are illegal. The rest just shows poor taste. Remember, you are preparing yourself for show biz. Dress the part!

Do your homework, get yourself to the trial on time, and watch the complete pattern a few times so you are familiar with where the exercises start and end. When it is your turn, take a deep breath, smile, walk in the ring with confidence, and do the best job you can on that day.

Don't forget your teammate! Focus only on the two of you and help him the best you can. If the performance doesn't go as you hoped, there is always another trial, and you can still take your dog home!

Be a good sport whether you win or lose. There will always be another trial! Good Luck!

Are you ready? Forward!

Appendix A: Balance Points

O n the following pages, you will find charts which show each of the AKC obedience exercises broken into *balance points* or separate pieces. The exercises are listed in the order they are performed in each class. The individual piece is on the left side of the chart and the chapter(s) in which we explain that piece is on the right side of the diagram.

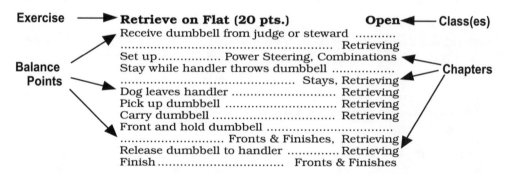

We hope this will give you a better understanding of how the teaching in each chapter fits into the bigger picture of a whole obedience class.

The Exercises

Heeling patterns are the most variable part of any obedience routine. A judge has a lot of leeway in how he puts a routine together. What follows is a common routine, but by no means the only possibility.

Heeling (40 pts.)   **Novice & Open**
Enter ring & move to starting line .... Heeling
Set up dog in heel position .... Power Steering, Combination Words

Heeling (cont.)

Forward (heel at Normal pace).................. Fundamental Words, Heeling
Halt .... Combination Words, Heeling
Forward .... Fundamental Words, Heeling
Left turn ....Power Steering, Heeling
Slow .... Heeling
Normal .... Heeling
About turn...Power Steering, Heeling
Halt .... Combination Words, Heeling
Forward .... Fundamental Words, Heeling
Right turn...Power Steering, Heeling
Fast .... Fundamental Words, Heeling
Normal .... Heeling
About turn...Power Steering, Heeling
Halt .... Combination Words, Heeling
Release .... Fundamental Words

Figure 8 (part of Heeling 40 pts.)   Novice & Open

Set up...Power Steering, Combination Words
Heel start.. Power Steering
Left circle.. Heeling
Hurry .... Fundamental Words, Heeling
Right circle .... Heeling
Halt .... Combination Words, Heeling

Stand for Exam (30 pts.)   Novice

Set up...Power Steering, Combination Words
Stand .... Fundamental Words
Stay .... Stays
Exam .... Stays
Handler's return .... Stays

Recall (30 pts.)   Novice

Set up...Power Steering, Combination Words
Sit-stay while handler walks to other end of ring .... Stays, Recalls
Come ....Fundamental Words, Recalls
Front .... Fronts & Finishes
Finish .... Fronts & Finishes

Group Sit-stay (30 pts.)   Novice, Open

Wait outside ring ....
Controlled walk into ring in line of 6-12 dogs and handlers .... Stays
Set up in tight quarters.. Stays
    Novice Sit-stay for 1 minute with handlers across ring .... Stays
-or- ....
    Open Sit-stay for 3 minutes with handlers out of sight .... Stays
Handler's return .... Stays
Optional release .... Stays

Group Down-stay (30 pts.)   Novice, Open
Set up in tight quarters....................Power Steering, Combination Words
Down on hip .... Fundamental Words, Stays
   Novice Down-stay for 3 minutes with handlers across ring .... Stays
-or-
   Open Down-stay for 5 minutes with handlers out of sight .... Stays
Handler's return .... Stays
Retrieve leash and armband; reattach leash.................................. Stays
Release .... Stays

Drop on Recall (30 pts.)   Open
Set up...Power Steering, Combination Words
Sit-stay while handler walks to other end of ring.............. Stays, Recalls
Come ....Fundamental Words, Recalls
Drop ....Fundamental Words, Recalls
Come from drop .... Recalls
Front .... Fronts & Finishes
Finish .... Fronts & Finishes

Retrieve on Flat (20 pts.)   Open
Receive dumbbell from judge or steward .... Retrieving
Set up...Power Steering, Combination Words
Stay while handler throws dumbbell .... Stays, Retrieving
Dog leaves handler .... Retrieving
Pick up dumbbell... Retrieving
Carry dumbbell.. Retrieving
Front and hold dumbbell .... Fronts & Finishes, Retrieving
Release dumbbell to handler .... Retrieving
Finish .... Fronts & Finishes

Retrieve Over the High Jump (30 pts.)   Open
Set up at correct distance from high jump ....
.... Jumping, Power Steering, Combination Words
Stay while handler throws dumbbell .... Retrieving
Dog leaves handler .... Retrieving
Jump the high jump ....Jumping, Retrieving
Pick up dumbbell... Retrieving
Carry dumbbell.. Retrieving
Jump the jump while carrying dumbbell ....Jumping, Retrieving
Front and hold dumbbell .... Fronts & Finishes, Retrieving
Release dumbbell to handler .... Retrieving
Finish .... Fronts & Finishes

Broad Jump (20 pts.)   **Open**

Set up at correct distance from broad jump .... Jumping, Power Steering, Combination Words

Sit-stay while handler walks to side of jump .... Stays, Jumping

Jump the broad jump .... Jumping

Turn and front .... Fronts & Finishes, Jumping

Finish .... Fronts & Finishes

Signal Exercise (40 pts.)   **Utility**

Set up ....Power Steering, Combination Words

Heel .... Heeling, Signals

Stand .... Fundamental Words, Signals

Stay .... Stays, Signals

Drop .... Fundamental Words, Signals

Sit .... Fundamental Words, Signals

Come ....Fundamental Words, Recalls, Signals

Finish .... Fronts & Finishes

Scent Discrimination (30 pts.)   **Utility**

Set up to watch articles placed by steward ..... Power Steering, Retrieving

Turn away from articles and set up in heel position near chair which

    holds articles that you will scent .... Power Steering, Combination Words

Sit in heel position during handler's article scenting .... Retrieving, Stays

Sit in heel position during article placement by judge............................. Fundamental Words, Scent Discrimination

    Turn to face pile and sit in heel position .... Combination Words, Scent Discrimination

    Dog leaves handler and goes to pile .... Retrieving

-or-

    Flying send .... Power Steering, Scent Discrimination

Dog leaves handler and goes to pile ...... Retrieving, Scent Discrimination

Scenting .... Scent Discrimination

Retrieving correct article .... Retrieving

Return to handler .... Retrieving

Front and hold article .... Retrieving, Fronts & Finishes

Release of article to handler .... Retrieving

Finish .... Fronts & Finishes

(Repeat from "Sit in heel position during handler's scenting" for 2nd

    article)

Directed Retrieve (30 pts.) **Utility**

Set up in middle of ring between jumps, facing away from where stew-
ard will place gloves ....
........................Power Steering, Combination Words, Directed Retrieve
Pivot to glove .... Combination Words, Directed Retrieve
Mark .... Fundamental Words, Directed Retrieve
Dog leaves handler and goes to correct glove .... Retrieving
Retrieve .... Retrieving
Return to handler .... Retrieving
Front and hold glove .... Retrieving, Fronts & Finishes
Release of glove to handler .... Retrieving
Finish .... Fronts & Finishes

Moving Stand (30 pts.) **Utility**

Set up where directed by judge .... Power Steering, Combination Words
Heel for about 10 feet.. Heeling
Stand and leave your dog .... Fundamental Words, Moving Stand and
Examination
Judge examines your dog............ Stays, Moving Stand and Examination
Call your dog to heel .... Fronts and Finishes,
Moving Stand and Examination

Directed Jumping (40 pts.) **Utility**

Set up at end of ring on center line ....
....Power Steering, Combination Words
Focus on go-out location .... Go-outs
Go-out .... Go-outs
Turn and Sit .... Go-outs
Taking direction .... Jumping
Jumping bar/high jump .... Jumping
Front .... Fronts & Finishes
Finish .... Fronts & Finishes
(Repeat from "Focus on go-out location" for 2nd jump)

Appendix B

Recommended Reading

American Kennel Club, Publisher, *Obedience Guidelines For Judges*, 51 Madison Avenue, New York, NY, 10010.

American Kennel Club, Publisher, *Obedience Regulations*, 51 Madison Avenue, New York, NY, 10010.

Booth, Sheila, with Gottfried Dildei, *Schutzhund Obedience Training in Drive*, Podium Publications, Box 171, Ridgefield, CT, 06877, 1993.

Cecil, Barbara & Darnell, Gerianne, *Competitive Obedience Training for the Small Dog*, T9E Publishing, Council Bluffs, IA, 1994.

Colflesh, Linda, *Making Friends, Training Your Dog Positively*, Howell, 1990.

Donaldson, Jean, *The Culture Clash*, James and Kenneth Publishers, Oakland, CA, 1996.

Handler, Barbara, *Successful Obedience Handling, The New Best Foot Forward*. Alpine Publications, Loveland, CO, 1991.

Lewis, Janet, *Smart Trainers, Brilliant Dogs*, Canine Sports Productions, Lutherville, MD, 1997.

Orlick, Terry, *In Pursuit of Excellence, How to Win in Sport and Life Through Mental Training*, Leisure Press, Champaign Illinois, 1990.

Pryor, Karen, *Don't Shoot the Dog*. Bantam Books, New York, 1984.

Reid, Pamela, *Excel-Erated Learning, Explaining in Plain English How Dogs Learn and How Best to Teach Them*, James and Kenneth Publishers, Oakland, CA, 1996.

Savioe, Jane, *That Winning Feeling! A New Approach to Riding Using Psychocybernetics*, Trafalgar Square Publishing, North Pomfret, VT, 1992.

Zink, M. Christine & Julie Daniels, *Jumping From A to Z, Teaching Your Dog To Soar*, Canine Sports Productions, Lutherville, MD, 1996.

Zink, M. Christine, *Peak Performance, Coaching the Canine Athlete*, Canine Sports Productions, Lutherville, MD, 1997.

Recommended Videos

Positively Fetching: Teaching the Obedience Retrieves Using Food

JABBY Productions
3676 W. Ellsworth Rd.
Ann Arbor, MI 48103
www.he.net/~jabby

Positively Fetching is also available from:
- J & J Dog Supplies (800-642-2050)
- Max 200 (800-446-2920)
- Direct Book Services (800-776-2665)
- 4-M Enterprises (510-489-8722)

For further information on Janice DeMello's *Around the Clock Method of Scent Discrimination*, write or call her at:

4525 Los Angeles Avenue
Somis, CA 93066
(805) 386-4427

Index

Positively Fetching

Teaching the Obedience Retrieves Using Food

A videotape by
Adele Yunck and Judy Byron

This 60-minute video:

√ Teaches you how to use a conditioned reinforcer.
√ Shows many dogs and handlers learning to retrieve.
√ The 48 page booklet provides an easy reference to the information in the video.
√ Includes in-depth examples at each stage of the retrieve process as well as problem solving.

Visit our web site at: http://www.he.net/~jabby

Video Order Form

Please send me _____ copy(ies) of the video (each video includes 1 copy of the booklet), for $50 per video, plus $3.50 for shipping and handling. Also send me _____ extra copy(ies) of the booklet, for $5 each.
Michigan residents: please add $3 sales tax per video and $.30 sales tax per *extra* booklet.
Canadian residents: please send US funds, and include $7.00 for shipping and handling ($57 total).

Name: _____
Address: _____
City, State, Zip: _____
e-mail address: _____

To order your copy of *Positively Fetching*, send a check made out to JABBY Productions to:

JABBY Productions • 3676 W. Ellsworth Rd. • Ann Arbor, MI 48103

You may make copies of this page.

You may make copies of this page.

Competition Obedience: A Balancing Act
Book Order Form

Please send me _____ copy(ies) of *Competition Obedience: A Balancing Act* for $30 per book, plus $3.50 for shipping and handling ($33.50 total).
Michigan residents: please include $1.80 for sales tax ($35.30 total).
Canadian residents: please send US funds and include $7 for postage ($37 total).

Name: _____

Address: _____

City, State, Zip: _____

E-mail address: _____

To order your copy of *Competition Obedience: A Balancing Act*, send a check made out to JABBY Productions to:

JABBY Productions • 3676 W. Ellsworth Rd. • Ann Arbor, MI 48103